Routledge Revivals

Victorian Culture and the Idea of the Grotesque

Originally published in 1999, *Victorian Culture and the Idea of the Grotesque* is the first fully interdisciplinary study of the subject and examines a wide range of sources and materials to provide new readings between 'style' and 'concept'. The book provides an original analysis of key articulations of the Grotesque in the literary culture of Ruskin, Browning and Dickens, where represents the eruptions, intensities, confusions and disturbed vitality of modern cultural experience such as the scientific revolution associated with Darwin and the nature of industrial society.

Victorian Culture and the Idea of the Grotesque

Edited by Colin Trodd, Paul Barlow and
David Amigoni

In memory of Paul Barlow (1962-2015)

First published in 1999
by Ashgate Publishing Ltd.

This edition first published in 2018 by Routledge
2 Park Square, Milton Park, Abingdon, Oxon, OX14 4RN
and by Routledge
711 Third Avenue, New York, NY 10017

Routledge is an imprint of the Taylor & Francis Group, an informa business

© 1999 Colin Trodd, Paul Barlow and David Amigoni

All rights reserved. No part of this book may be reprinted or reproduced or utilised in any form or by any electronic, mechanical, or other means, now known or hereafter invented, including photocopying and recording, or in any information storage or retrieval system, without permission in writing from the publishers.

Publisher's Note
The publisher has gone to great lengths to ensure the quality of this reprint but points out that some imperfections in the original copies may be apparent.

Disclaimer
The publisher has made every effort to trace copyright holders and welcomes correspondence from those they have been unable to contact.

A Library of Congress record exists under LCCN: 98035002

ISBN 13: 978-1-138-47893-0 (hbk)
ISBN 13: 978-1-138-48689-8 (pbk)
ISBN 13: 978-1-351-04447-9 (ebk)

Victorian Culture and the Idea of the Grotesque

Edited by Colin Trodd, Paul Barlow and
David Amigoni

ASHGATE

© The individual contributors 1999

All rights reserved. No part of this publication may be reproduced, stored in a retrieval system, or transmitted in any form or by any means, electronic, mechanical, photocopying, recording, or otherwise, without the prior permission of the publisher.

The authors have asserted their moral rights.

Published by　　　　　　　　　Ashgate Publishing Company
Ashgate Publishing Limited　　Old Post Road
Gower House　　　　　　　　 Brookfield
Croft Road　　　　　　　　　　Vermont 05036–9704
Aldershot　　　　　　　　　　　USA
Hants GU11 3HR
England

British Library Cataloguing-in-Publication data

Victorian culture and the idea of the grotesque
1. Grotesque in art   2. Art, Victorian – Great Britain   3. Art, British
I. Trodd, Colin   II. Barlow, Paul   III. Amigoni, David
709.4'1'09034

Library of Congress Cataloging-in-Publication data

Victorian culture and the idea of the grotesque/
edited by Colin Trodd, Paul Barlow and David Amigoni
　　　p.　cm.
　Includes bibliographical references (p. 197) and index.
　ISBN 1-85928-380-2 (hb : alk. paper)
　　　1. Great Britain–Civilization–19th century.   2. English literature–19th century–History and criticism.   3. Grotesque–Great Britain–History–19th century.   4. Great Britian–History–Victoria, 1837–1901.   5. Grotesque in literature.   6. Grotesque in art.
I. Trodd, Colin, 1959–   . II. Barlow, Paul, 1962–   .
III. Amigoni, David.
DA533.V53   1998
941.081–dc21   98–35002
                                                                              CIP

ISBN 1 85928 380 2

Typeset in Palatino by IML Typographers, Chester

Contents

Acknowledgements		ix
List of contributors		xi
List of figures		xiii
Introduction: Uncovering the grotesque in Victorian culture		1
1	'Borrowing Gargantua's mouth': biography, Bahktin and grotesque discourse – James Boswell, Thomas Carlyle and Leslie Stephen on Samuel Johnson *David Amigoni*	21
2	Thomas Carlyle's grotesque conceits *Paul Barlow*	37
3	Culture and energy: Ford Madox Brown, Thomas Carlyle and the Cromwellian grotesque *Colin Trodd*	61
4	'Griffinism, grace and all': the riddle of the grotesque in John Ruskin's *Modern Painters* *Lucy Hartley*	81
5	Grotesque obscenities: Thomas Woolner's *Civilization* and its discontents *Paul Barlow*	97
6	'Entangled banks': Robert Browning, Richard Dadd and the Darwininan grotesque *Nicola Bown*	119

7	Monsters and monstrosities: grotesque taste and Victorian design *Shelagh Wilson*	143
8	Turning back the grotesque: G.F. Watts, the matter of painting and the oblivion of art *Colin Trodd*	173
Bibliography		197
Index		207

All art consists in being dazzled by the truth: the light upon the grotesque mask as it shrinks back is true, and nothing else.

Kafka

Acknowledgements

The editors would like to thank the following for their valuable assistance in this project: Liz Astandoust, **Stephanie Brown**, Fiorna Cairns Smith, Colin Campbell, Hugh Dixon, **Jan Dodshon**, Trisha Dodsworth, Edna Edwards, Richard Jefferies, Joan Jones, Libby Kemp, Francis Law, Alison Lloyd, Janet Mclean, Rose Pearson, Susan Smith.

Contributors

DAVID AMIGONI lectures in English at Keele University and is reviews editor of the *Journal of Victorian Culture*. He is the author of many essays and articles on Victorian culture, whose most recent publications include *Victorian Biography and the Ordering of Discourse* (Harvester-Wheatsheaf, 1994) and *Re-Reading Darwin*, co-edited with Geoff Wallace (Manchester University Press, 1995). Currently completing research concerning Darwin, Wordsworth and ecology, he is also writing a manuscript which addresses Victorian ideas about literature, science and culture.

PAUL BARLOW is Lecturer in the History of Art at the University of Northumbria at Newcastle. He has published widely on many aspects of Victorian art, aesthetics and cultural theory. His most recent publications include essays on the formation of the National Portrait Gallery and Ford Madox Brown's Manchester Murals. He is currently preparing for publication a book on Holman Hunt and problems of pictorial space in mid-Victorian painting. In addition, essays on Millais, Leighton and Henry O'Neil appear in 1999. Future plans include a book on the interplay between Carlylean culture and Victorian art, and *Governing Cultures: Institutions of Art in Victorian London*, a volume of essays to be co-edited with Colin Trodd.

NICOLA BOWN, who lectures in the History of Art at the University of Birmingham, received her doctorate from the University of Sussex in 1997. Her essay in this collection is part of a wider research project involving the interplay between literary, artistic and scientific discourses in the formation of Victorian fairy culture.

LUCY HARTLEY lectures in English Language and Literature at Southampton University. She is currently revising her doctoral thesis, *Physiognomic*

Perceptions: Science and the Natural Order in Nineteenth-Century England (University of Oxford, 1996), for publication. The essay in this collection is part of a study of national ethics and national art in the Victorian period.

COLIN TRODD is Senior Lecturer in the History of Art at the University of Sunderland. The author of a number of articles and essays on nineteenth-century art, culture and cultural institutions, he is currently co-editing *Academic Cultures*, to be published by Manchester University Press in 1999. Recent publications include 'The Authority of Art: Cultural Criticism and the Idea of the Royal Academy in Mid-Victorian Britain' in *Art History* (1997) and 'The Laboured Vision and the Realm of Value: Articulations of Identity in Ford Madox Brown's *Work*' in E. Harding (ed.), *Reframing the Pre-Raphaelites* (Scolar, 1996). He is at present writing a work that addresses problems associated with the institutionalization of visual culture in England between 1850 and 1890.

SHELAGH WILSON is Senior Lecturer in Design History at the University of Northumbria at Newcastle. Her wide range of research and publication interests include the Victorian jewellery trade in Birmingham and the connections between fast food, modernism and design culture. She is currently writing a book on nineteenth-century societies devoted to the promotion of contracts between art, commerce and trade.

Figures

2 Thomas Carlyle's grotesque conceits

2.1 E. J. Sullivan, 'Teufelsdröckh in Monmouth Street', 1898, illustration to Carlyle's *Sartor Resartus*

2.2 E. J. Sullivan, 'The Flourishing of the Fleur de Lis (Marie and Marat)', 1910, illustration to Carlyle's *The French Revolution*

2.3 E. J. Sullivan, 'The Sword of Damocles', 1910, illustration to Carlyle's *The French Revolution*

3 Culture and energy: Ford Madox Brown, Thomas Carlyle and the Cromwellian grotesque

3.1 Ford Madox Brown, *St. Ives AD 1630: Cromwell on his Farm*, 1874, oil on canvas, 141 × 105.5 cm, The Board of Trustees of the National Museums and Galleries on Merseyside (Lady Leverhulme Gallery, Port Sunlight)

3.2 Ford Madox Brown, *Cromwell, Protector of the Vaudois*, 1877, oil on canvas, 86 ×107 cm, Manchester City Art Galleries

3.3 George Cattermole, *Cromwell Viewing the Body of Charles I*, 1841, engraving

3.4 George Cattermole, *Cromwell Consulting the Lawyers*, 1841, engraving

4 'Griffinism, grace and all': the riddle of the grotesque in John Ruskin's *Modern Painters*

4.1 Ruskin's Theory of Art (diagram)

4.2 John Ruskin, 'Noble and Ignoble Grotesque', from *The Stones of Venice*

4.3 John Ruskin, 'True and False Griffins', from *The Stones of Venice*

5 Grotesque obscenities: Thomas Woolner's *Civilization* and its discontents

5.1 Thomas Woolner, *Puck*, 1847, engraving

5.2 Thomas Woolner, *Civilization*, 1856–1866, Wallington Hall, Northumberland

5.3 Thomas Woolner, *Civilization*, detail: 'Druids Sacrificing Victims in a Wicker Cage'

5.4 Thomas Woolner, *Civilization*, detail: 'Barbaric family group'

5.5 Thomas Woolner, *Civilization*, detail: 'Attacking charioteer'

XIV FIGURES

5. 6 F. W. Fairholt, 'Illustrations of Medieval Grotesques', from T. Wright, *A History of Caricature and Grotesque*, 1863–1865

5. 7 The O'Shea Brothers, *For Scolding Women*, c1863, Manchester Assize Courts

5. 8 John Ruskin, 'Grotesques from Rouen Cathedral', from *The Seven Lamps of Architecture*

6 'Entangled banks': Robert Browning, Richard Dadd and the Darwinian grotesque

6. 1 Richard Dadd, *The Fairy Feller's Master-Stroke*, 54 × 39 cm, c1855–1864, Tate Gallery, London

6. 2 Richard Dadd, *Songe de la Fantasie*, 38 × 31.5 cm, 1864, Fitzwilliam Museum, Cambridge

7 Monsters and monstrosities: grotesque taste and Victorian design

7. 1 Robert Wallace Martin, *Grotesque Fountain*, detail, 1906, Pitshanger Museum, Ealing

7. 2 Robert Wallace Martin, *Grotesque Fountain*, detail, Pitshanger Museum, Ealing

7. 3 The Martin Brothers, *Examples of Martin Ware*, 1882, engraving

7. 4 Earrings made from mounted humming birds, c1875

7. 5 H. Ploucquet, *The Schoolmaster at Home*, tableau exhibited at the Great Exhibition, 1851

7. 6 'Man-eating tiger mounted as an Arm Chair', from *The Strand* magazine, 1896

7. 7 'Types of animal furniture', illustration from *The Strand* magazine, 1896

7. 8 Majolica glazed 'Vulcan and Python' teapot, 1879

7. 9 Henry Cole, design for a tea service, c1845

7. 10 Design for a grotesque gas bracket, 1849

7. 11 Christopher Dresser, *Old Bogey*, 1867

7. 12 Contrasting grotesque frogs: (a) Christopher Dresser's *Frog Frieze*, 1871 and (b) Wallace Martin's *Frog*, c1900

7. 13 E. J. Sullivan, 'Omar with the Ungainly Vessels', illustration to Fitzgerald's *The Rubáiyát of Omar Khayyám*, 1913

8 Turning back the grotesque: G. F. Watts, the matter of painting and the oblivion of art

8. 1 G. F. Watts, *She Shall be Called Woman*, oil on canvas, 257.8 × 116.8 cm, c1875–1892, Tate Gallery, London

8. 2 G. F. Watts, *Experientia Docet: Tasting the First Oyster*, oil on canvas, 72 × 93 cm, 1885, Watts Gallery, Compton, Surrey

8. 3 G. F. Watts, *Love and Death*, oil on canvas, 151 × 75 cm, 1875, Bristol City Art Gallery

8. 4 G. F. Watts, *The Sower of the Systems*, oil on canvas, 66 × 53 cm, 1902, Watts Gallery, Compton, Surrey

8. 5 G. F. Watts, *Eve Repentant*, oil on canvas, 257.8 × 116.8 cm, 1892, Watts Gallery, Compton, Surrey

8. 6 G. F. Watts, *Evolution*, oil on canvas, 70 × 64.5 cm, c1890–1895, Watts Gallery, Compton, Surrey

8. 7 G. F. Watts, *The Genius of Greek Poetry*, oil on canvas, 66 × 53.3 cm, c1857–1878, Watts Gallery, Compton, Surrey

Introduction:
Uncovering the grotesque in Victorian culture

Colin Trodd, Paul Barlow, David Amigoni

Fascinated by the competing definitions of the grotesque in Victorian culture – its oscillation between the quotidian and the numinous, its representation as growth, vitality and power, its association with the decay of form, its articulation as the buried body of historical meaning, its correspondence with biological development, its presentation as the violation of beauty, its definition as worthless elaboration, its registration as incoherent intensity or energy – this book examines the critical spaces in which cultural discourse generates interpretations of the marginal, the aberrant, the uncanny, the liminal, the vital and the excessive. As such, the essays that follow are at once historical and theoretical: they examine the articulation, circulation and organization of the grotesque in order to uncover the processes that enabled it to hover between different cultural and social registers. Linked by a desire to engage with the complex nature of the grotesque and its discursive spaces, the contributors to this book seek to disinter the subject, thus to explain its significance within modern cultural history.

In addition to re-theorizing well-known and established subjects, this book deals with a range of little-known, under-researched and extremely important archival materials. By examining painting, sculpture, poetry, literature and design; by engaging with art criticism, cultural history, literary history, historical biography, evolutionary biology and design theory, the authors seek to render the grotesque less obscure, thus demonstrating its entanglement in social, aesthetic, scientific and political thought. Writing across different disciplines, the authors knit together a multiplicity of grotesques: the grotesque as violating profusion; the grotesque as stylized body; the grotesque as cultural critique; the grotesque as primal force; the grotesque as physical mutation. Each essay deals with the double identity of the grotesque as imprisonment and liberation, elimination and elaboration; and this recognition that there is no locus of the grotesque enables contributors to examine its paradoxical nature as the movement between, and mingling of, opposites.

We have approached the grotesque by acknowledging the idiosyncrasies it generated in Victorian culture. Although the following essays present original research, we have, each in our own way, recognized the highly selective nature of this project. We have tried, in other words, to do justice to our subject by resisting some of its most obvious manifestations: Hood's use of the grotesque 'comic-vernacular' in the popular literature of the 1830s; Rossetti's use of the 'Faustian' grotesque in his early graphic work; Dickens's realist transmutation of caricature as monstrosity; Gustav Doré's conflation of grotesque illustration and London topography; Beardsley's extraordinarily knowing assimilation of the grotesque and aestheticism; the 'monster' literature of the 1890s. We realize that other authors might have given prominence to these themes, but we have deliberately selected a set of topics that enable us to study the elliptical profusions and mutations of this most mutant of cultural forms. Because the contributors to this volume have not set out to produce a survey of 'the grotesque' as a cultural term in Victorian society, the result is a book that, mirroring the nature of the grotesque aesthetic, is intensive rather than comprehensive, detailed rather than definitive. We look closely and critically, but we certainly have not exhausted this archival network.

Nevertheless, the essays in this volume do seek to identify interlocking, or at least interrelated, problems and to uncover in the archive material which offers access to points of difficulty within Victorian cultural experience. The multiple and aberrant nature of the grotesque as a cultural phenomenon places it in a problematic position as an evaluative, or even descriptive, term. As an aesthetic of the *irreconcilable*, the grotesque here is construed not simply as an aesthetic position or method adopted by writers and artists, but as a means to realize experience which tends to overwhelm, or fundamentally to dismember, representations. For this reason several essays consider the problem of the 'Victorian' itself as a cultural label, a means to name the cultural forms of nineteenth-century Britain. As Shelagh Wilson points out in Chapter 7, for Modernist designers the Victorian *was* grotesque, a point of aberrance, incoherent profusion and stylistic incongruity. It was an 'impossible' experience of taste.

Philip Thomson, identifying the grotesque as 'the unresolved clash of incompatibles in work and response', claims that it is characteristic of cultural moments when inconsistency is experienced without a faith in the dynamic of transformation itself, when irresolution and duality are the content of the experience.[1] Fragmentation without disintegration, in which each fragment stands equally present and in which stasis is forced on contradiction: this is a powerful form through which Victorian commentators and artists represented their cultural condition. Carlyle is in this respect the presiding genius of the grotesque. His protean personifications (monster, chimera, satirist, sage) appear throughout this book, and are discussed in detail by David Amigoni, Paul Barlow and Colin Trodd. Unable to identify a knowable logic in history, he stands against the figure of Marx, for whom contradiction was subject to science, which knew it and harnessed it. As Paul Barlow argues, for Carlyle modernity was grotesque precisely because contradiction collapsed claims to knowledge, constantly generating the form of its own perversion. Carlyle's work invites both humour and horror, neither response being adequate nor effacing the other. To quote Thomson's definition of grotesque writing again, it insists on 'a confusion between a sense of the comic and something – revulsion, horror, fear – which is incompatible with the comic.'[2] Thomson is commenting on Kafka, but he points to a problem necessary to the appreciation of the Carlylean grotesque, the oscillation between the monstrous and the ridiculous.

This oscillation arises from the complex history of 'grotesque' as an aesthetic category. In marking the continuing and shifting significance of this category, it is necessary to address the cultural dynamics that Carlyle, Marx, Ruskin and their contemporaries encountered. To think about the historical semantics of the grotesque one can turn to the work of Raymond Williams. As we will suggest, Williams all but overlooks the term; but he does present us with a framework for thinking about the ways in which words can be either activated or marginalized by cultural formations. For Williams the vocabulary of 'culture and society' consists of clusters of words which might originally have had quite particular or specialized meanings, but which, from the beginning of the nineteenth century, came increasingly to vary in meaning as they became organized by separate domains – principally 'art' and 'society' – which underpinned urgent debates over value.[3] For Williams, it was important to trace the relationship between words, their variable meanings, and those historically specific mediating formations through which 'different ... distributions of energy and interest' were deployed.[4] But given the predominantly social-realist formations that Williams himself extended, the 'grotesque' was not represented as active in Williams's influential account of the 'culture and society' tradition and its Victorian origins.

Yet, active it had been, in England and elsewhere. During the 1960s American-based scholars such as Frances K. Barasch were alert to this activity, acknowledging the significance of the term for formations such as the New Critics. Barasch dealt with historical semantics in a way strikingly similar to Williams in suggesting that 'new perceptions and conceptions of the grotesque occurred with every new generation of artists and critics; each created its own grotesque art, understood the past in its own way, and invested the word with its own meanings'.[5]

Barasch's studies of the historical semantics of the 'grotesque' – in her book,

The Grotesque: A Study in Meanings (1971), and her introduction to the reprint of a book by the Victorian antiquarian Thomas Wright, *A History of Caricature and Grotesque in Literature and Art* (1968) – trace a history of active and transforming meanings. Like Thomson and other commentators, Barasch locates the coining of the 'grotesque' and the aesthetic that it came to evaluate in the fifteenth century and the discovery of the fantastic hybrid images adorning the reopened ancient Roman Titus Baths. By the fifteenth century these ancient structures were well below street level, and so came to be associated with underground grottoes. The semantics of 'grotesque' (literally 'grotto-like') continued to be informed by this connection with the grotto.[6] The hybrid forms discovered in the Titus baths led to the association of the grotesque with both antiquity and fantastic artistic licence. Even at this point, the term began to connote different values depending on its field of aesthetic activity: following the recycled Classicist strictures of Vitruvius the term develops pejorative, decadent associations in architectural theory, whilst in painting Vasari, in *Lives of the Painters*, accepts it as a legitimate style.[7] This classical grotesque, identified by its wilful rejection of proper continuities in the representation of objects, may be said to have provided the conditions for the later association between the grotesque and caricature which was of such importance to Wright, working in the 1860s. Here nature is reduced to fractions or signs of objects, their elimination of material density permitting a dislocation from real experience. This form of fancy was specifically to be rejected by Ruskin, for whom Raphael's grotesques in the Vatican constituted a form of amorality, or refusal to encounter the necessary struggle to constitute fact as image.[8] Nevertheless, Ruskin's own account of the grotesque as disordered conflations of fragmentary knowledge ultimately draws on these originating instances of the grotesque.

The ambivalence of monstrosity and humour may be said to emerge from this uncertain relation between the grotesque and the real, a concern of crucial importance to Ruskin and Carlyle. The late Renaissance forms of the grotesque did however provide another important source for Victorian articulations of the category. As Naomi Miller points out in her book *Heavenly Caves*, by the sixteenth century the Classical grotesque had generated forms of grotto and fountain design in which fantastical shapes were connected to imagery of natural prodigality, dynamic and generative processes which reordered and expanded given forms. Here mythic figures were combined with the oddities of nature (bizarre animals, fungal growths). Figures, creatures and strange motifs would adhere to walls, covered in plastered 'calcification'. Aggressive vitality would be signalled in demonic forms spurting water. Such grottoesque motifs provide the origin of conceptions of the grotesque as violent deformity, notions which began to take their modern form in the nineteenth century. These images had, however, a pre-Renaissance origin, derived from

Gothic marginalia, bestiaries and the gargoyles of fifteenth-century cathedrals.[9] For Victorian culture, in which the debate between the Gothic and the Classical was crucial, these conflations of Gothic structures with Classical forms became a point of contention: themselves a moment of unresolved contradiction.

The Renaissance grotto provided a means to name the Gothic itself as grotesque, to return the term to a point prior to the discovery of the Classical decorations valued by Raphael and Vasari. Victorian critics of architecture and design consistently described the use of the gargoyle and of humorous or bizarre imagery in decoration as 'grotesque'. The phrase 'grotesque architecture' does continue to suggest fanciful grottoes and other garden designs into the early nineteenth century, but by the Victorian moment (from about 1840), 'grotesque' is predominantly associated with the use of decoration in Gothic revival buildings, in which Ruskin was very closely concerned.[10] The grotesque here becomes entwined in complex and varied ways with the claims of Ruskin regarding the function of the pre-industrial craftsman and, in particular, with the identities of the labourer and of undeveloped or incomplete modes of consciousness. The complexity of this function of the grotesque is discussed here in the contributions of Lucy Hartley and Colin Trodd.

The Renaissance grotto is also, however, a crucial historical condition for the application of the concept of the grotesque to the forms of natural excess discussed by Nicola Bown in Chapter 6. Bown's supple commentary on the Darwinian grotesque in art and literature draws attention to its articulation through the violence, bodily transformation and flows of natural energy that Renaissance grottoes and fountains realized. Paul Barlow's accounts of the sculptures of Woolner and the O'Sheas mark the same connection, as does Shelagh Wilson's analysis of the grotesque fountain constructed by the anti-Darwinian potter Wallace Martin. Wilson also emphasizes the importance granted to the 'scientific' interest in natural history evidenced in the Renaissance grotto, in particular with the influence of the sixteenth-century ceramicist and grotto designer Bernard Palissy, lauded by the Victorians as an heroic Protestant martyr and as a pioneer natural scientist.[11] The grotesque, then, provided a means to visualize the aesthetic form of the new natural sciences, having since the Renaissance itself provided the models for the incorporation into its structures of fossils, growths and apparently aberrant bodily configurations.

In literature, the grotesque has experienced a slightly different history, but one equally important to the development of its Victorian formations. In *Keywords* Williams notes the complex relations of many English words to their continental originals,[12] and Barasch's researches into the semantics of the 'grotesque' yield a similar insight. The first recorded English usage occurs in a 1561 inventory in which it is still restricted to visual art, describing the style of paintings given to the Royal Household, and spelled in the French form, 'crotesque'. In 1598 John Florio, in *A Worlde of Words*, continued to treat 'grotesque' as though it were a foreign word.[13] In line with Florio's position, 'grotesque' was regularly translated as 'anticke' in English until the actual word started to be used in the seventeenth century, but with many of its original discriminations intact. Sir Henry Wotton's use of the term in 1624 (*The Elements of Architecture*) finds the grotesque acceptable in painting but not in architecture.[14] Here, again, early usage refers to the visual arts. The English 'anticke', however, had more extended use. In its Shakespearean sense of 'mad' and as the origin of the modern word 'antique', its connotations signal the relevance of the grotesque to the forms of word-play and deliberate linguistic archaisms characteristic of Shakespearean and Metaphysical literature, which were themselves important sources for the grotesque styles later to be adopted by Carlyle and Browning.[15]

Barasch traces two crucial developments in the seventeenth century which came to have important ramifications for the eighteenth and nineteenth centuries. First, 'grotesque' developed a figurative sense in English, meaning 'monstrous' or 'fantastic'.[16] It thus came to absorb some of the broader connotations of 'anticke'. It also, more specifically, became increasingly associated with satirical characterization in drama as well as the visual arts – a trend in low humour that came to be particularly strong in the eighteenth century. Second, endowed with figurative mobility, the 'grotesque' began to penetrate other spheres of thought and discourse.[17] Upon arrival in another sphere, the grotesque could be evaluated quite differently, as was the case with literary criticism and poetry, where grotesque motifs were sometimes held to be 'transparent shrouds for moral meaning, not merely created to achieve spectacular effects'.[18] This increasing critical seriousness was further reflected in Burke's division of the grotesque into the sublime and ridiculous in *On the Sublime and Beautiful* (1757).[19] But, as Barasch points out, this seriousness should be set alongside the simultaneous development of popular forms of caricature in the eighteenth century also known as 'grotesque'.

Barasch's 1968 genealogy of the grotesque aims at uncovering the meanings at play in one of the most important Victorian studies of the grotesque, Thomas Wright's book *A History of Caricature and Grotesque in Literature and Art*, chapters from which appeared as articles in the *Art Journal* during 1863, but which was published in full in 1865. Barasch argues that when Wright was constructing his field, 'grotesque' and 'caricature' – 'key words' as Barasch refers to them – were closely related terms, a merger consequent upon widespread and divergent uses of the word 'grotesque' in the seventeenth century. Moreover, a sense of the theory and practice of caricature in the eighteenth century (which Wright knew in scholarly depth) is another meaning of 'grotesque' at work in the book, as, in addition, is Wright's anthropological sense of the grotesque as a manifestation of the human instinct for mirth and satire.

What we see in Wright's book, with the aid of both the researches of Barasch and Williams's framework, is the presence of historical formations which have elaborated and put in circulation various meanings of the grotesque. By the date at which Wright published his book, these formations had developed into a number of powerfully contending accounts. Wright's own work emerges from antiquarian traditions. Working with his colleague and illustrator William Fairholt, Wright's procedure was to collect a 'cabinet of curiosities': to construe history as an accumulation of moments of eccentricity, of deviations from a given norm. As antiquaries, Wright and Fairholt's research is defined by encounters with the 'antique' – a concept which at this time still retained elements of its origin in 'anticke'. Writing books on such subjects as *Eccentric and Remarkable Characters* (Fairholt, 1849), or *Gog and Magog, the Giants of Whitehall* (Fairholt, 1859), in addition to their various studies of the grotesque itself, Wright and Fairholt's antiquarian scholarship forms part of an important strand of Victorian thinking, one which stems from Scott's *Antiquary* and which stretches through Dickens's *Old Curiosity Shop* and even into the late Victorian city of Sherlock Holmes.[20] The grotesque is interwoven with this antiquarian discourse in varied ways. Wright's version of the antiquarian grotesque constructs a demotic history, addressing the popular and the (often literally) marginal. In seeking to conflate antiquarian traditions with an anthropological account of universal human needs and pleasures, Wright takes his place alongside Dickens, in whose work the grotesque is similarly allied to a humanist ethic, which seeks in deviations and eccentricities a means to destabilize the rationalizing and systematizing functions of the bureaucratic systems of knowledge.

This use of the grotesque to identify instabilities in knowledge as spectacle is closely related to the idea of the city (Carlyle's famous image of a monstrous hat trundling through London streets). Oscillations between spectacular disturbances of social space and processes of containment function in contending 'humanistic' and 'scientific' claims, evident in the tensions at work in the projects of Stephen, Carlyle and Cole, as discussed here by David Amigoni, Paul Barlow and Shelagh Wilson. Sherlock Holmes, the 'scientific' detective, is continually assailed by the antiquarian grotesque: endless quirks and oddities which threaten to overwhelm systematic analysis. In the 'Adventure of Wisteria Lodge' Holmes identifies his task as the study of the grotesque, for 'the grotesque often deepens into the criminal'.[21] Grotesque criminality forces him to displace scientific system for antiquarianism in order to counter this threat. Bizarre incidents and inexplicable fractions of fact are reconstituted as knowledge by drawing on a store of increasingly esoteric learning. Doyle's stories were first published in *The Strand* magazine, which consistently maintained a fascination with modern 'cabinets of curiosities', as Shelagh Wilson here shows.[22]

By the nineteenth century, then, the forms through which the concept 'grotesque' had passed were remarkable for their fissiparous multiplicity, generating their own tensions and contradictions: the condition of the category itself. The association of the term with forms of popular satirical drama and caricature continued. Comic and novelty entertainments are commonly advertised as 'grotesque' performances in the mid-century.[23] The seriousness with which the grotesque began to be treated as a form of allegory also developed its own dynamic. Much of the writing on this theme derives from the influence of German philosophy and critical theory, which sought to incorporate the grotesque into Romantic aesthetics. Burke's association of the grotesque with the problem of the sublime is developed by the Schlegels and others. The work of Wolfgang Kayser and Lee Jennings has explored these ideas in detail.[24] For Victorian culture, the importance of this connection is complex and varied. Early Victorian thinking on the grotesque often associates it with Germanic culture. Carlylean grotesque owes much to Jean Paul Richter and to Hoffmann, a connection discussed by David Amigoni in Chapter 1. Likewise, the influence of German illustration in a neo-Gothic style was strong in the 1840s and was associated with the popularity of supernatural and folk literature, influences which are clearly evident in publications such as S.C. Hall's *Book of British Ballads* (1842), to which Richard Dadd, discussed in Chapter 6 by Nicola Bown, contributed his early grotesque illustrations. Opponents of the early work of the Pre-Raphaelites likewise sought to associate their style with the eccentricities of pre-Renaissance Germanic and Netherlandish art.

All these associations emerge from Romantic critiques of Classical aesthetics, and from attempts to identify alternative aesthetic forms that mark cultural complexity and multiplicity. Drawing on the work of the Schlegels and Hegel, Victor Hugo's seminal Preface to *Cromwell* (1827) attacks the Aristotelian dramatic unities, identifying in Shakespeare an anti-Classical theatre of the grotesque. The importance of Hugo's ideas in relation to the work of Carlyle and F.M. Brown is examined in depth by Colin Trodd in Chapter 3. Trodd traces intricate patterns of aesthetic and political allegiance into which the violating figure of Cromwell intrudes as the embodiment of inescapable but aberrant energy.

The political implications of this Romantic grotesque are also explored by Lucy Hartley, David Amigoni and Paul Barlow. In a sense, Carlyle's is a radical attempt to affiliate the antiquarian and Romantic grotesque, seeking to drag from aggregations of oddities which constitute the antiquarian gaze the dynamic and clashing 'presence of things'. This connection between the grotesque and the political is closely allied to the imagery that emerged from the late eighteenth century, especially from the forms of caricature discussed by Wright, in which the grotesque becomes a tool of party conflict and a mark of the desanctification of authority, a point which led Wright to associate the prevalence of caricature and the grotesque with liberal society.[25] For Wright, as for Dickens and Brown, the grotesque realism of Hogarth's paintings and prints provides the aesthetic model for a modern, critical and engaged culture fusing the popular and the serious.[26]

However, it is important to note that the antiquarian grotesque functions in tandem with imagery of the eruptions and contradictions generated by the dynamics of socio-political radicalism and industrialization. For Ruskin, industrial Manchester was to be imagined as an alien, irreconcilable growth on the body of the nation, turning nature against itself. Carlyle and Marx both used the concept of the grotesque to describe the perverse experience of objects constituted by advertising and commodification.[27] For Carlyle, as Paul Barlow suggests in Chapter 2, mechanization and mobility engendered a deranged 'dance' of arbitrary social fragmentation and recombination.

Both conservative and liberal imagery often uses the grotesque against the picturesque.[28] The integrated, panoramic variety of the picturesque scene is replaced by the multiple, shape-shifting forms of modernity. Assertive forms of urban, lower-class identity and popular culture are described as grotesque destabilizations of the panoramic picturesque gaze. This political function of the grotesque aesthetic has been discussed in detail by Isobel Armstrong in her substantial study of Victorian poetry and aesthetics.[29] For the contributors to this book, however, this account of the grotesque as a form of energy that continually violates and intrudes on the orderly surface of social experience is connected to other Victorian experiences of radical ruptures in the social and cultural ordering of things. Colin Trodd analyses the attempts by G.F. Watts to construct an aesthetic which resanctified – and so Classicized – as authoritative the necessary violence and gross physicality of Evolution. Likewise, Lucy Hartley and Nicola Bown examine the dense relationship between theories of organic growth and the logics of classification and codification, a problem, in different ways, for both Ruskin and Darwin.

For Darwin – as for Leslie Stephen and Sherlock Holmes – the grotesque was a continual threat to his scientific claims. As Gillian Beer has pointed out, the 'ludicrous' idea that one animal might become another led Darwin's critics to satirize passages such as the one in which he appears to claim that a bear could easily turn into a whale.[30] These were identified quite specifically as flights of fancy, a fantastical jumbling and dismembering of real forms. Ruskin's attack on Raphael's grotesques adopts the same logic as Professor Sedgwick's denunciations of Darwin and of the pre-Darwinian evolutionist Robert Chambers, author of *Vestiges of Creation*:[31] arrogant fantasy, disregard for the real, wilfulness. Sedgwick finds *The Origin of Species* both repulsive and hilarious, sliding between caricature and monstrosity.³² This sense of the danger of the grotesque, lying in the tension between libertine speculation and obedient reverence for fact, is shared by such diverse texts as *The Origin, Sartor Resartus* and *The Hound of the Baskervilles*.

Darwin's comments on sexual selection in *The Descent of Man* also occupy this hazardous terrain. He treads warily when invoking the grotesque, suggesting that apparently strange, excessive bodily growths in some animals may have developed from female experience of 'beauty' in males competing to attract them. Apparently grotesque distortions of European ideas of beauty serve a comparable purpose, for example, the tattooed faces of Maoris. More bizarrely, African tribesmen knock out their front teeth, giving the face 'a hideous appearance owing to the prominence of the lower jaw; but these people think the presence of the incisors most unsightly, and on beholding some Europeans, cried out, "Look at the great teeth!"'³³ In such accounts of clashing cultural identities the grotesque slides uncertainly between a description of *experience* – the encounter with radically alien aesthetic values – and the ascription of distortion and aberrance to 'savage' identity itself.³⁴ This anthropological ambivalence is also implicit in Ruskin's theorization of the psychology of the grotesque, as discussed by Lucy Hartley. It is present in Victorian anxieties about the proper ordering of taste and physicality in design, analysed by Shelagh Wilson in Chapter 7, and is central to Woolner's attempt to visualize the clash of 'civilized' and 'barbaric' aesthetics, described by Paul Barlow in Chapter 5.

The grotesque, then, was connected to problems of orderliness, legitimacy and cultural debasement. As an aesthetic practice and critical category it was judged in relation to orders of art and the legitimacy of modes of knowledge. Although few commentators denied its application or veracity within specific contexts, its wider legitimacy was often associated with lowly genres or popular culture. If most critics of the grotesque were concerned to control the nature of its appearance, this arose from their desire to monitor the places of its articulation. It is therefore useful to consider in some detail Victorian critical commentary on the grotesque which attempts to theorize some of the cultural difficulties we have just outlined.

The process of resisting the lure of the grotesque is noticeable in the writings of Arnold, Lewes and Bagehot, three of the most distinguished critics in the period between 1850 and 1875. The articulation of the grotesque as a sign of the ruination of authentic culture by a sentimental, democratic popular realism – a realism which seeks experiential plenitude through the swarming of expressive detail – is caught by G.H. Lewes in his 1872 essay 'Dickens in Relation to Criticism', published in the *Fortnightly Review*. Dickens, we are informed, lacking the capacity to make proper judgements, is obliged to produce a fantastic, delusional art of power and fantasy. He is not much of a thinker; his work is galvanized by the visions it records. This hallucinatory intensity generates an art rich in imaginative detail, but weak in psychological insight. However, his genius, which is also a form of deception, is the communication to a body of readers of the imagery of his imagination as the *subject* of art. His writing makes vivid the contents of his mind to his audience in a form of seductive rapture: 'He presented [his vision] in such relief that we ceased to think of it as a picture. So definite and insistent was the image, that even while knowing it was false we could not help, for a moment, being affected, as it were, by his hallucination.'[35]

Lewes's position is not simply that Dickens is attracted to deformity, but that his is a deforming aesthetic: it is because his demonstration of human character is portrayed with 'a mingled verisimilitude' that he cannot detect the difference between the grotesque and his own 'grotesqueness'.[36] He is simply unaware that he is infected by his own art; his representations of the world coil round his self-referential imagination; his expansive but inarticulate vision leads to the erosion of conceptual power.

It should be noted that one of the characteristics of this reading is its tendency to sever Dickens from those transformative powers Ruskin and Carlyle associated with the grotesque. For Lewes, the vitality of a Dickens novel denotes mechanical repetition, non-reflexive action. Here the grotesque is a form of policing or suppressing of life as natural growth. 'His characters', claims Lewes, 'are so predictable' that one is reminded of the 'frogs whose brains have been taken out for physiological purposes, and whose actions henceforth want the distinctive peculiarity of organic action, that of fluctuating spontaneity ... It is this complexity of the organism which Dickens wholly fails to conceive; his characters have nothing fluctuating and incalculable in them.'[37]

However, a certain image of organic form is re-introduced by Lewes in order to confirm that Dickens assimilates life into formulaic movement. In this sense excessive imaginative power is taken to lead, not to extraordinary creative vision, but to the obsessional conflation of the individual life with the representative type. Dickens's devotion to the grotesque suppresses Life in the name of Order. It is, therefore, a desire to standardize and organize even as it pursues apparent differences. Dickens denudes life of its authentic vitality by transmuting it into the false vitalism of his art. At the same time, Lewes's desire to see in the grotesque the imprisoning of life by the reproduction of mechanical form is made by a language that insists on the uncanny nature of Dickens's vision. Dickens's reduction of character to automata is also an alchemical process in which dull matter is vivified. In this world where representation is given a ludic intensity, subjects are bearers of an invisible materialism; objects are transmuted into radiant forms. And yet, in this penetration of matter, Lewes discovers the essential confusion and grotesqueness of Dickens's art. Bringing to the surface of life the internal forms of the body, Dickens cannot express psychological motivation, the critical object of literature, because his art is 'a reckless twisting of known facts into impossible relations', the creation of a 'jumbled web' of endless entanglements.[38] Failing to produce a clear articulation of the relationship between physiological structures and cognitive patterns, his art entangles subjects in the skeins of habit that are their bodies. Personality is reduced to the mechanical facticity of behaviour, character becomes the repetition of organic life at the level of action, and subjects are conflated with the structures they are taken to carry.

If Dickens reduces the living density of the individual to the performative rhetoric of the self, a self that is endlessly staged as a concatenation of dramatic acts, this is because he has lost himself in a landscape of 'masks', 'caricatures' and 'distortions'.[39] Losing control of the authentic resources of literary culture, Dickens is trapped by a grotesque art that cannot express the real connection between surface and depth. Or again, unable to establish a proper division between the sentient and the inert – desiring, instead, to democratize matter – Dickens is subsumed by a process that moves between the mechanical and the organic, mingling life and its representation in a confused amalgam of the animate and the inanimate.

For Lewes, the failure of Dickens's art lies in the intensity of his vision: the appalling power of his grotesqueness derives from the mysterious fusion of the image and the world it ostensibly represents; the attempt to capture the complexity of life transmutes art into a fragmented structure, a disfiguring form. His use of 'verisimilitude' not only mingles the real and the fantastic, it also entangles his reader within his optic; and the visual intensity of such art is compounded by the formal incoherence of a method that is as sensible, rational and intelligible as the stylistic conjunction of the invention of Michelangelo and the drawing of Giotto.[40] This assimilation of creative power by primitive vision is identified as the manifestation of an 'animal intelligence'; Dickens's attempt at the 'bourgeois epic' degenerates through his 'exquisite susceptibility to the grotesque'.[41]

Lewes's dislike of the grotesque, which he identifies as an ineluctable expression of popular culture, is also found in the writings of Bagehot and Arnold, both of whom characterize it as a dominant element within the modern cultural formation. Bagehot's article on Dickens in the *National Review* (1858), emphasizing the 'irregularity and confusion' of his work, adopts the critical framework Lewes was to develop in his reading.[42] At the end of his essay 'Wordsworth, Tennyson and Browning; or, Pure, Ornate and Grotesque Art in English Poetry' (1864), Bagehot continues to look for evidence of the rootedness of such 'miscellaneous' or 'ubiquitous' art in the common culture of Victorian life.[43] Identifying the literary grotesque as a deformed and deforming style, he finds evidence of its disease in the nature of the 'headless'

Victorian middle class. The grotesque mirrors this class because both are aberrant or half-formed: the grotesque, in substituting action for purpose, sanctions the unwarranted fusion of things that should remain separate; the middle class, in surrendering culture for entertainment, supports a sensational rather than an expressive or measured aesthetic. The middle class is grotesque because its expansion is a form of truncation, an erosion of culture, learning and taste. The literary habits of such a class provide the conditions for the manufacture of a parodic and parasitic art of glittering surfaces whose glare traps the reader in its elaborative but depthless spaces. Reading becomes a surrender to effects rather than the experience of values, a surrender to the author as star rather than an engagement with the author as self-effacing sage.[44] It is, he claims, 'singularly characteristic of this age that the poems which rise to the surface should be examples of ornate art and grotesque art, not of pure art. We live in the realm of the *half*-educated.' Grotesque art 'arrests the eye for a moment', but ultimately 'fatigues it'. Unable to emulate the achievements of 'pure' art, this grotesque mode may stimulate excitement, but its fragmented and incoherent nature forces out aesthetic value.[45]

Both Lewes and Bagehot see in the grotesque a cultural, ethical and political failure: it is the registration of action without transformative power or developmental logic (Lewes); it is the fragmentation and proliferation of sensation that denudes experience of its essential character (Bagehot). The generative powers of the grotesque fragment or mutilate representations, weakening their capacity to authenticate forms of knowledge or truth. Dissolving unities, abolishing hierarchies and imploding structures in their endless self-consuming circulation, the entangling forms of the grotesque confirm that modern culture lacks the capacity to articulate a central political body, or a common national culture. For Lewes and Bagehot, popular culture is grotesque because it surrenders authentic aesthetic and ethical values to a mass-produced literature of false intensities in a process that dismembers experience as it is announced.

In *Culture and Anarchy*, Arnold, like Bagehot, associates contemporary middle-class society with the grotesque: its 'illusions' and 'narrow and twisted growth' are responsible, he claims, for the mutilation of humanity.[46] Elsewhere, in two more key texts of this decade, 'On the Study of Celtic Literature' (1867) and 'On Translating Homer' (1861), he, like Lewes, sees in the grotesque a form of manic activity severed from proper thought or coherent meaning. Although Arnold finds the grotesque in the deviant shapes of modernity, he discovers its roots in Celtic culture, of which he writes: 'chafing against the despotism of fact, its perpetual straining after mere emotion, has accomplished nothing'.[47] Identifying Celtic culture as a perverse localism, he sees in its residual manifestations a target for the centralizing logic of the modern nation-state. This double definition of the grotesque – as the instrumentalized form of modernity that deracinates culture and authority; as the residual primitivism that modernity, in the form of the nation-state, must eliminate – is central to Arnold's account of cultural formation.

Arnold's approach to Celtic culture takes the form of presenting a model that accounts for the social marginality of 'Celtic races'. In this reading the primitive is identified as the failure to complete expression or authenticate articulation as unified form. Cultural fragmentation is an analogue of social fragmentation. So, in the spheres of poetry, painting and sculpture, the achievements of the Celts are fragmentary because they turn all their powers to the pursuit of endless elaboration; and consequently the world is imprisoned by the pursuit of technical accomplishment, by the absorption of the matter of art rather than the representation of life. Deficient in the sense of measure, Celtic art is marked by its 'first dash of a quick, strong perception', which results in the conflation of easy sentiment and technical skill.[48] The Celt, he writes, is 'undisciplinable, anarchical, and turbulent by nature';[49] and he generates a self-nihilating art that diminishes the idea of the impalpable in its desire to grasp or picture it. The ideal is defaced by the processes of articulation, and inscription becomes a form of mutation, in a style that, hovering between the real and the ideal, collapses them into pictorial, conceptual and formal confusion.

Although Arnold's peculiar account of the nature of the grotesque is detailed more consistently in *On Translating Homer*, it clearly derives from his need to connect it with cultural and national identity. *On the Study of Celtic Literature* makes a number of truly bizarre assumptions. For instance, ignoring the characteristics of German Romanticism identified by Scott and Carlyle – the wildness of subject matter, the irrationality of its style, its fascination with the dark and uncanny forces of nature – Arnold proposes that the 'German races' are recognized by 'their honest love of fact ... their steadfast pursuit of it [and] their fidelity to nature'.[50] Claiming that German culture is measured, lucid, harmonious and rational, whereas Celtic culture is 'wild', incoherent and deforming, he is obliged to find evidence of this interpretation in contemporary art.[51] At this point he identifies the rather unlikely figure of Sir Joshua Reynolds, the first president of the Royal Academy, with the oblivion that is Celtic culture. Reynolds's failure to accomplish the purest form of composition, he claims, is due to his assimilation by Celtic culture with its devotion to 'magic' and the 'inexpressible'. Like Turner, with whom he is interchangeable in Arnold's text, Reynolds is 'overbalanced by soul and feeling'.[52] Arnold believes that the grotesque quality of such art is occasioned by its inability to overcome the uncertainty it feels in the face of its subject; instead it transmutes this anxiety into the expressive content of the work. The world is buried by a mode of representation that becomes self-directing; this is an art where the need for interpretation is transmuted into the intensity of technique.

It seems perverse that Arnold can find signs of the grotesque in Reynolds, but not in German Romanticism; and it should be remembered that the identification of nature with magic rather than beauty is not a noticeable feature of the *Discourses*. However, although his choices are unconvincing, Arnold's position is, as one would expect, the standard Classical critique of the grotesque: in place of mimetic theory, which selects and combines the beautiful elements of higher nature in order to create an ideal form, the grotesque aesthetic is enchanted by a 'weird power' it will liberate by performing its incantations before common nature.[53] It will fuse, in other words, representation and its subject. It is, of course, this mingling of high art and vulgar matter that he cannot countenance. The grotesque, then, collapses and confuses the difference between art and the world: seeing objects in isolation, it cannot understand, as he writes of the Pre-Raphaelites, 'that the peculiar effect of nature resides in the whole and not in the parts'.[54]

Where Arnold calls for the rejection of the grotesque by an authentic culture rooted in the Classical tradition, other commentators, echoing one of the central claims of *Culture and Anarchy*, see in mid-Victorian society the suppression of cultural tradition by a grotesque modernity. This view of the grotesque as the mutilation of art and its objects could be enforced by examining the characteristics of contemporary culture. Arnold's division between an art that sees the object (Homer) and an art that sees its own style (Pope) is found in readings of modern painting.[55] In the early accounts of Pre-Raphaelitism we find commentators criticizing its elaborative surfaces as examples of ornamental waste or obsessional repetition. Instead of measuring and ordering the world through the deployment of an aesthetic that makes of matter something elegant and harmonious, it is claimed that such images become entangled in the materials of the world, lost in style and buried by an anti-aesthetic that liquidates morality. A tormenting art, Pre-Raphaelitism tears nature into competing, conflicting and confusing elements. Thus in 1852, *The Times*, referring to the 'grotesque illuminations of Mr. Millais and his friends', asserts that Pre-Raphaelite paintings are marked by the 'absence of any real sense of beauty'; that Millais's treatment of Ophelia 'robs' her of 'all pathos and beauty'; that Hunt's *Hireling Shepherd* is 'ludicrous and repulsive'.[56]

Of course, this identification of the grotesque as a form of diseased vitality was not unique to the critical literature surrounding the Pre-Raphaelites. Here one can cite the case of William Blake. If Alexander Gilchrist, Blake's Victorian biographer, set out to rescue his hero from the charge that he was insane, he felt obliged to acknowledge that his work was very often grotesque. His drawing, we are informed, was 'almost always powerful, expressive and sublime, as the sketches of Raffaelle or Albert Durer'.[57] However, many of his productions 'range under the category of the impossible; are crude, contorted, forced, monstrous'.[58] He rescues Blake's imaginative profusion from the charge that it signals madness by claiming that it generates 'incoherence and wildness'.[59] Here the grotesque is the elaboration of formal and stylistic confusion. Blake's art, it would seem, disappears beneath a frantic activity that is always incomplete because it loses itself in its revisionary processes. As profusion is a form of compositional blockage that incites interpretative energy, acting as a barrier to conceptual plenitude, the grotesque is the disfiguring material presence of an image where inscription functions as erasure. Stylistic fecundity generates interpretative mutilation. Expression turns against meaning in an art where bodies are both purely physical and totally spiritual, and where the grotesque is the ruination of matter, the infection of animation. Like many of his contemporaries, Gilchrist is bemused by an art that is at once corporeal and ethereal, an art that is a confusion of opposites, a mingling of contradictory elements. In the face of Blake's inexhaustible stylistic abundance, where energy and substance are one continuous non-volumetric mass, Gilchrist finds a visionary style condemned by the conceits of its ludic form.

Gilchrist, discovering in Blake a transcendental desire imprisoned by its commitment to the corporeal, generates a rhetoric that is more often associated with Victorian attitudes to the religious cultures of non-European societies. Commentators like Ruskin could project the Oriental grotesque as a failure to generate clear articulations of the relationship between the physical and the spiritual, a descent into a mock-metaphysical realm of pure solipsism. From such a premise it was possible to associate such cultures with a form of mindless cultural lassitude, an expressivity that retreats into empty playfulness by playing with ideas of the sacred or the terrible. Or, in the manner of Thomas Wright, the grotesque could be figured in terms of the resilience of the humorous in the face of mere caricature or brutally repulsive representations.

Something resembling a fusion of these two positions is found in Harry Tilly's article on Burmese art, which was published in *The Magazine of Art* (October and November 1892). Tilly defines the grotesque as 'the presentation of a superstition in a half-ludicrous light; that is often a playing with the terrors of religion, and is sometimes a conversion of the innocent forms of nature into symbols of those terrors'.[60] Popular and didactic, the grotesque is authentic when it reaches out to embrace the world through its assimilation into the shared symbolic order of religion. The grotesque is legitimate when it bodies forth 'parables' or registers the nature of evil. However, with the demise of 'personified evil', the grotesque loses its 'inner meaning' and becomes the 'delineation of the outward forms of vice'.[61]

The registration of vice entangles the grotesque in the 'debased' art of caricature.[62] Burmese art, we are informed, deals with the 'grosser forms' of vice.[63] Although the analysis of such art is extremely rudimentary in an essay that eschews the most aggressive attacks on non-European culture, the nature of Tilly's conceptual model is evident from his general response to the artefacts he describes. The fascination with all forms of social experience creates 'excitable and demonstrative' people and a restless, frenetic art.[64] Confronted with such an elaborate style, Tilly retreats into descriptive journalism, avoiding stylistic analysis or critical exposition. It is as if he is trapped by the proliferating energy of this mode of representation. Although Tilly acknowledges that the depiction of the body is the main subject of this form of the grotesque, he seems to conclude that the nature of Burmese culture is to make bodily presence incoherent; that this culture seems to bury authentic art in its conflation of design and form; that it reduces innovation to the repetition of organic confusion; that it substitutes the terrible for the evil. Representation turns away from the world to inhabit its own universe, generating compositions festooned with lattice-like forms where bodies become pulsating skeins of energy or sinuous arabesques.

Such material, which addresses a subject that seems to oscillate between aestheticism and asceticism, points us to the realm of Symbolism and the art of Decadence, where the grotesque is sanctified as the most supremely oxymoronic of forms; that which affirms the absolute physicality and self-directedness of pleasure and desire; that which celebrates individual gratification through the oblivion of social contact. At once of the body and negating public intercourse, the grotesque enters late Victorian discourse as an ambiguous presence, claiming for culture a metaphysical purity or authority, the experience of which is the registration of the perverse, absurd, incoherent and monstrous nature of life. That this entangling of the grotesque in the diabolical, the violating and the uncanny, the most obvious example of which is the self-mutilating art of Aubrey Beardsley, is also a feature of earlier conceptual models of the grotesque, is one of the points that emerges from this book. The following essays demonstrate that if we look at a range of material outside the cultural spaces associated with Pater, Wilde and Beardsley we find writers and artists locked into ways of embodying or realizing experience as dense, chaotic, contradictory, deforming, overpowering, disorientating and aberrant.

Notes

1. Thomson, P., *The Grotesque*, London: Methuen, 1972, p. 21.
2. *Ibid.*, p. 7. Thomson describes the opening of Kafka's *Metamorphosis*, having just made the same point about Beckett's *Watt*. Writing in 1972, Thomson's bias is towards Modernist writing, with the emphasis on the then fashionable literature of the Absurd. His comments on Victorian culture are few and slight. He discusses Nonsense verse, Ruskin and Bagehot (pp. 25–28, 39, 65). For other general explorations of the definition of 'grotesque', see Fingesten, P., 'Delimiting the Concept of the Grotesque', *Journal of Aesthetics and Art Criticism* 42, Summer 1984, pp. 419–26; Harpham, G. G., *On the Grotesque: Strategies of Contradiction in Art and Literature*, Princeton, N.J.: Princeton U.P., 1982.
3. Williams, R., *Keywords: A Vocabulary of Culture and Society*, London: Fontana, 1983, p. 14.
4. *Ibid*, p. 11. Williams embarked on his researches in historical semantics when he resumed his university studies at the end of the Second World War. He was prompted to do so because he was struck

by significant shifts away from the concerns of the 1930s in conversational and intellectual vocabularies. Williams based his eventual selection comprising *Keywords* (1976, new edn 1983) on words that he had observed in active and variable use. 'Culture' was the key contested word with a massively complex history: it could mean, for one formation, superiority based on learned refinement, whilst, for another formation of artistic practitioners, in for example the theatre, it could mean what they saw themselves to be producing. It is in this latter sense and field of use that the 'grotesque' was visible as a still-active word with a rich, varied and transnational semantic history. Indeed, Williams glimpsed it in his account of Luigi Pirandello – part of his study of Modernist and avant-garde theatre – in which Pirandello's transgressive practice was traced to the work of Luigi Chiarelli and his Teatro del Grotesco, with its parodic exaggeration of Romantic conventions (Williams, R., *Drama from Ibsen to Brecht*, Harmondsworth: Pelican, 1973, p. 176; originally published as *Drama from Ibsen to Eliot*, 1952).

5. Barasch, F.K., *The Grotesque: A Study in Meanings*, The Hague: Mouton, 1971, p. 152.
6. Though most authors identify the origin of the term 'grotesque' with the excavated wall paintings of these buildings, it is worth noting that Alberti suggests reviving ancient grotto decorations prior to these discoveries (Amico, L.N., *Bernard Palissy: In Search of Earthly Paradise*, Paris, New York: Flammarion, 1996, pp. 49–52). Alberti's recommendations of 'rustic' or organic forms, and the designs to which they gave rise, perhaps provide a more useful indication of the sources for the later, broader development of the word. The specific forms of the 'grotesques' discovered in the Titus Baths and other first-century buildings continue to this day to form a definite and limited meaning of the word within art and design (West, S. (ed.), *Guide to Art*, London: Bloomsbury, 1996, p. 487). Writing in 1856, Owen Jones likewise insists on this reduced usage, expelling from design all other connotations of the term 'grotesque' (Jones, O., *The Grammar of Ornament*, London: Day & Son, 1856, pp. 123, 136). In contrast, Thomas Wright's 1865 history of the grotesque, which he construes as a specific form of caricature, makes no mention at all of grottoes or of the first-century wall paintings (Wright, T., *The History of Caricature and Grotesque in Literature and Art*, London: Virtue, 1865).
7. Wright, T., *A History of Caricature and Grotesque in Literature and Art*, with an introduction by F.K. Barasch, New York: Frederick Ungar, 1968, p. xxv.
8. M. Russo's recent *The Female Grotesque* (London and New York: Routledge, 1994) perversely (grotesquely?) misrepresents Ruskin in its opening pages by referring to his views on Raphael as evidence that Ruskin considered the grotesque an innately trivial aesthetic (pp. 5–6). For Russo, this alleged account of the grotesque associates it with the culturally 'feminine'.
9. Wright (*op. cit.* at note 6, pp. 40ff) traces the medieval history of such imagery from the earliest post-classical examples onwards. Animalistic and demonic motifs in French Romanesque architectural decoration also begin to become increasingly important as the Gothic revival proceeds, emerging as a powerful influence from the mid-nineteenth century (Eastlake, C.L., *A History of the Gothic Revival*, London: Longman, Green, 1872).
10. William Wrighte's book *Grotesque Architecture, or Rural Amusement*, originally published in 1767, was republished in 1790 and in 1802. Wrighte's subtitle clearly indicates that for him the term 'grotesque' was synonymous with 'picturesque'. The book gives designs for 'huts, retreats, summer and winter hermitages, terminaries, Chinese, Gothic and natural grottos ... many of which may be executed with flints, irregular stones, rude branches and roots of trees' (*Grotesque Architecture, or Rural Amusement*, London: Taylor, 1802, title page). By the end of the century, writers on architecture generally assume that the term predominantly applies to demonic figures derived from medieval church carvings (Rathbone, P.H., *Realism, Idealism and the Grotesque in Art: their Limits and Functions*, Liverpool: Lee and Nightingale, 1877, pp. 18–21; Scudder, V.D., *The Grotesque in Gothic Art*, privately printed, 1887; Wildridge, T.T., *The Grotesque in Church Art*, London: Andrews, 1899).
11. The French potter's fame in Victorian Britain was great. Palissy (1510–1590) was a model of 'self-help', having struggled to build his own business by hard work and technical innovations. He was a Protestant hero, having died in a French prison for his beliefs; he was a precursor of Darwin, having helped create natural history as a science, organizing the first conference on the subject since Classical antiquity. In particular, he was credited with having initiated the scientific study of fossil remains. His own ceramics contain fossil-like casts of snakes, frogs, fish and other animals (Amico, *op. cit.* at note 6, *passim*; Arts Council of Great Britain, *Great Victorian Pictures: Their Paths to Fame*, London: Arts Council, 1978, pp. 85–86).
12. Williams, *op. cit.* at note 3, p.20.
13. Wright, *op. cit.* at note 7, p. xxix.
14. *Ibid.*, p. xxxii.
15. The modern words 'antique' and 'antic(s)' both derive from 'anticke'. The connection arises from the implication that old-fashioned styles (in costume, for example) appear odd or absurd. This correlation between the culturally obsolete and the fanciful is implicit in Renaissance grottoes, which often

incorporate imagery designed to imply antique origins. The action of time is signalled by accretions and deposits over the 'stone'. The suggestion of a partially obliterated, lost or alien cultural meaning is also sometimes present; the grotto is imagined as the visible but illegible remains of pagan or folk traditions and rituals.

16. Wright, *op. cit.* at note 7, p. xxxiv.
17. *Ibid.*, p. xxxvii.
18. *Ibid.*, p. xli.
19. *Ibid.*, p. xlii.
20. Scott's novels often begin with apparently odd fragments of history which are then woven into a narrative that seeks to return them to lived experience: to rid them of antiquity. Thus, *Old Mortality* (1816) is named from 'an eccentric and remarkable character' who wandered the Lowlands repairing the graves of Covenanters. The antics of this ancient specimen, dislocated from the historical energies of which he is a relic, constitute him as a suitable object of antiquarian enquiry – an identity from which the fictive realm of the novel rescues him. For a detailed discussion of the relation between antiquarian, picturesque and grotesque perception in Dickens's *The Old Curiosity Shop* see Hill, N., *A Reformer's Art: Dickens' Picturesque and Grotesque Imagery*, Athens, Ohio, and London: Ohio U.P., 1981, pp. 98–111.
21. Conan Doyle, A., *His Last Bow; Some Reminiscences of Sherlock Holmes*, London: John Murray, 1917, pp. 1–2.
22. Typically, the 1897 volume of *The Strand* contains an article on 'the Romance of the Museums', illustrating skeletons of the Irish Giant and Sicilian Dwarf; another article, on 'Dandy Dogs', includes a photograph of a bejewelled miniature sedan chair containing a skull (inside are the ashes of a pampered pet). An article on medieval trials of animals is illustrated with cartoons of outsize fleas and worms standing in the dock. The flea wears hobnailed boots.
23. Examples of such usages include H.J. Byron's *Robinson Crusoe, or Harlequin Friday: a grotesque pantomime opening* (1861), W.S. Gilbert's *Thespis, or The Gods Grown Old: an entirely original grotesque opera* (1871) and J.F. MacArdle's *Puss in Boots: an entirely new and original grand, gorgeous and grotesque Christmas pantomime* (1874). This stock theatrical usage may have influenced H.G. Wells's subtitle for *The Invisible Man* – 'a grotesque romance'.
24. Kayser, W., *The Grotesque in Art and Literature*, trans. U. Weisstein, Bloomington: Indiana U.P., 1963; Jennings, L.B., *The Ludicrous Demon: Aspects of the Grotesque in German Post-Romantic Prose*, Berkeley: University of California Press, 1963.
25. Wright, *op. cit.* at note 6, p. 183.
26. Hill, *op. cit.* at note 20, pp. 44–79.
27. Carlyle, T., *Works*, 30 vols, ed. H.D. Trail, London: Chapman and Hall. 1896–1901, vol. 6, p. 50; Marx, K., *Selected Writings*, ed. D. McLellan, Oxford: O.U.P., 1977, p. 124.
28. Hill, *op. cit.* at note 20; Steig, M., 'George Cruikshank and the Grotesque: A Psychodynamic Approach', in Patten, R. (ed.), *George Cruikshank: A Revaluation*, Princeton: Princeton U.P., 1974, pp. 189–213.
29. Armstrong, I., *Victorian Poetry: Poetry, Poetics and Politics*, London: Routledge, 1993.
30. Beer, G., *Darwin's Plots*, London: Routledge and Kegan Paul, 1983, p. 105.
31. Hull, D., *Darwin and his Critics: The Reception of Darwin's Theory of Evolution by the Scientific Community*, Cambridge, Mass.: Harvard U.P., 1973, pp. 159–70.
32. Parts of the *Origin* made Sedgwick 'laugh until my sides were almost sore'. See Hull, *op. cit.* at note 31, p. 157. Sedgwick also referred to 'wild machinery' of this 'eminently amusing' book. Beer's account of Darwin neglects the problem of the grotesque, but it does discuss extensively Darwin's struggle with affective language. See Beer, *op. cit.* at note 30, pp. 80–81ff. It is interesting to note that anthropomorphic phraseology continually intrudes into Darwin's accounts of animal behaviour. Thus, he draws on Orientalist conventions when he contrasts the slave-using behaviour of a vigorous, if 'tyrannic', species of (British) ant with that of its decadent continental relatives, who have evolved into 'abject dependence' on slavery to fulfil their needs (Darwin, *The Descent of Man and Selection in Relation to Sex*, London: John Murray, 1871, pp. 341–42). This imagery of insects behaving in contrasting human-like ways appears in the grotesque caricatures of J. J. Grandville, Ernest Griset or even Edward Lear, where it is intended to be 'eminently amusing'. (Hood, T., *Griset's Grotesques: or Jokes Drawn on Wood*, London: Routledge, 1867; Lambourne, L., *Ernest Griset: Fantasies of a Victorian Illustrator*, London: Thames & Hudson, 1979.) Pro-evolutionists also drew on the grotesque to attack opponents. Philip Gosse's *Omphalos* (1857) suggests that God created the bones of dinosaurs, rock stratification and

other signs of a non-existent past at the moment of a Biblical creation. Critics condemned the idea that God might play monstrous jokes on humanity by making the exercise of reason impossible and by creating the equivalent of physically 'real' caricatures of absurd beings that never existed.

33. Darwin, C., *op. cit.* at note 32, p. 876.
34. Similar problems are evident elsewhere. Thus, Owen Jones's *The Grammar of Ornament* (*op cit.* at note 6, p. 12) begins by discussing the decorative work of 'savage' peoples. The purpose of the book is to liquidate history for design: to offer up to modern manufacturing an abstract and atemporal grammar of pattern negating its historically and culturally diverse sources. Its account of savage modes of adornment is, however, caught between the atemporal frame of grammar and the historicizing act by which such adornment is designated primitive. The point is significant because, as Shelagh Wilson explains in Chapter 7, the project of design reform proposed by Jones and his allies was the detachment of design from the body: a refusal of physicality, constituting design as the aesthetic expression of mechanized manufacture itself. Savage design is discussed in just this manner, but, uniquely, a threatening physicality is implied by an engraving of the flayed face of a tattooed Maori, the bodily humanity of which grotesquely clashes with the abstraction of the tattooed pattern.
35. Lewes, G.H., 'Dickens in Relation to Criticism', *Fortnightly Review*, 1872, pp. 141–54, p. 145.
36. *Ibid.*, p. 148.
37. *Ibid.*
38. *Ibid.*, p. 147.
39. *Ibid.*, p. 145.
40. *Ibid.*, p. 148.
41. *Ibid.*
42. Bagehot, W., *The Collected Works*, 12 vols, ed. N. St-John Stevas, London: The Economist, 1974, vol. 1, p. 79.
43. *Ibid.*, vol. 1, p. 83.
44. *Ibid.*, vol. 1, pp. 365–66.
45. *Ibid.*, vol. 1, p. 366.
46. Arnold, M., *The Works*, 15 vols, London: Macmillan, 1903, vol. 6, p. 33.
47. *Ibid.*, vol. 5, p. 85.
48. *Ibid.*, pp. 85–87.
49. *Ibid.*, p. 90.
50. *Ibid.*, p. 100.
51. *Ibid.*, p. 113.
52. *Ibid.*, p. 101–2.
53. *Ibid.*, p. 132.
54. *Ibid.*, p. 166.
55. *Ibid.*, pp. 173–74.
56. *The Times*, 1 May 1852, p. 16.
57. Gilchrist, A., *Life of Blake*, 2 vols, London: Macmillan and Co., 1863, vol. 1, p. 3.
58. *Ibid.*
59. *Ibid.*, p. 329.
60. Tilly, H., 'Burmese Art and Burmese Artists', *The Magazine of Art*, October 1892, pp. 415–20, p. 415.
61. *Ibid.*
62. *Ibid.*
63. *Ibid.*, p. 418.
64. *Ibid.*, p. 419.

1

'Borrowing Gargantua's mouth': biography, Bakhtin and grotesque discourse – James Boswell, Thomas Carlyle and Leslie Stephen on Samuel Johnson

David Amigoni

I

'"Why, Sir"', says Samuel Johnson to Boswell and the architect Gwyn in Boswell's *Life of Johnson* during a discourse which 'satyrised statuary', '"you would not value the finest head cut upon a carrot."'[1] Johnson's sense of values suggests a distaste for the grotesque and the discordances that this aesthetic generates. Frances K. Barasch has argued that 'in eighteenth-century England, ... the new "Augustans" waged their most powerful campaign against the grotesque'.[2] One of the sources legitimating this campaign was the Augustan architect Vitruvius's original judgement on the grotesque in his *De Architectura*, which reminds us of the very origins of the term.[3] Commenting on the emergent Roman fashion of hybrid arabesque patterns which mixed human and plant forms, Vitruvius demanded to know 'how can a tender shoot carry a human figure, and how can bastard forms composed of flowers and human bodies grow out of roots and tendrils?... Such things ... never existed, do not now exist, and shall never come into being.'[4] Vitruvius's criteria for questioning the probity of the grotesque in the field of visual ornamentation are analogous to Samuel Johnson's later and well-known neo-Augustan complaints against the metaphysical conceit in the field of poetry as set out in his biography of Abraham Cowley (*Lives of the Poets*, 1781).[5]

And yet, as Barasch admits, there is another story to tell about the neo-Augustan period, in which the origins of the Victorian grotesque become visible:

The eighteenth century was certainly a period of polished wit and refined taste, and native Gothic tendencies were eschewed to make way for Palladian grandeur, Horatian decorum, and Longinian sublimity. But this era was also a way station between two romantic periods, and the native English appetite for forms that were 'unregulated' and 'unnatural' to a handful of critics survived in popular taste as a kind of underground railroad running from the Renaissance to the nineteenth century.[6]

It could even be said that aspects of Johnson's own criticism played a part in keeping the grotesque train on the tracks. The 'Preface' to his edition of Shakespeare (1765) defends the 'serious and ludicrous' irregularity of Shakespeare's dramaturgy.[7] Moreover, if we focus on Barasch's sense of the Augustan age as an epoch sandwiched between two Romanticisms, then we should remember that the most powerful monument to Johnson's life and reputation, James Boswell's *Life of Johnson*, appeared at the point (1791) at which the later Romantic movement was coming into being.

The point of this chapter will be to explore the presence of grotesque discourses in Boswell's *Life of Johnson*, and to trace their transmission to and refashioning within Victorian representations of Johnson. First, which canons of grotesque discourse am I referring to? A good starting point is Boswell's image of Johnson's table manners:

When at a table, he was totally absorbed in the business of the moment; his looks seemed rivetted to his plate; nor would he, unless when in very high company, say one word, or even pay the least attention to what was said by others, till he had satisfied his appetite, which was so fierce, and indulged with such intenseness, that while in the act of eating, the veins of his forehead swelled, and generally a strong perspiration was visible. To those whose sensations were delicate, this could not but be disgusting; and it was doubtless not very suitable to the character of a philosopher, who should be distinguished by self-command.[8]

Boswell presents us with a body absorbed in a Gargantuan act of consumption. This is a body which makes the secrets of its interior systems of circulation visible, even in polite company, with veins protruding from the forehead. Rather than keeping its secrets to itself, this body secretes. Indeed, the necessity of bodily excretion – and so the dissolution of the boundary between inside and outside – is apparent in copious amounts of perspiration. Conversation is suspended while Johnson stuffs food into himself. Boswell rehearses 'disgust' on behalf of the reader: yet the energy of the description suggests that repulsion and attraction are contending against one another in equal strength.

The canon of grotesque discourse that is encountered here, with its emphasis on the earthy body of exaggerated proportions and its excessive appetites, takes us back to the Renaissance as reconstructed by M. Bakhtin in his seminal work *Rabelais and His World* (1965). This 'grotesque realist' body – a key image of Medieval European popular culture which Rabelais textualized in the sixteenth century – broke out of its 'underground' habitat, and coupled itself to Romantic main-line inflections of the grotesque. Together they transported an image of Johnson to Victorian critics and biographers.

In an act analogous to the archaeological recovery of Roman ornamental grotesques during the Renaissance, Bakhtin's aim in *Rabelais and His World* was to rescue Rabelais's 'canon' of grotesque body imagery from the layers of cultural re-inscription that had obscured the liberatory potential he claimed for it. But Bakhtin also acknowledged the paradoxically anti-canonical historical dynamics at work in a canon of imagery:

> in the art and literature of past ages we observe two such [canons], which we will conditionally call grotesque and classic... in history's living reality the canon was never fixed and immutable. Moreover, usually the two canons experience various forms of interaction: struggle, mutual influence, crossing and fusion.[9]

Struggle, crossing and fusion. In this chapter, which reflects on an aspect of the movement of grotesque discourses between eighteenth- and nineteenth-century literary cultures, I shall trace the way in which Victorian critics and biographers such as Thomas Carlyle and Leslie Stephen came to generate a variety of meanings from the grotesque image of Johnson which they inherited from Boswell. It is important to emphasize the variety of meanings: Michael Hollington has stressed that the grotesque is a 'mixed aesthetic... compounded of opposite and indeed contradictory sensations',[10] and a key aim of this chapter will be to explore the ways in which writers 'borrow' or appropriate canons of representation from one another, crossing and fusing them and generating new oppositions as they deploy them in new contexts. It is for this reason that it is illuminating to explore an aspect of the Victorian grotesque through its late eighteenth-century, proto-Romantic precursor. Moreover, such a focus suggests that Bakhtin's somewhat dismissive attitude to the meanings of the grotesque in the nineteenth century can be challenged from the perspective of a more nuanced cultural history which examines in turn Victorian readings, recyclings and uses of eighteenth-century discourses.

My title – 'Borrowing Gargantua's mouth' – is borrowed from Boswell's *Life of Johnson*. Boswell borrowed it from Johnson, as Johnson had borrowed it – via an anonymous journalist – from Shakespeare's *As You Like It*: Shakespeare had, of course, borrowed the figure of Gargantua from Rabelais. In Boswell's text, the idea appears in the context of an account of Johnson in conversation with members of his circle, the subject being a newspaper-led fashion of 1778, whereby public figures were described by means of words from Shakespeare:

> Somebody said to Johnson, across the table, that he had not been in those characters. 'Yes (said he,) I have. I should have been sorry to be left out.' He then repeated what had been applied to him,
> 'I must borrow GARGANTUA'S mouth.'
> Miss Reynolds not perceiving at once the meaning of this, he was obliged to explain it to her, which had something of an aukward and ludicrous effect. 'Why, Madam, it has a reference to me, as using big words which require the mouth of a giant to pronounce them. Gargantua is the name of a giant in Rabelais.'[11]

Immediately raising the cultural and mythic stakes whilst seeking to restore Johnson to the Classical pantheon, Boswell (as a character in the text) attempts to liken Johnson to Neptune and Jove, but Johnson notably refuses: 'There is nothing marked in that. No, Sir, Gargantua is the best.'

There are three points that can be drawn from this which will help to clarify the arguments of this chapter. First, there is an acknowledgement that the representation of biographical identity is subtly interwoven with fictional schemes of representation. Second, a cultural knowledge of François Rabelais – which would be recognizable to Bakhtin – is demonstrated (notwithstanding that the 'knowledge' is filtered through Shakespeare).[12] Although, for the purpose of this episode, Boswell plays Classicist stooge and Johnson opts for a Rabelaisian self-identification, Boswell understood very well Rabelais's place on the cultural map. The fact that the ludicrously grotesque Gargantua is defined in opposition to the Classical images of Neptune and Jove suggests that Boswell's understanding of the complex struggle between grotesque and classic canons of representation was similar, if not identical, to that displayed in Bakhtin's account of it.[13] Drawing upon Bakhtin's reading of Rabelais, I shall argue that this canon of so-called 'grotesque realism', when blended with a so-called 'Romantic grotesque' canon, shaped Boswell's image of Johnson, and in turn the image of Johnson fashioned by the Victorian critics Thomas Carlyle and Leslie Stephen. Third, the connection that Johnson draws between his Gargantuan identity and the size of the words that he utters – a connection crystallized by Shakespeare's line – will be appropriated by Leslie Stephen's late Victorian reading of Johnson, in which the grotesque image of Johnson will be further embedded in physiognomic and biological discourses, and used pathologically to explain cultural history. We shall see that, for Stephen, the grotesque is materialized in the historically mutable signs of language as well as in the economies of the body. And in turn I will explore the ways in which the mutable signs of the grotesque are deployed by Boswell and Stephen as their subjectivities entwine, in some ideological discomfort, with their own historical and cultural situations.

II

Following Samuel Johnson's death in 1784, a contest to be first to press with either a memoir or a biography ensued amongst those closest to him. James Boswell did not bring his biography to press until 1791.[14] The last to appear, it was Boswell's work that became a central and much discussed text in Victorian culture. Why was this so, and what part did Boswell's handling of grotesque discourse contribute to its powers of attraction?

Allan Ingram's study of Boswell's practice of image-construction demonstrates how Boswell's *Life of Johnson* is a delicate 'balancing act', appropriating and counter-inflecting the field of imagery manufactured by its opponents in an attempt to produce the most multi-faceted portrait of Johnson in which the struggle between Classical and grotesque figured prominently.[15] This strategy enables the reader to perceive 'all the shades which mingled in the grand composition', as Boswell put it – notably in the painterly language of portraiture – in his Dedication of the biography to Sir Joshua Reynolds.[16] This helps to explain Boswell's image of a contradictory Johnson whose 'figure was large and well formed', and who possessed a

countenance of the cast of an ancient statue; yet his appearance was rendered strange and somewhat uncouth, by convulsive cramps, by the scars of that distemper which it was once imagined the royal touch could cure, and by a slovenly mode of dress ... He was afflicted with a bodily disease, which made him often restless and fretful; and with a constitutional melancholy, the clouds of which darkened the brightness of his fancy, and gave a gloomy cast to his whole course of thinking ... .[17]

or, the finest head cut upon a carrot. Boswell's image of a statuesque Johnson fuses the opposition between Classical and grotesque which is conventionally polarized: in Boswell's Johnson Classical and grotesque are embodied contradictorily in one subject.[18]

In opposition to rival, unflattering representations, Boswell stresses the complex relationship between Johnson's mind and body.[19] This is dramatically demonstrated in the course of the narrative by Boswell's elaborate staging of Johnson's mastery in speech and public debate, but which itself sits in stark contrast to the ludicrous image of Johnson's body on a horse: 'he had no command or direction of his horse, but was carried as if in a balloon'.[20] Boswell's great achievement was to fashion an image of Johnson which reconciled the contradiction between the outwardly ludicrous diseased body and the inwardly generated eloquence of speech. Thus, whilst the Rabelaisian grotesque realist body constitutes one canon of imagery, the grotesque effect woven by Boswell arises out of the relationship of tension between these contrasts.

These contrasts are inflected further by Johnson's 'melancholic' interiority which 'gave a gloomy cast to his whole course of thinking', and which checks the laughter which Johnson otherwise invokes.[21] For Boswell, Johnson's 'restless and fretful' body – his tics, uncontrollable gestures and spasmodic limb movements – could be read physiognomically[22] as the semiotic markers of a melancholic mind perpetually on the brink of maddening torment:

His mind resembled a vast amphitheatre, the Colisaeum at Rome. In the centre stood his judgement, which, like a mighty gladiator, combated those apprehensions that, like the wild beasts of the *Arena*, were all around in cells, ready to be let out upon him. After a conflict, he drove them back to their dens; but not killing them, they were still assailing him.[23]

Boswell articulates Johnson's mental anguish through Classical and heroic figures; and yet the image of an unrelievedly tormented and incarcerated subjectivity propels Boswell's Johnson towards modernity through an historical canon which Bakhtin has described as 'the Romantic grotesque': 'in folk grotesque, madness is a gay parody of official reason ... In Romantic grotesque ... madness acquires a sombre, tragic aspect of individual isolation.'[24] Boswell represents Johnson as a subject tortured by bodily disease and melancholia who maintains a vigorous and heroically articulated social and moral outlook despite his individual anguish. Victorian critics and biographers were to become fascinated by this grotesque-realist and Romantic-grotesque image of Johnson, and re-worked its antinomies in relation to new, specifically Victorian configurations of literary, historical and scientific discourse, as we shall see as we look at Leslie Stephen's biography of Johnson.

Before doing this, however, I want to identify an additional complex of grotesque discourse in Boswell's image of Johnson. For there are points in Boswell's writing when the knowing, strategic manipulation of grotesque canons that I have so far described breaks down. One such moment occurs in the *Journal of a Tour to the Hebrides* (1786), a narrative in which, significantly, a measure of Boswell's own subjectivity – his imaginativeness, his conflict with his father (a stern judge), his dislike for the profession forced on him (the law) – is explicitly revealed.[25] The *Journal* is, in a sense, the record of a Romantic political pilgrimage during which Johnson was to be returned by Boswell to the remnants of the last stand of the Jacobite cause – to which, it was assumed, Johnson was covertly attached.[26] Indeed, it is at this point, when Johnson has just slept in the very bed formerly occupied by Charles Edward Stuart in the house of Flora MacDonald on Skye, that Boswell's image of the scene is disrupted:

> The room was decorated with a great variety of maps and prints. Among others, was Hogarth's print of Wilkes grinning, with the cap of liberty on a pole by him. That too was a curious circumstance in the scene this morning; such a contrast was Wilkes to the above group. It reminded me of Sir William Chambers's Account of Oriental Gardening, in which we are told all odd, strange, ugly, and even terrible objects, are introduced, for the sake of variety.[27]

Boswell's desire to capture a moment of romantic historical resonance is undone by the presence of Hogarth's representation of another grotesque, the maverick John Wilkes, Johnson's great political adversary of the 1770s.[28] I have not the space to explore the uncomfortably ironic parallels between rebellious and legitimate forces that stared Boswell down. But the upshot is that Boswell cannot make sense of the pencilled Latin inscription which the departed Johnson leaves for him.[29] And, pointedly, he turns, via Sir William Chambers, to the grotesque ('odd, strange, ugly ... terrible objects') to help articulate that 'which it is not easy for words to describe'.[30] We will see that, almost one hundred years later, different inhibitions to subjectivity and articulation will arise for Leslie Stephen during his more distant 'encounter' with Johnson. But he will have the basis of Boswell's grotesque, contradictory image of Johnson on which to play them out.

III

In such a strange case was imprisoned one of the most vigorous intellects of the time. Vast strength hampered by clumsiness and associated with grievous disease, deep and massive powers of feeling limited by narrow though acute perceptions, were characteristic both of soul and body.[31]

Thus Leslie Stephen in his biography of Samuel Johnson, the first in Macmillan's series of brief lives of British authors entitled 'English Men of Letters'.[32] Ludicrous, diseased body: sharp, vigorous mind – the antinomies are from Boswell. But Stephen has also borrowed from Carlyle's famous review of the Croker edition of Boswell's *Life of Johnson* (1832):

Nature had given him a high, keen-visioned, almost poetic soul; yet withal imprisoned it in an inert unsightly body: he that could never rest had not limbs that would move with him, but only roll and waddle: the inward eye, all-penetrating, all-embracing, must look through bodily windows that were dim, half-blinded ... he was eminently social; the approbation of his fellows was dear to him, 'valuable', as he owned, 'if from the meanest of human beings'; yet the first impression he produced on every man was to be one of aversion, almost of disgust.[33]

It is important to remember that Carlyle elaborated, through his biographical sketches and his work on modern German literature, a complex commentary on the grotesque in early Victorian culture. The essay on the Croker edition of Boswell's *Life of Johnson* focuses on Boswell, and presents a grotesque-realist portrait of Boswell's 'stomachic character' and his physiognomy: 'those bag-cheeks, hanging like half-filled wine-skins ... The under part of Boswell's face is of a low, almost brutish character.'[34] Carlyle's biographical sketches of Boswell and Johnson need to be seen in relation to his sketch of the German writer E.T.W. Hoffman (1827). Together these can be read as explorations of contrasting ways of embodying and living the grotesque. Hoffman's mind, 'swarming with beautiful or horrible chimeras', produced an art which emphasized 'extravagances and ludicrous distortions'; but Carlyle renders Hoffman's death symbolic by emphasizing the gradual seizure advancing from, significantly, the lower body towards the head.[35] By contrast, Carlyle claims, Johnson's intellect and sense of sociality ultimately transcend the ludicrously distorted, out-of-control body which struggles to imprison them. It is precisely this, Carlyle argues, which the physically and morally grotesque Boswell recognizes, and which demands the saving grace of worship which Boswell bestows upon his hero.[36]

Carlyle's impact on Stephen thus needs to be noted. But whilst there are lexical continuities between Carlyle and Stephen – 'imprisonment'/'imprisoned' take their lead from Boswell's Romantic-grotesque image of Johnson's incarcerated mental torment – it is important to stress that Stephen has veered away from Carlyle's discourse of hero-worship. Carlyle's image of Johnson's mental faculties is organized by the language of sight and the prophetical office of the seer, whilst Stephen's emphasizes the activity of the 'vigorous intellect', which implies a sense of intellectual purpose. And Carlyle's rendering of the imprisoning bodily form in the metaphor of 'dim, half-blinded windows' becomes in Stephen a body racked with 'grievous disease'. Following Boswell's lead, both Carlyle and Stephen work within a physiognomical framework, employing a semiotics of the invisible to produce a reading of the relationship between external signs and interiority. But whereas Carlyle's physiognomical reading is avowedly poetic, Stephen's discourse is clinical and pathological: 'sometimes he seemed to be obeying some hidden impulse ... the queer convulsions by which he amazed all beholders were probably connected with his disease'.[37]

Stephen also borrows the Rabelaisian canon of grotesque imagery from Boswell's narrative, evident in Stephen's appropriation of Boswell's image of Johnson eating: 'He was not a pleasant object during this performance. He was totally absorbed in the business of the moment, a strong perspiration came out, and the veins of his forehead swelled.'[38] Stephen is attracted to the bizarre acts of his 'uncouth monster',[39] which is clear from the pleasure he takes in narrating an episode in which Johnson, out walking and aged fifty-four, observing that it has been a long time since he had enjoyed 'a good roll', falls deliberately to the ground and rolls to the bottom of a hill. For Stephen this episode promotes 'laughter' which, nonetheless, should be tempered by the realist's sense of the body's physical limits and vulnerabilities: 'we may believe ... that his performance in this kind was so strange and uncouth that a fear for the safety of his bones quenched the spectator's tendency to laugh'.[40]

Stephen's biography of Johnson fuses Romantic and Rabelaisian canons of the grotesque with discourses on disease pathology and the intellectual function – the latter signified in the language of types employed by Stephen (Johnson 'represents the secular rather than the ecclesiastical type, a disciple of Socrates rather than St. Paul').[41] These canons of the grotesque body, disease pathology and intellectual types coalesce into a discourse which finds its context in Foucault's observation that 'it's the body of society which becomes the principle in the nineteenth century ... the social body ... needs to be protected in a quasi-medical sense',[42] a set of concerns which in the case of Britain crystallized in that project known as Social Darwinism.

In this discourse, existing physiognomical sciences developed new explanatory ambitions: on the basis of bodily traits and moral dispositions human subjects were classifiable into types, some varieties of which, according to the law of natural selection, contributed to the survival chances of society, otherwise known as 'the social organism', and some of which did not.[43] In a sense it would be more accurate to describe Stephen as a cultural Darwinist insofar as his work was concerned to construct relationships between the extinction and emergence of 'species' of thought and conditions of intellectual leadership and influence. Indeed, one of the concerns of Stephen's biography of Johnson is for the way in which the moral sentiments of an intellectual leader 'may be transmuted into a permanent source of nobler views of life and the world'.[44]

In other texts, published around the writing of *Johnson*, Stephen sought answers to this question by focusing on language. His *Science of Ethics* (1882) was a Darwinian account of the evolution of the moral sense, which Stephen socialized and materialized in arguing that 'we may be said to feel through signs as well as to reason by signs'.[45] Stephen's sense of the social-semiotic basis of thinking and feeling was historicized in *The History of English Thought in the Eighteenth Century* (1876), where Stephen constructed a history of thought which was characterized by 'the gradual emancipation of the mind from the errors spontaneously generated by its first childlike attempt at speculation', and beset by the problem that 'old conceptions are preserved to us in the very structure of language'.[46] Stephen thus presents a theory of the tendency of intellectual progress through the mutability of thought, checked by the contradicting conservatism latent in the conventions of linguistic structure.

This contradiction is explored in Stephen's opening allusion to the significance of Hume, whose bold philosophical work, in confronting the established conventions of thought between 1739 and 1752, 'fell dead-born from the press', yet whose same work in the course of time 'transformed the history of thought'. Stephen finds an 'explanation of the apparent contradiction' in the fact that Hume 'appealed to a few thinkers, who might be considered as the brain of the social organism'.[47] Notably, Stephen finds the intellectual explanation for this social phenomenon in a cerebral, but still organic, bodily metaphor.

Stephen's Johnson offers a contrasting perspective within this grand narrative representation of the evolution of eighteenth-century thought and its contradictory tendencies:

Johnson denies ... that the business of life can be carried on by the help of rose-coloured sentiments and general complacency. The world is, at best, but a melancholy place, full of gloom, of misery, of wasted purpose, and disappointed hopes ... Make up the heavy account of suffering, of disease, vice, cruelty, of envy, hatred and malice, of corruption in high places, of starvation and nakedness amongst the low, of wars, of pestilences and famines, of selfish ambition trampling on thousands, and wasted heroism strengthening opposition by its failure, of petty domestic tyranny, of lying, hypocrisy, and treachery, which run all through the social organism like a malignant ulcer, and see how far your specious maxim will take you.[48]

The implication is that if Hume courted the brain of the social organism, then Johnson's thought, conditioned by his 'constitutional depression',[49] was attuned to its lower – physically and morally – diseased regions. The mediating link here, between Johnson's diseased, melancholic individual body and the 'malignant ulcer' afflicting the social body, is, as we will see, language, or the signs through which reason and feeling are structured and experienced.

My brief account of Stephen's work on language and its place in the history of thought is a useful context for reading Stephen's inflected appropriation, from Boswell, of Johnson's self-identification with the Rabelaisian Gargantua. It occurs towards the end of the biography when Stephen is remarking on Johnson's prose style:

> The mannerism is strongly marked, and of course offensive; for by mannerism, as I understand the word, is meant the repetition of certain forms of language in obedience to blind habit and without reference to propriety in the particular case. Johnson's sentences seem to be contorted, as his gigantic limbs used to twitch, by a kind of mechanical spasmodic action. The most obvious peculiarity is the tendency which he noted himself, to 'use big words and too many of them.' He had to explain to Miss Reynolds that the Shakespearean line
> > You must borrow me Gargantua's mouth,
> had been applied to him because he used 'big words which require the mouth of a giant to pronounce them.'[50]

An episode which, in Boswell's writing, played with questions of naming and identity has become, in Stephen's text, a pathology of Johnson's style. Johnson's explanation for his likeness to Garagantua – that he used big words which required the mouth of a giant to pronounce them – is retained from Boswell, but it has been transformed by being linked to self-censure: that the big words are too many in volume. This turns out to be a manifestation of Stephen's observation of 'mannerism' in Johnson's prose, which Stephen defines as 'repetition of certain forms of language in obedience to blind habit', and here one can see continuities between Stephen's account of the history of thought, built around an inhibiting custom and convention inscribed in the very structure of language, and his account of Johnson. Above all, and to complete this physiognomic pathology of Johnson's prose, the reader is given the grotesque image of Johnson's body and the 'gigantic' spasmodic twitching limbs, which have become metonyms for the contorted structure of Johnson's prose, which is itself viewed as grotesque.[51] Stephen reminds the reader that such bodily derived linguistic habits are 'of course offensive'. There are grounds for treading carefully around Stephen's meaning here: in his biography of Swift for 'English Men of Letters' Stephen makes it clear that he finds Swift's scatology (a definitive element in Bakhtin's grotesque-realist aesthetic) to be truly offensive.⁵² By contrast, in his account of Johnson he negotiates 'offensiveness' and, rather as we saw with Boswell's image of Johnson eating, where attraction and repulsion were present in equal measure, we need to look more closely at Stephen's investment in, and surreptitious attachment to, this image.

What does Stephen derive from appropriating and inflecting this episode by crossing it with other discourses? Put another way, what is played out in borrowing discourse from Gargantua's mouth and other grotesque sources? I have shown how a discourse of the grotesque is articulated in Boswell's narrative of Johnson on Skye at a moment of subjective political and ideological ambivalence. Consequently edited and negotiated canons of grotesque representation play an analogous role in Stephen's evaluation of Johnson: an evaluation of Johnson's conservatism which Stephen – an ostensibly liberal, progressive intellectual, yet with pessimistic, anti-feminist tendencies – articulates publicly through the ambivalent antinomies of the grotesque.

Stephen states that Johnson's 'dogged conservatism has both its value and its grotesque side'.⁵³ In Stephen's *History of English Thought in the Eighteenth Century* the liberal intellectual argues that 'the stubborn adherence of Johnson, and men such as Johnson, to solid fact, and their unreasonable contempt for philosophy, goes far to explain how it came to pass that England avoided the catastrophe of a revolution'.⁵⁴ Given Stephen's intimation of a metonymic relationship between the diseased body of society, the diseased body of Johnson and his conservative thought, there is a sense in which the diseased body of the individual intellectual helps preserve and protect the body of society from the 'catastrophe' of revolution. Yet, as Stephen admits here, it is an unreasonable contempt for speculative advance which produces the very maintenance of order that he values, which suggests a blurring of the absolute dividing line that Stephen attempts to maintain between the 'valuable' and 'grotesque' sides of conservatism.

A sense of Stephen's surreptitious attachment to the conservative grotesque and its canons of representation is evident in a letter written to C.E. Norton (Dec. 23 1877), which is about the very act of appropriating from Boswell's *Life of Johnson* for Stephen's own 'English Men of Letters' volume:

My chief employment at this time is doing a little book on Sam. Johnson ... I am half ashamed of the business in one way, for it seems wicked to pick the plums out of poor old Bozzy, and yet that is all there is to be done; and the plums are very fine ones. I don't fancy I am like S.J. in any way and that he would hardly have attracted me very much in his life-time; but I don't know anyone whom I enjoy so much, 'in the subjective stage of existence,' as the positivists say. His unreason is so incomparably better to my taste than Macaulay's good sense: eg: I quite agree with him that the young woman who thinks for herself about religious matters is an odious wench, though I should not dare to say it in public, and, in fact, preach quite the contrary – in a sense.⁵⁵

Reflecting upon the act of appropriation simultaneously raises complex questions of identification for Stephen which, from his allusion to Comte's theory of the 'subjective stage of existence', he takes to be led by bodily sensations before rational intellectual engagement.[56] Against his rational judgement, Stephen is led to identify with Johnson's 'unreason' which, like Johnson's 'unreasonable' contempt for speculative advance, stands implacably opposed to radical solutions. Given Stephen's claim in *The History of English Thought in the Eighteenth Century* that the Johnsonian pestilential vision of a world of misery and vice is a 'thoroughly masculine ... determination to see the world as it is',[57] it is striking that at his deepest and most private moment of identification with Johnson's 'unreason', Stephen should choose, in his complaint against odious thinking wenches, to remind us of what is, perhaps, Johnson's best-known coining of a grotesque image: 'Sir, a woman's preaching is like a dog's walking on his hinder legs. It is not done well, but you are surprized to find it done at all'.[58]

It is important to stress that Stephen's identification with Johnson's conservatism as related to gender is (at least before the publication of Maitland's biography) a private moment of confession: Stephen admits that he dare not make his comment about odious thinking wenches in public, where he preaches 'quite the contrary'. Thus, in borrowing Gargantua's mouth, Stephen is appropriating an edited Rabelaisian canon of grotesque representation which permits the indirect articulation of this view in public. In doing this, Stephen could be seen to be aligning himself with a canon of representation which had strong links with a misogynist, anti-feminist urge – a formation that Wayne C. Booth has reminded us of in his critique of Bakhtin's celebration of Rabelaisian carnival.[59]

Bakhtin's political aim in *Rabelais and his World* is to restore the unified folkish, popular understanding of the image of the grotesque-realist body which had been silenced by the individualizing drive of Enlightenment and Victorian discourses: for Bakhtin, it was nineteenth-century biologism and physiologism which rendered Rabelais's imagery unreadable in modern contexts.[60] Yet, as Bakhtin also admits – in a move which problematizes his quest for the recovery of a unified folk culture and its ambivalent laughter – canons of representation are complex and subject to fusion and crossing as they are appropriated in subtle processes of intellectual struggle. Indeed, the biographical image of Samuel Johnson which was produced by and after Boswell exemplifies this process of fusion and crossing of Rabelaisian grotesque, Romantic grotesque and discourses of biology and physiognomy. Consequently, Augustan, Romantic and Victorian appropriations of the grotesque manifest at once an interwovenness and a degree of discursive and affective variation. Above all it is important to stress the variety of effects produced by grotesque discourses and images: for Boswell the grotesque 'complexifies' his portrait of

Johnson, but also marks the limit of his articulacy regarding his and Johnson's political identifications. For Leslie Stephen – self-conscious about the role played by language in the making of cultural history – the grotesque encodes a way of publicly articulating a private confession which marks the limit of the liberal cultural historian's willingness publicly to endorse (feminist) movements for social change. To argue this is not to invalidate Bakhtin's radical cultural excavation and re-reading of the grotesque; it is, however, to read significance and complexity in those aspects of the story – the eighteenth and nineteenth centuries, and the Victorian period's reading of its precursor – that Bakhtin was inclined to dismiss as mere cultural accretions.

Notes

1. Boswell, J., *The Life of Johnson*, Oxford: O.U.P, 1980. p. 689.
2. Wright,. T., *A History of Caricature and Grotesque in Literature and Art*, with an introduction by F.K. Barasch, New York: Frederick Ungar, 1968, p. xxix.
3. The origins of the term are Italian and were first coined during the Renaissance. *La grottesca* and *grottesco* refer to *grotta* (cave), and were coined to signify a particular arabesque style of ornamentation which first became apparent during fifteenth-century excavations of the Baths of Titus in Rome; these adornments were found to correspond to styles which were negatively evaluated by Vitruvius, and prompted Renaissance humanist scholars such as Vasari to re-map their sense of the 'progress' of Roman aesthetics. See Kayser, W., *The Grotesque in Art and Literature*, trans. U. Weisstein, Bloomington: Indiana U.P., 1963, p. 20, and Barasch, F.K., *The Grotesque: A Study in Meanings*, The Hague: Mouton, 1971, pp. 25–31.
4. Kayser, *op. cit.* at note 3, p. 20.
5. Johnson, S., *Prose and Poetry*, selected by Mona Wilson, London: Rupert Hart-Davis, 1963, p. 789.
6. Barasch, *op. cit.* at note 3, p. 96.
7. Johnson, *op. cit.* at note 5, p. 494. See also Arieh Sachs's anthology, which traces manifestations of the grotesque in British writing from Langland to Joyce, and which includes in this canon Johnson's review (1757) of Soame Jenyns's *A Free Inquiry Into the Nature and Origin of Evil*, in which by dint of being the sport of the gods, the differences between human and animal traits are collapsed: 'To swell a man with a tympany is as good sport as to blow a frog'. (Sachs, A., *The English Grotesque*, Jerusalem: Israel U.P., 1969, p. 153; Johnson *op. cit.* at note 3, p. 365.)
8. Boswell, *op. cit.* at note 1, p. 331.
9. Bakhtin, M., *Rabelais and his world*, Bloomington, Indiana: Indiana U.P., 1984, p. 30.
10. Hollington, M., *Dickens and the Grotesque*, London and Sydney: Croom Helm, 1984, p. 24.
11. Boswell, *op. cit.* at note 1, p. 920.
12. See *As You Like It*, III, ii, lines 239–42: Celia: 'You must borrow me Gargantua's mouth first: 'tis a word too great for any mouth of this age's size.'
13. It appears that Boswell understood Rabelais's orientation in the way that Bakhtin came to do, as a prophet of the low, excremental dimension of the symbolic and its connection to carnival laughter: in one of Boswell's so-called 'French Themes', written during his trip to Holland in 1763–64, Boswell writes that he is composing following the example of 'all those people of unbridled imagination', and he cites Rabelais as being one of these. Unbridling his imagination, and taking as his topic Lord Bute's royal office of Groom of the Stole, Boswell embarks on a parodic etymological reverie which takes him to the 'Groom of the Stool' and 'his Majesty['s visit to] the temple of Cloacina' (see Pottle, F.A. (ed.), *Boswell in Holland: 1763–4*, Yale edition of the Private Papers of James Boswell, London: Heinemann, 1952, pp. 67–68). Such an excremental vision was linked to a popular philosophy of the body, politics and representation. As Peter Stallybrass and Allon White have pointed out, Bakhtin's reading of the body in works such as Rabelais' *Gargantua and Pantagruel* (1532–34) needs to be seen in

the context of a system of poetics organized around two fundamentally contrasting images and concepts of the body. The Classical body finds its image in the Renaissance statue: originating in Greek and Roman aesthetic models, this is a circumscribed, closed and individualized figure. The grotesque-realist body, by contrast, cannot be circumscribed by individualizing markers; it is social, multiple – indeed, collective – and linked homologically to the material reproduction of society through the substances it eats and excretes (Stallybrass, P., and White, A., *The Politics and Poetics of Transgression*, London: Methuen, 1986, pp. 21–22).

14. Hesther Piozzi, formerly Thrale, who published in 1786 an anecdotal memoir covering the last thirty years of Johnson's life; Sir John Hawkins, who in 1787 produced a full life (Piozzi, H.L., *Anecdotes of the Late Samuel Johnson LL.D. during the Last Thirty Years of His Life*, ed. S.C. Roberts, Cambridge: Cambridge U.P., 1925; Hawkins, J., *The Life of Samuel Johnson LL.D.*, London: published by subscription, 1787). All of Johnson's earliest biographers agreed on one point: that their subject possessed a huge and strangely distorted body which barely seemed to be his to control. Hesther Piozzi, in her *Anecdotes of Dr Johnson*, broached the subject of Johnson's body only towards the end of her account as 'that which contained the soul'. Johnson's container was:

remarkably high, and his limbs exceedingly large: his strength was more than common I believe, and his activity has been greater than ... such a form gave one reason to expect. His features were strongly marked, and his countenance particularly rugged, though the original complexion had certainly been fair, a circumstance somewhat unusual. (Piozzi, *op. cit.* above, p. 189.)

In Sir John Hawkins's biography, the narrator's language continues to observe the degree of measure and politeness established by Piozzi. Other voices he quotes, however, give a stronger impression of the peculiarity of Johnson's body and its wild gestures: Lord Chesterfield's character sketch reports that 'His figure (without being deformed) seems made to disgrace or ridicule the common structure of the human body. He throws any where, but down his throat, whatever he means to drink...' (Hawkins, *op. cit.* above, pp. 189–90). Boswell argues that the 'respectable Hottentot' described in Lord Chesterfield's letter does not refer to Johnson, but to 'a late noble Lord' (Boswell, *op. cit.* at note 1, pp. 188–89).

15. Ingram, A., *Boswell's Creative Gloom: A Study of Imagery and Melancholy in the Writings of James Boswell*, London: Macmillan, 1982, p. 161.

In 1783 Gillray published a caricature alluding to the reception of Johnson's *Lives of the English Poets*: captioned 'Apollo and the Muses inflicting Penance on Dr. Pomposo, round Parnassus', it depicts Johnson being scourged by Apollo and the Muses for his treatment of Milton, Otway, Waller, Gray, Shenston and Lyttleton. The contrasting images of the bodies are significant: Apollo's muscular, Classical body is defined in opposition to Johnson's obese, flabby torso, bared to receive the lash. The meanings of the opposition between the Classical and the grotesque are at work here in formulating a statement about Johnson's right to exert cultural authority: Johnson's subordination is signified by the grotesque which, in this context, strips him of authority (the Johnson figure utters, 'I acknowledge my transgressions and my sins are ever before me'). See Clark, J.C.D., *Samuel Johnson: Literature, Religion and English Cultural Politics from the Restoration to Romanticism*, Oxford: O.U.P, 1994, plate 8, p. 242.

16. Boswell, *op. cit.* at note 1, p. 2.

17. *Ibid.*, pp. 1398–1400.

18. Boswell fashioned the statue image over a number of years; it first appears in his *Tour to the Hebrides* (1786): 'His person was large, robust, I may say approaching to the gigantick, and grown unwieldy from corpulency. His countenance was naturally of the cast of an ancient statue, but somewhat disfigured by the scars of that *evil*, which, it was imagined, the *royal touch* could cure' (Boswell, J., *The Tour to the Hebrides*, in Birkbeck Hill, G., and Powell, L.F. (eds), *Boswell's Life of Johnson*, 6 vols, Oxford: Clarendon Press, 1950, vol. V, p. 18). For the rhetoric of contradiction as a governing trope in Boswell's biography, see 'Man is in general made up of contradictory qualities; and these will ever shew themselves in strange succession...' (Boswell, *op. cit.* at note 1, p. 1399).

19. In his 1789 publication *The Art of Criticism as Exemplified in Dr Johnson's 'Lives of the Most Eminent Poets'*, Robert Potter wrote that Johnson's mind was 'in some respects as narrow as a crane's neck', and that this could be explained by reference to Johnson's body:

But the coarseness of his constitution, his vigorous mind being perhaps vitiated or degraded by the grossness of his body, vibrated not to the delicate touches of a Shenstone and a Hammond, nor even to the stronger hand of a Gray, but gravitated by the weight of that in which it was enclosed to the earth.

(See Boulton, J.T. (ed.), *Johnson: The Critical Heritage*, London: Routledge and Kegan Paul, 1971, pp. 308–10.) For Potter, Johnson's coarse, earthy body weighed upon the lugubriousness of his mind, and the aim was to use the body to undermine Johnson's intellectual and moral authority.

20. Boswell, *op. cit.* at note 1, p. 1398.

21. See Boswell's recollection of Garrick's comment 'Rabelais and all other wits are nothing compared with him. You may be diverted by them, but Johnson gives you a forcible hug, and shakes laughter out of you, whether you will or no' (Boswell, *op. cit.* at note 1, p. 520). See Vance, J.A., *Boswell's Life of Johnson: New Questions, New Answers*, Athens: University of Georgia Press, 1985, pp. 204–24, 'The Laughing Johnson'. As Boswell's private journals testify, he, like Johnson, was a life-long sufferer from the condition of 'Hypochondria', or attacks of melancholia. Boswell wrote a series of essays entitled *The Hypochondriack* for *The London Magazine* between November 1777 and August 1783. In *Hypochondriack* **39** (Dec. 1780), 'On Hypochondria', Boswell provides specific descriptions of the effects of attacks of melancholia on the sufferer – one of which is, in addition to the darkness and loss of self-worth, that 'he begins actually to believe the strange theory, that nothing exists outside the mind'.

22. See G.S. Rousseau, 'Towards a Semiotic of the Nerve: the Social History of Language in a New Key' in Burke, P. and Porter R. (eds), *Language, Self and Society: A Social History of Language*, Cambridge: Polity, 1991, pp. 213–75; physiognomy was 'the truest universal science, precisely because it established links between the seen and the unseen, based on a semiotics of the invisible' (p. 246). Boswell knew of physiognomy but was not working as a polemicist promoting a physiognomy defined principally as the analysis of facial countenance: Towards the end of the *Life of Johnson*, Boswell compiles a note which acts as an inventory of all the portraits and visual memorials of Johnson: 'As no inconsiderable circumstance to his fame, we must reckon the extraordinary zeal of the artists to extend and perpetuate his image' (Boswell, *op. cit.* at note 1, p. 1395). In recording these details Boswell acknowledges that one image of Johnson (number 18 in Boswell's catalogue) can be found in '[J.K.] Lavater's *Essay on Physiognomy*, in which Johnson's countenance is analysed upon the principles of that fanciful writer' (p. 1396). For a broader sense of the importance and general currency of physiognomy we need to consider the important work of Ludmilla Jordanova, who defines physiognomy as 'a broadly environmentalist view of health and disease, an interest in language, a belief in the general validity of moving from visible signs to invisible qualities' (Jordanova, L., 'The Art and Science of Seeing in Medicine: Physiognomy 1780–1920', in Bynum, W.F., and Porter, R. (eds), *Medicine and the Five Senses*, Cambridge: Cambridge University Press, 1993, pp. 122–33, p. 130). As Bynum and Porter note in their 'Introduction', Jordanova's work 'extend[s] the conventional reading of physiognomy after Lavater as simply a series of footnotes to him' (p. 4). For the relationship between physiognomy and the grotesque aesthetic tradition see Hollington, *op. cit.* at note 10, pp. 14–15.

23. Boswell, *op. cit.* at note 1, p. 427.

24. Bakhtin, *op. cit.* at note 9, p. 39.

25. Boswell, *op. cit.* at note 18, pp. 51–52.

26. Much is made by Boswell of Johnson's anti-Scottish attitudes; their first meeting in the *Life* is built around this (Boswell, *op. cit.* at note 1, p. 277). Yet Johnson's Toryism held an ideal of Scottish feudal landlordism in high regard when compared to Whiggish English arrangements; though Boswell, heir to his father's estate, points out that Johnson's sense of a Scottish landlord is an anachronism – 'of late years ... Highland Chiefs have destroyed, by means too well known, the princely power which they once enjoyed' (p. 290). The ramifications of the '45 are a subtle but important factor in the Boswell/Johnson relationship.

27. Boswell, *op. cit.* at note 18, p. 186.

28. For an account of the differing ideological positions occupied by Wilkes and Johnson, see Sennett, R., *The Fall of Public Man*, London: Faber and Faber, 1993, p. 105. It is worth reflecting on Sennett's description of Wilkes as a grotesque comprising contradictory characteristics: 'Cross-eyed, afflicted with a bulging forehead and a receding upper lip, this strikingly ugly man was a personage of great charm and wit' (p. 99).

29. 'Quantum cedat virtutibus aurum' ('With virtue weighed, what useless trash is gold!'). In the second edition, Boswell added an explanation provided by 'an ingenious friend', that Johnson 'meant by these words to express his admiration of the Highlanders, whose fidelity and attachment had resisted the golden temptation that had been held out to them' (Boswell, *op. cit.* at note 18, p. 187).

30. *Ibid.*, p. 186.

31. Stephen, L., *Samuel Johnson*, English Men of Letters, London: Macmillan, 1878, p. 4.

32. For an account of the formation of this series, see Bruce Nadel, I., *Biography: Fiction, Fact and Form*, London: Macmillan, 1984. Stephen's specific role has been traced from a bibliographical point of view by Gillian Fenwick in 'Nourishing the Curiosity: Leslie Stephen and the English Men of Letters Series', *Nineteenth-Century Prose* **22:2**, Fall 1995, pp. 95–114. See also Amigoni, D., *Victorian Biography and the Ordering of Discourse*, Hemel Hempstead: Harvester-Wheatsheaf, 1993.

33. Carlyle, T., *Works*, ed. H.D. Trail, 30 vols, London: Chapman and Hall, 1896–1901, vol. 28, pp. 91–92.
34. *Ibid.*, pp. 69–70.
35. *Ibid.*, vol. 2, *German Romance*, pp. 18–19.
36. *Ibid.*, vol 28, p. 74.
37. Stephen, *op. cit.* at note 31, p. 3.
38. *Ibid.*, p. 55.
39. *Ibid.*, p. 93.
40. *Ibid.*, p. 4.
41. *Ibid.*, p. 10.
42. Foucault, M., *Power/Knowledge*, trans. Colin Gordon, Brighton: Harvester, 1980, p. 55.
43. Jordanova, *op. cit.* at note 22, p. 123.
44. Stephen, *op. cit.* at note 31, p. 7.
45. Stephen, L., *The Science of Ethics*, London: Smith, Elder and Co., 1882, p. 63.
46. Stephen, L., *The History of English Thought in the Eighteenth Century*, 2 vols, London: Smith, Elder and Co., 1876, vol. 1, p. 5.
47. *Ibid.*, pp. 1–2.
48. *Ibid.*, pp. 371–72.
49. *Ibid.*, p. 374.
50. Stephen, *op. cit.* at note 31, pp. 167–68.
51. Kayser gives a contrasting (non-biological) account of 'verbal grotesques' – or 'language which gets out of hand' – which finds the concept to be most active in Romantic and Modernist aesthetics; it has its origins in the sixteenth century (Kayser, *op. cit.* at note 3, p. 155).
52. Stephen, L., *Swift*, English Men of Letters, London: Macmillan, 1882, pp. 179–80.
53. Stephen, *op. cit.* at note 31, p. 184.
54. Stephen, *op. cit.* at note 46, vol. 2, p. 376.
55. Maitland, F.W., *Life and Letters of Leslie Stephen*, London: Duckworth, 1906, p. 305.
56. Auguste Comte states that 'The first condition of unity is a subjective principle; and this principle in the Positive system is the subordination of the intellect to the heart' (Comte, A., *A General View of Positivism*, trans. J.H. Bridges, London: Trubner, 1865, p. 13): in other words, and applying this to the context in which Stephen uses the idea, identification and the concomitant spread of social sympathy is generated out of a mind/body split, in which the intellect is the subordinate partner to the power of feelings and sensations.
57. Stephen, *op. cit.* at note 46, p. 376.
58. Boswell, *op. cit.* at note 1, p. 327.
59. Booth addresses the long-standing critical debate about the anti-feminist status of images of women in Rabelais (in a text in which episodes of humiliation are frequent, women are usually subjected to its most degrading forms), and challenges Bakhtin's contention that 'moralistic' readings overlook the quality of the laughter that is offered. Booth takes this one step further: 'I am suggesting, then, that Rabelais' work is unjust to women not simply in the superficial ways that the traditions have claimed but, to some degree, in its fundamental imaginative act' (Booth, W.C., 'Freedom of Interpretation: Bakhtin and the Challenge of Feminist Criticism', *Critical Inquiry* **9: 1,** 1982, pp. 45–76; pp. 65–66). In other words, for Booth, women are objectified and left outside of the community of dialogic relations. For my part, I would not want to write off the historical significance of the 'traditions' that Booth holds to be superficial.
60. Bakhtin, *op. cit.*, at note 9, pp. 17–18.

Thomas Carlyle's grotesque conceits

Paul Barlow

Still the question returns on us: How could a man occasionally of keen insight, not without keen sense of propriety, who had real Thoughts to communicate, resolve to emit them in a shape bordering so closely on the absurd?

Sartor Resartus

His criticisms were often grotesque caricatures. They abounded in contradictions ... and much of the teaching, so far as it is intelligible, is preposterous and impracticable.

The Times, Obituary of Thomas Carlyle, 1881

Carlyle as a grotesque

Grinning, gap-toothed, lounging on a rail, Thomas Carlyle leers out at the viewer in Ford Madox Brown's painting *Work* (1857–1865). Notionally a figure who embodies authority, the full observational and analytical power of the intellectual, Carlyle is relegated to the margins of the image, forced into passivity when confronted by the transformative power of labour. His sardonic, Mephosphelean grin mirrors that of an anarchic, wilful urchin, who is depicted messing with a wheelbarrow while labourers, absorbed in their work, reconstruct the substance of the city, digging deep into its foundations.[1] Carlyle here is a grotesque, his position that of the playful, perverse marginalia of the Gothic prayer book.[2] The workers' single-minded action is countered by his ironic self-consciousness, which threatens to disturb their efficient performance of allotted tasks. Implicating the viewer in inquisitive detachment, like the disruptive boy Carlyle turns the workers' tools into objects of play.

Brown's image draws attention to a paradox. Carlyle's ideas are often characterized as a 'Victorian' belief in the work ethic and the endorsement of authoritarian leadership to enforce it. Yet here he is depicted as inactive and powerless. Carlyle certainly claimed that absorption in labour is sacred. He argued that the healthy body is 'unconscious of itself' and that self-awareness is a 'symptom of derangement' – a sign of the Fall. He thus seems to advocate a condition from which his own advocacy necessarily alienates him, as Brown shows. This grotesque Carlyle experiences knowledge as disorder, writing as a form of disease.[3] The paradox was not lost on many of Carlyle's critics. From the publication of his first major work, Sartor Resartus, commentators identified a form of self-destruction operating in his texts, a tendency to erase their own insights and to constitute an incoherence from within their logic. For Lord Jeffrey, Carlyle's 'genius' was vitiated by his 'odd, broken and ostentatiously irregular' style, and made distasteful by a 'tone of mockery and Mephistophelic humour'.[4] For Thackeray, reviewing *The French Revolution*, Carlyle's 'extraordinary powers' were 'disfigured by grotesque conceits and images'.[5] Both Thackeray and Jeffrey find themselves experiencing 'power' which seems wilfully to distort itself, to construct a 'shape bordering ... on the absurd'. Carlyle's grotesque desecrates his own texts and violates his thought. The identity of his writing is constructed at the expense of its legibility. Carlyle alienates himself from his own meaning.

By the end of his life, Carlyle's opponents were convinced that his very identity as a thinker had become grotesque. Leslie Stephen, writing authoritatively in the *Dictionary of National Biography* complained that Carlyle's 'language of grotesque exaggeration' made his work unintelligible; the reader found it 'difficult to distinguish between the serious and the intentionally humorous'. For Stephen, the publication of the notoriously illiberal *Latter Day Pamphlets* (1850) marked the destructive triumph of the grotesque in Carlyle's mind. His 'excitement carried him away into astonishing displays of grotesque humour and vivid imagination, while his hearers listened in silence or were overpowered by his rhetoric. The pamphlets gave general offence.' Stephen's own excremental image of Carlyle 'pouring out' the offensive 'matter' of the pamphlets indicates the extent to which he, like Brown, sees Carlyle himself as a grotesque body.[6] Another writer, Patrick Proctor Alexander, satirized Carlyle's last major work, his biography of Frederick the Great, in a parody of its author's own style. Alexander's 'Sauerteig' (Carlyle) appears as an embodied oxymoron, 'luminous-tenebrific, sagacious-inept'.[7] Sauerteig/Carlyle gleefully describes hangings ordered by his Frederick-like hero 'Grimwold': 'Singular dance upon nothing going on there in the summer dawn, the opening heavens smiling down upon it; singular! Picturesque enough! lively! naturally – each poor losel having his whim of it – with much convulsed variety of *step*.'

This wild, delighted dance of death epitomizes the image of Carlyle as a 'moral desperado' – in Matthew Arnold's phrase – thrilled by violent transgressions of ethical norms. Certainly the imagery is typical of him. *Latter Day Pamphlets* abounds in deranged dances 'upon nothing'. Towns are 'set-a-dancing' by the railway, their populations jumping about in new, unpredictable steps. Money and paper – pieces of 'scrip' – cause objects to jerk around as if by magic. This failure to find a *ground* for rational analysis is archetypally Carlylean, and it is always associated with the power of the grotesque. For it was not only his critics who considered him grotesque. Carlyle's own first and most important literary persona, Diogenes Teufelsdröckh, the imaginary German philosopher in *Sartor Resartus*, is presented in the book as equally authoritative and ludicrous. His jumbled Latin-Germanic name – translatable as 'Godborn Devilshit' – attests his grotesque identity. Furthermore, it was in the grotesque that contemporaries such as Dickens and Madox Brown identified Carlyle's capacity to speak of the distinctively Victorian (for them 'modern') condition. Both saw in Carlyle an assault on the passive 'picturesque' gaze by which social experience is rendered spuriously harmonious. When Carlyle's 'Picturesque tourist' in *Past and Present* finds his view disrupted by the alienated presence of the unemployed, the Victorian grotesque vision is born. It is the logic of this vision, and of Carlyle's apparently absurd position as a grotesque philosopher, that I wish to consider here.

Stephen's liberal-democratic distaste for Carlyle has characterized twentieth-century responses to Carlyle, who is construed as a disturbed presence in intellectual history.[8] However, the ruptured, ironic, self-cancelling structures to which Stephen's critique draws attention identify a collapse of referentiality and of legible 'master narratives', a position now commonly identified with Postmodern, rather than Victorian, cultural thinking. The connections between Carlyle's work and the characteristic gestures of Postmodernism are complex and problematic. What is important here is that Carlyle's critique of the liberal-Enlightenment project takes the form of an assault on theory, on claims to *write* knowledge. One of the ironies of Postmodernist thought is its tendency to attack 'foundational' arguments for knowledge by proliferating theory.[9] What I wish to suggest here is that for Carlyle, in contrast, the grotesque is constituted by the necessary failures of knowledge. It is, therefore, Carlyle's substitute for theory or, in his own terminology, for 'formulas' or 'mechanisms'.[10] The grotesque is anti-theory. All writing which recognizes its own position as a sign of disease must become grotesque. This is why Stephen was right to identify the grotesque as the visible form of Carlyle's power and also as the source of his 'general offence'. Carlyle's grotesque marks the world as inaccessible to articulation, as that which cannot be mastered by narrative. His tendency to desecrate, or write over, his texts identifies the violence and imposture that is implicit in writing itself. However, it also signals the disjunction between what is intelligible and what is experienced. This is also part of the imposture of writing, its inevitable misrepresentation. The urgently disruptive, anarchic energy that so disturbed Stephen is the attempt to identify the dynamic towards which writing can gesture, but of which it cannot speak.

In his early essay 'On History' (1830) Carlyle expounds his anti-scientific account of history as the continual generation of complex patterns of action irreducible to intelligible chains of cause and effect. The totality of human behaviour forms an unknowably dense 'chaos of being' from which observable historical events emerge into visibility. History-in-itself remains inaccessible to the historian, who must construct representations of events in the knowledge of their instability and fragmentary inadequacy. A complete history would be a 'perfect monster': simultaneously ideal, impossible and oppressive.[11] For Carlyle, then, the body of history is dynamic, transgressive of boundaries, constantly regenerating itself. The historical text is inevitably dislocated, distorted, a caricature. For historical writing to articulate its own relation to the past of which it speaks, it must recognize itself as grotesque.

Such views ally Carlyle with Victor Hugo, who had argued that the 'grotesque' structure of Shakespearean tragi-comedy properly represented historical action as a layering of multiple, unresolved and contradictory moments. Hugo's thinking itself drew on the theory and practice of German Romantic drama, in which Carlyle himself was thoroughly immersed. But Carlyle identifies the grotesque as a manifestation of ruptured, discontinuous experience: an alienation of language from truth.

Of course, this concern with the fragmentation that overcomes language when encountering conditions which require its endless regeneration is a familiar theme in Romantic accounts of the relation between the Sublime and the Beautiful. Carlyle's deployment of the grotesque is, as we shall see, continually allied to his account of the possibility of the Sublime. However, Carlyle clearly identifies in *Sartor Resartus* the psychological and cultural failure of the Sublime as the source for a new grotesque form of philosophical and social engagement. In *Sartor* this point is made at the juncture between the biographical and philosophical components of the text. The structure of *Sartor* is the most complex engagement with the grotesque in Carlyle's work. It will therefore be necessary to consider in detail the role of the form of *Sartor* in the construction of Carlyle's theory of the grotesque.

Sartor Resartus: grotesque language, grotesque form

Mad loves and mad hatreds, church bells and gallows ropes, farce-tragedy, beast-godhead.

Sartor Resartus: 'Old Clothes'

Sartor Resartus is a structurally complex work which operates through the form of proliferating marginal commentary. The text continually emerges from and returns to writing about other, more substantial, texts. In this respect, Carlyle refers back to medieval modes of academic writing, in particular those which function to illuminate and glorify literature of sacred or authoritative status. This pre-modern structure functions as a means to resist the claims of scientific or, more particularly, Utilitarian, modernity. Throughout *Sartor* Carlyle seeks to disrupt the characteristic values and gestures of contemporary intellectual discourse: linear clarity, inductive logic, functional efficiency. Thus *Sartor* works against the 'mechanical' tendencies of the age and provides the conditions to reaffirm the sacred. However, *Sartor* differs fundamentally from its medieval models, because in this instance the marginal comments overwhelm and eviscerate the texts which they claim to elucidate. The heart of the book is an absence: a 'Centre of Indifference' in which all values are suspended. *Sartor*'s aspiration to the sacred is built on an experience of faithlessness. It is this structural inversion that gives such importance to the grotesque, as embodied by the book's own grotesque sage, Diogenes Teufelsdröckh.

Sartor begins with a lengthy, tortuous sentence, in which the authorial voice speaks of the progress of knowledge under the figure of the 'Torch of Science', its light now spreading into every once-dark corner of the world. The sentence already generates linguistic disturbance as the metaphor of the Torch becomes increasingly strained by elaboration to include 'innumerable Rush lights and Sulphur Matches', as it attempts to cover the modern proliferation of knowledge. Already, Carlyle articulates the potential failure of language, its encounter with a multiple, uncontainable dynamic. The unity of the metaphor of light begins to break into fragments, and with it the very claim of 'science' to picture the world completely.

This convoluted opening sentence is followed by a paragraph in which the progress of knowledge is unwittingly acknowledged as fragmentary. Demonstrating the scope of modern science, the author describes successful disquisitions on 'the Social Contract, on Standards of Taste, on the Migrations of the Herring'. Here the grotesque begins to enter the text as a consequence of the forms of knowledge described, in which the aspiration to totality reveals the arbitrary conjoining of the irresolvably alien. The irony and absurdity of these juxtapositions is lost on the 'author', whose position as embodiment of an objective science is thus threatened by the emergence of the grotesque. It is the author's failure to *hear* the grotesque within his own voice that alienates that voice from the reader. The authorial voice loses its authority and moves towards a conditional rather than absolute claim on the reader: it becomes a 'character' in the book, rather than the book itself.

At this point *Sartor* begins to constitute *itself* as grotesque. The loss of authorial authority generates a split in the body of the text. The weakened voice of the author calls on a new voice as authority: that of Teufelsdröckh, whose comprehensive exposition of the 'Philosophy of Clothes' is proffered to the reader as an all-encompassing body of knowledge. However, Teufelsdröckh's own text, *Die Kleider ihr Wirden und Werken* ('Clothes: their Origin and Influence') is only available to the reader as 'translated' fragments. The textual body of truth is permanently alienated from *Sartor*, which can never fully assimilate it. Each attempt to do so ends in failure, as the 'editor' – the original author demotes himself to this role – seeks to pin down Teufelsdröckh's elusive claims. The text can never speak, but must always be spoken of. Its knowledge is continually deferred. The Philosophy of Clothes itself mirrors this condition, being defined by the absence of the body – of naked truth.

Expounding the Philosophy of Clothes, the editor quotes Teufelsdröckh's claim that 'Clothes have made Men of us, they are threatening to make Clothes-screens of us.'[12] The naked condition of the postulated 'aboriginal savage' is construed as animalistic. Clothing constructs consciousness and internality. For Teufelsdröckh, however, this desire for clothing is not a fall from Edenic communion with divine purpose, but rather a necessary act, constituting 'individuality, distinctions, social polity'. However, clothing's capacity to generate internality and difference also threatens to negate or screen the body, and to efface the subjectivity it has brought into being. Clothing substitutes for identity, forcing humans to function as aggregations of signs. Thus clothing is the source of both the Sublime and the grotesque; it simultaneously spiritualizes and caricatures humanity. The structure and content of *Sartor* play on this double function of clothing.

The baroque complexity of the book's structure corresponds to Teufelsdröckh's own comments on the history of costume and on the lure of what he calls the 'Dandiacal Body'. The early chapters discuss perverse and improbable developments in fashion as signs of the contortions through which human psychology has passed. Teufelsdröckh's commentary partakes of these very contortions as he ascribes moral significance to ruffs, aprons and hooped skirts. The disturbed character of the Clothes philosophy is apparent at this stage, as it obscures the distinction between the spiritual and caricatural functions of clothing. Reading clothes as pointers to human mental states, Teufelsdröckh turns his own philosophy into a parody of itself. Like the conjoined theories of Taste and Herring migration, Teufelsdröckh's attempt to read the morality of aprons becomes grotesque. Teufelsdröckh seems, as much as the original authorial voice, unaware of the absurdity of his claims. Clothing the vanity of Dandyism with his philosophical rhetoric, Teufelsdröckh conceals its very tendency to negate subjectivity. In order to recognize the danger of Teufelsdröckh's interpretative rhetoric, the reader has to 'see through' the Clothes philosophy, to rid it of its own concealing layers and reveal the absence of the body beneath.

In the chapter called 'The Dandiacal Body', the reader is invited to do just this. After an analysis of Dandies as members of religious sects engaged in a form of devotion that requires them to 'keep themselves unspotted from the world', Teufelsdröckh contrasts this with the alternative sect of 'Poor Slaves' (the destitute), dedicated to lives of poverty and obedience. The editor is unsure whether Teufelsdröckh genuinely understands these two groups as religious sects, or whether he intends a Swiftian satire on inequality and the very *absence* of binding spiritual values in modern society. In the end he is forced to abandon the prospect that Teufelsdröckh's own voice be granted authorial authority, insisting that 'his irony has overshot itself; we see through it, and perhaps through him'. Thus Teufelsdröckh himself is revealed as an absence: an empty suit.

This chapter comes after several in which the Clothes philosophy has been offered as an agent of spiritual transformation, as a means to read the world as signs and thus to see Creation itself as a 'vesture', an elaborate, complex, embroidered design. Here the Sublime moment of revelation is transformed by the grotesque reduction of its form into a means to mis-recognize social and cultural facts. The philosophy re-clothes rather than reveals. If the universe itself is a 'Dandiacal Body', then the philosophy may be as misplaced in this respect as in others. Certainly *Sartor* itself is recognizable as Dandiacal in form, wilfully over-refined, exaggerated, self-regarding.

Here, then, is the essential significance of the grotesque for Carlyle. The reader must not be *persuaded* by the Clothes philosophy, for to become so would be to be trapped by its text: to be spoken by language, which is conceptual clothing. Clothing only generates internality by alienating the subject from the body. The grotesque is the making visible of this alienation. It displays writing as an aberrant, illicit body. The narcissistic Dandy becomes the grotesque 'incroyable'. Throughout *Sartor*, Carlyle presents Teufelsdröckh's voice as potentially seductive, that of a wordsmith and sentimentalist. Here Carlyle indicates his debt to Sterne, whose novels *A Sentimental Journey* and *Tristram Shandy* are important models for *Sartor*.[13] As in *A Sentimental Journey*, the urge to experience emotional authenticity is presented as a form of connoisseurship which by definition precludes what it seeks.[14] Early in the book, the editor writes of his visit to Teufelsdröckh. He describes a moment when Teufelsdröckh, walking home with him, expressed his feelings about the city at night in an effusive speech.[15] The speech itself is self-consciously purple prose, woven from contrasting vignettes ('Riot cries aloud, and staggers and swaggers in his rank dens of shame; and the mother, with streaming hair, kneels over her pallid, dying infant, whose cracked lips only her tears now moisten', etc.) It is, in fact, an exercise in literary Sentiment. It epitomizes

Teufelsdröckh's double identity: he is either divinely inspired or full of shit. After the speech, says the editor, 'we looked into his face', but 'no feeling might be traced there'. Teufelsdröckh remains empty of identity: a speaker of diverse texts.

But the speech is important. It is defined by its ability to codify experience; each activity is neatly pigeon-holed, given its own literary flourish. However, it is the proximity of the alien worlds it encapsulates that is emphasized: 'All these heaped and huddled together, with nothing but a little carpentry and masonry between them.' The text seeks to move from a Picturesque vision of the sleepy town to a Sublime vision of transcendental totality. It is, however, caught between these two aesthetic moments. Instead, it describes the forced conjoining of opposites 'heaped' together. It is, therefore a grotesque vision. Seeking to dissolve the walls between people, Teufelsdröckh cannot deliver the universality necessary to sustain sublimity. Breaking the picturesque image, he forces into being a vision that is trapped by its own aspirations.

Here, then, is the particular character of the grotesque vision in *Sartor*. It is defined by the experience of entrapment. Teufelsdröckh is potentially in thrall to his own rhetoric. By structuring the book as a series of marginal commentaries, Carlyle alienates the reader from the very literary forms he uses. Hence the fact that the book lurches unpredictably from one literary genre to another, each of which breaks up just as it begins to fulfil readers' expectations. The central instance of this is Teufelsdröckh's experience of failed romance. Blumine, Teufelsdröckh's faithless beloved, seems to offer the prospect of a Romantic communion transcending the alienating entrapments of social signs. The chapter 'Romance', in which she appears, is at the centre of the book. As Isobel Armstrong points out, it is both an instance of the Romantic aesthetic and a critique of its values.[16] The chapter is Romantic by virtue of its refusal of narrative resolution in the face of an untranslatable experience. It negates, however, the Romantic affirmation of such experience. Teufelsdröckh appears to achieve transcendent communion at the very moment he is rejected in favour of a another suitor. Impulsively kissing Blumine before he leaves her, 'their lips were joined, their two souls, like dew drops, rushed into one, for the first time, and for the last'.[17] This florid moment of seemingly authentic intensity is rendered grotesque by the reader's knowledge that Blumine's rejection is caused by nothing more serious than a desire to cut an impressive figure in high society, in other words, by the victory of Clothing over Subjectivity.

Within the moment of Romantic transcendence, then, is the triumph of clothing: the defeat of the sublime by the grotesque. For Carlyle, it is the condition of literary form that this absurd triumph be continually enacted by the text. The only authenticity the text can achieve is its parody of the sublime moment it seeks. Romanticism constitutes itself as kitsch, generating satirical pastiche of its own rhetoric. Teufelsdröckh's very experience is defined by its 'clothing'. As he re-enacts the role of a Werther-like tragic lover, he finds himself trapped by the conventions from which he seeks to free himself.

In *Sartor*, then, the text generates gaps through which the rituals and mechanics of social interaction are seen to be rhetorical; but while the prospect of the sublime is continually engendered, such moments are always recuperated by the text as grotesque, as in the cases of Teufelsdröckh's night speech and his fantasized Romantic intimacy. Each triumph is a move towards caricature and thus to the negation of consciousness. As all forms of communication abstract themselves as patterns of signs, they become a vision of empty clothing jerking with its own mechanical life: the animation of inanimate screens as a Dance of Death. Teufelsdröckh moves through a world of caricatures. His only means of reconstituting subjecthood is to accept this parade of signs. Visiting London, Teufelsdröckh passes through Monmouth Street, where he identifies a Jewish second-hand clothes dealer as a transfigured Biblical patriarch. Wearing three hats on his head and holding out his arms to drape cloth over them as he advertises his wares, he becomes an impossible Angel of Apocalypse. This incarnation of allegory proffers his clothes as Revelations.[18] Here the relation between caricature and sublimity is defined by the loss of the authoritative Biblical master-text. The archetypally sublime figures from the Apocalypse, 'clothed with the sun', epitomize the triumph of the symbolic over the material, as the material form of the universe itself is reconstituted as Signs spoken by the text. However, in conditions in which all text generates the grotesque, such a moment can only be reduced to Teufelsdröckh's typically absurd need to translate the Dandiacal figure of the merchant into a spiritual being. Identifying the importance of the emerging rhetoric of advertising, Carlyle plays off the merchant's and Teufelsdröckh's conception of signs. In the absence of the truly Revelatory text, the mercantile circulation of desires – 'mad loves and mad hatreds' – becomes the only actual master-text at work: one in the service of the clothes-screen. In order to see the truth, Teufelsdröckh must miss it. He must become absurd. In this respect, Colin Cameron's recent claim that Carlyle's work can be illuminated by reference to Kierkegaard's thought is entirely justified.[19] The biographical structure of *Sartor* functions to emphasize the existential moment from which choice emerges. Teufelsdröckh's act of interpretation is both necessary and grotesque: a failure which generates action.

The necessary conclusion to this existential dilemma is that Teufelsdröckh, seeking to enter history, must silence himself in order to avoid his continual entrapment in the inevitable grotesque position of a 'modern philosopher', whose discourse constantly becomes pastiche, a form of 'kitsch' intellectuality. The silence of the philosopher as actor in history leads us to consider the problem of writing history itself, and Carlyle's conception of the role of grotesque thinking in the work of the historian.

The French Revolution: history as farce-tragedy

> Incongruity fronting Incongruity, and, as it were, recognising themselves incongruous, and staring stupidly in each other's face.
>
> *The French Revolution*, vol. 2

If *Sartor* articulates the grotesque as a problem of modern consciousness, continually tending towards the 'kitsch', *The French Revolution* construes the grotesque as a necessary means to provide the literary form to speak of complex and unresolved social transformation. Here the grotesque belongs to the problem of reading history itself. Carlyle's use of the grotesque, I will suggest, is inseparable from the act of narrating historical process itself, from the need to both construct and resist the imposition of legibility. In this respect, *The French Revolution*, like *Sartor*, examines the limits of language both as an agent in history and as the means to know it. If *Sartor* explores the problem of authentic experience for the modern subject, *The French Revolution* addresses history itself as a dynamic in which the sublime continually tends to generate the grotesque.

In this respect, Carlyle's writing can be fruitfully compared with Karl Marx's attempt to both recognize and negate the grotesque as a mode of reading history. Marx, as is well known, uses the term 'grotesque' when describing the form of the commodity under capitalism. The mechanisms of capitalist production alienate the commodity from its own materiality and function, generating fantastic or 'mystical' identities. As an ordinary wooden table is transfigured into a commodity it 'not only stands with its feet upon the ground, but, in relation to all other commodities, it stands on its head, and evolves out of its wooden brain grotesque ideas, far more wonderful than "table turning" ever was'.[20] Like Carlyle's, Marx's grotesque manifests itself through parody of the prospects of transcendence and of subjectivity. The image of the animated table draws directly on the anthropomorphized houses and furniture found in the grotesquery of cartoonists such as Cruikshank.[21] But Marx's satirical rhetoric plays against the scientific claims of his own discourse. Marx both ridicules and invokes the 'misty realm' of theology as a necessary but aberrant agency of explanation, through which the commodity can be spoken of by philosophy. Theology is an alien body of thought within the Materialist text, just as the 'ideas' emerging from the wooden mind of the table are both a reality and an impossibility. Thus Marx's own philosophical language becomes an instance of the grotesque, of a conflated and incompatible form. Capitalism, by the form of the commodity, continually forces the persistence of illicit Idealist thinking in the very text which seeks to expel it.

Of course, for Marx, it is necessary to contain this tendency, to identify the grotesque as a phenomenon of which his text has possession, to separate his own voice from grotesque identity. Whereas for Carlyle in *Sartor*, the philosophical voice and body *are* grotesque (absurd, scatological, incoherent), for Marx, as for Stephen, the textual voice must suppress the grotesque in order to affirm its legitimacy. In *Capital*, Marx begins by analysing the commodity, its grotesque identity subjected to the philosophical voice, negated by the torch of science. If the opening of *Sartor* realizes the collapse of the text in the eruption of the grotesque, *Capital* proclaims the text's irresistible force by dissipating the grotesque ideas, ejecting them from their wooden brains.

This point is relevant to Carlyle's *French Revolution* because it marks the problem of narration for both Carlyle and Marx. As we have seen, Carlyle's 'On History' had implied that the historical text must of necessity continually overwrite itself, cancel its own knowledge and dramatize its alienation from the conditions it describes. In doing so, it can never attain to 'science', as Marx seeks to do. Instead, it seeks the Shakespearean form of tragi-comedy, or the grotesque.

As a means to approach the French Revolution this invocation of drama is of particular significance. As Paul Hindson and Tim Gray have shown in their study of Burke's use of dramatic metaphor, for Burke the revolution in France was both aesthetically and politically illicit *because* it took the form of tragi-comedy.[22] If, for Hugo, the tragi-comic grotesque proffered a fullness which transcended theatrical orderliness, for Burke, it marked a drama from which control had slipped away. The structure of tragi-comedy is unpredictable and absurd.

Carlyle inherits Burke's critique of the Revolution, in particular his claim that the conditions which constitute a stable political culture can never be constructed anew on abstract principles of justice without generating unpredictable destabilizing dynamics. For Burke, the cultural patterns of expectation and behaviour which sustain social relations depend on facts which are themselves finally unknowable.[23] The metaphor of drama allows him to develop a language to describe this conception of politics as the *enactment* of roles. Dramatic terminology operates to indicate the ways in which social functions are performances, that roles are occupied and sustained by the exercise of rhetoric. It demonstrates that power is both ritual and locked into patterns of conflict. For Burke (unlike Marx) a political theorist is concerned with structural rather than causal relations. Dramatic form is concerned with the accommodation of the particular (and its specific causes) to patterns which allow a continual assimilation of conflict by ritual and reconstitution of ritual through conflict. A grotesque structure is one through which the formal possibilities for such a process are inaccessible. It is open, arbitrary, multiple.

Burke's concern with dramatic form is consistent with Carlyle's metaphor of clothing in *Sartor*. As we have seen, *Sartor* also deploys a dramatic structure as part of its purpose to articulate the theatre of splits, conjunctions and ironies that constitute a grotesque body of thought. Clothing itself stands for the function of ritual in *Sartor* in a way that works both to identify the workings of social myths and to mark their absolute alienation from the moments of free choice that constitute pure subjectivity. For Carlyle, as Cameron shows, this conflict continually generates moments of existential freedom environed by the theatrical mechanics of various forms of 'clothing'.

Carlyle's radicalism in this respect is wholly alien to Burke's conception of structural orders through which dramatic action is realized. *Sartor* continually emphasizes that social myths are grotesque because it insists on the possibility of dislocation from them. For Burke, in contrast, it is necessary to maintain rituals of political action and therefore to recognize the formal limits of their dramatic roles. Carlyle's account of the French Revolution is Burkean in two important senses. Firstly, it accepts Burke's claim that causal explanations are of limited relevance to an understanding of the logic of political conflict. Throughout *The French Revolution* Carlyle narrates events with a specifically dramatic emphasis. Problems emerge and enter into the performance of political conflict. He does not seek to marshal causation in order to negate dramatic action. Secondly, Carlyle accepts Burke's belief that the revolution is tragi-comic in structure. For Carlyle, however, as we have seen, the tragi-comic is the necessary formal condition for radical social and cultural transformation.

The apparently contradictory character of this Burkean radicalism explains Carlyle's language in *The French Revolution*. The nature of this project is first articulated in Carlyle's early essay 'Signs of the Times'. Carlyle describes a ship at anchor as an image of the state. The crew imagine that their position is stable, tied to the rock beneath the sea. But they cannot *know* what their anchor is attached to. Its being is inaccessible to them. Only their experience of stability leads them to assume that the sea-bed itself is stable. But if the 'rock' awakes, if it is not dead matter but a living, dynamic creature with its own desires and aspirations, the creature may begin to move; the ship will thrash about. Soon it will lurch through the ocean, its destination unknown, its crew helpless. This, claims Carlyle, is the condition of modern political culture, caught between energy unleashed from a powerful but unknowable source and the visible antics of those who claim to command the vessel. Those who can see ahead cannot understand the journey. The helmsman may seem to be directing the movements of the ship. Foolishly, he may even believe that he is, refusing to acknowledge the monster below, declaring it to be a myth. But such surface rhetoric is only a 'sham'.

This image of social change is specifically grotesque. Indeed, it takes the form of allegorical political caricature familiar from the late eighteenth century. Political power is reduced to flailing gestures encountering forces visualized as monstrous figures; it cannot articulate a hidden Reality struggling to constitute itself in history. For Carlyle, then, caricature is an important means to label the very condition of intellectual helplessness in which the theorist finds himself when confronted by social transformation. Unlike Marx, however, Carlyle does not claim access to a position capable of resisting the 'chaos of being', a position from which these historical dynamics can be known and spoken about by 'science'. Rather, he writes from within the chaos, constituting a form of post-scientific writing which attempts to dramatize the continual attempts to generate formal coherence from monstrous figures. It is this refusal of the academic discourse of knowledge that forms Carlyle's grotesque mode of writing.

The revolutionary conditions described by Carlyle in *The French Revolution* are the continual generation of the grotesque. Sustainable social and cultural representation is impossible. A proliferating struggle of clashing 'formulas' attempts to replace the lost cultural intelligibility of the Age of Chivalry, but reason cannot control a dynamic which springs from a complex of processes constantly overtaking their articulations. The opening sentence of the book refers to this process: 'President Henault, remarking on Royal surnames of honour, how difficult it often is to ascertain not only when, but even why they were conferred, takes occasion, in his sleek official way, to make a philosophical reflection.'[24] The odd syntax is characteristically Carlylean. The structure of the sentence forces the reader to participate in Henault's confusion when confronted with obscure titles separated from the conditions which generated them. Such 'surnames of honour' are often difficult to explain; the source, and even the meaning, is often obscure, lost in the mist of time. The theatre of royal authority is revealed as an aggregation of occluded histories. Henault, President of the Paris Parlement, sleekly glosses over the problem by claiming transparency for Louis XV's newly acquired title of 'Well Beloved'. Monarchy's rituals now have meaning in an Age of Sentiment. Louis is King of Hearts. However, though the 'sleek' language of the official asserts the continuity (and constant regeneration) of rhetorical honours, it reveals their dangerously extended supply lines. The language of chivalry presents itself as alien, its forms and terms begin to border on the absurd.

We are, then, in the same territory as in the opening passage from *Sartor*. Language attempts to maintain an unbroken ritual of affirmation. Just as 'science' extends its knowledge in a continual expansion of light, so monarchy accumulates through history endless affirmations of its value. But these signs of value have developed into a baroque rhetoric. They have become empty clothes. No one knows why the monarch was granted this or that 'honour', or what it is that is being honoured.

If this aspect of *The French Revolution* signals the transformation of myths of royal power ('the Age of Chivalry') into absurdities and caricatures, then the eruption of the power of the sansculottes implies a very different form of grotesque. Here the image of the monstrous force which seeks to find its language, but is forced to accumulate fragments of political and cultural rhetorics as a sign of its very alienation from cultural coherence, is central to the text. The multitudinous body of the sansculottes is stressed throughout the book. Individual figures separate themselves from the mob, sink back into it, shift its form.

The culminating moment of the grotesque in the narrative is the intrusion of a sansculottic mob into the royal apartments in 1792. As the Duke of Brunswick's invading army approaches Paris, threatening the Revolution, the King finds himself represented as a contradictory body. He is sought out by the sansculottes as a figure of the revolutionary nation, to become a King of Revolution. Likewise he is claimed by Brunswick as the sign and body of legitimacy, in the name of which he invades and ravages France. The former figure brings the Carnival moment of the 'peasant King' into the being of history, forcing it from popular ritual into conflation with actual monarchy. The latter claim marks legitimacy as treason, authority as anarchy. As the sansculottes break into the royal apartments to meet the royal family the fantasy of the organic 'feudal' community is forced to enact itself. The relation of king and people has been localized, but fails to come into being. Incongruity fronts incongruity and 'recognizes themselves incongruous'. The moment is comic precisely because it is a revelation of the grotesque. There can be no feudal affirmation of a king entering the body of his people, as fantasized in Scott's *Ivanhoe*, a novel to which Carlyle refers implicitly and explicitly on several occasions in his writings.[25] The signs of revolution are forced into a montage with those of royalty. The Phrygian cap is placed on the king's head; the sansculottes attempt to chat informally with the royal family. But neither identity can speak to the other. Each is rendered 'stupid' by the moment.

For Carlyle, then, this is the moment when history becomes comedy. It is also the moment which generates the 'monstrous' forms of the September Massacres and the Terror. Thus the comic and the monstrous constitute one another as the fulfilment of the grotesque. Earlier in the history Carlyle writes of concepts entering into the real ('Patriotism, passing that way, fired a volley in the Felon-world'). Bodies of people come into historical visibility by generating conceptual identities. Concepts struggle to enter into social being, to make the world representable once more, but in their struggle the world is a grotesque body. 'Patriotism' is continually oscillating between realization and vacuity. Just as the ceremony of kingship slides into caricature as it is revealed to be a sham – chivalry is theatrical costume and incredible claims – so the new formulas fail to function as symbols. During Robespierre's celebration of 'the Supreme Being' the grotesque condition of 'rational faith' is marked by the attempt to embody reason itself. One 'Madame Barboux' personifies Reason. Carlyle describes her toothless smiles to the crowd, but then seeks to speak from her own experience (to become 'the voice of Reason') as she travels home from the festival, forced back into the confusion from which she should be aloof.

For Carlyle, then, the comic monstrosity manifested by revolution is the only possible position from which a 'philosophical' discourse of history can speak. In a dynamic age neither the legitimacy of representation nor the identity of the real can be known. The impossible position of embodied 'Reason' is itself a sign of the inadequacy of a Humean or Burkean voice. This point leads us back to a consideration of *Sartor Resartus*, as an attempt at a mode of writing in which 'philosophy' can speak in the absence of conditions for rational exchange. The work entails, as we have seen, an account of the conditions of academic discourse, as it sets Empiricism against Transcendental Idealism, while denuding both of the ground of their claims.

Grotesque philosophy and the grotesque philosopher

These points lead us back to the figure of Carlyle and to Stephen's ascription of grotesque identity to the writer himself. As we have seen, in *Sartor* only the philosopher can escape the grotesque, not the philosophy. To achieve existential authenticity he must silence himself. In *The French Revolution* the only escape from the parody of monarchy, religion and its symbols lies in the figures of Mirabeau and Danton, both 'realities', who are presented as Gargantuan figures, 'swallowing all formulas' with insatiable appetites. This inclusive grotesque counters the reductive, parodic, caricature into which 'Reason' enters when it attempts to realize itself as a Sign. Both *The French Revolution* and *Sartor* deal with the conditions of representation. In particular they are concerned with the epistemology of history. As 'philosophical' accounts of history, however, both texts refuse academic conventions and, indeed, assert their inapplicability in modern conditions. Like Marx, Carlyle seeks to avoid 'interpreting' the world, insisting on the act of changing it. If, for Stephen, Carlyle himself became grotesque, this was because this willed failure of interpretation so alienated him from the conditions he sought to illuminate that his texts generated struggles against themselves. It is a criticism that has been repeated regularly since. It is true that Carlyle, following Burke, attacks 'grand narratives' of historical development. In *Sartor* Hegel is treated satirically. Teufelsdröckh is a kind of anti-Hegel. Like Marx, he turns Hegel on his head but, unlike Marx, he then proceeds to roll him over again.

Carlyle's inversion of Hegel is the key to his conception of the necessity of grotesque style as an affirmation of freedom. It is a very different proposition from Marx's. A comparison of two passages articulates this difference and draws attention to the philosophical rationale for his deployment of the grotesque. The first is from Marx, the second from Carlyle. In his satirical critique of Napoleon III, *The Eighteenth Brumaire of Louis Napoleon*, Marx begins with the famous sentence that 'somewhere in Hegel' it is remarked that history repeats itself, but that Hegel 'forgets to add' that the first time it is as tragedy, the second as comedy. The sentence is fascinating, and much commented upon. Marx finds this phrase 'somewhere' in Hegel. Amid the coherent, all-encompassing theorization of history that is Hegel, this statement is made. It has a role, a logic, wherever it is, but this logic has slipped Marx's mind. It is somewhere, but where? Correspondingly, Hegel also nods. He too forgets; it just doesn't occur to him to mention that the comic follows the tragic.

Marx and Hegel here drop out of philosophical discourse. They become subject to their own bodies and to history (to 'mortality'): things slip their minds. At this point Marx's text becomes a parody of itself. It is tempting to say that at this point Marx becomes Carlyle. Marx's attempts to speak the language of philosophical analysis fail with his memory. The tragic becomes the comic. Marx is no longer the master of the narrative of history, but rather an observer, or, in part, a victim of its ironies. His text is tragic for *being* a comedy, comic as a defence against the assault on the legitimacy of its claims to speak at all. The 'Eighteenth Brumaire' of Napoleon III cannot *be* history. It has already been history; it is a distraction.[26] Marx must recover his mastery by attempting to create a logic from aberrance. He must repress the grotesque eruption of Napoleon III, a parody of the 'real' Napoleon. He must demonstrate that history is not the mere aggregation of conflated instances, but that it is a realization of a logic spoken by 'scientific' discourse.[27]

This is the position of Carlyle/Teufelsdröckh. The moment when history becomes comedy, when it ceases to be dynamic and intelligible, and also when it negates its *being*; it becomes unhistorical. The Philosophy of Clothes is this condition, a series of surfaces replacing a logic of development.

And this is how Hegel appears in *Sartor*. The English editor, trying to locate Teufelsdröckh's ideas in the debates of German philosophers, finds that he has read everything, consumed the tragic and the comic, the profound and the trivial, Classical and ephemeral. He is unable to place Teufelsdröckh amid this flurry of texts. Teufelsdröckh 'strangely' places Hegel and Bardili 'under a common ban' (that is, he rejects Hegel and Bardili for the same reasons – Hegel and Bardili are at some level 'the same' for him). What are we to make of this? Who is Bardili? One of Hegel's tutors, Bardili was also a theorist of logic, but his work has since been forgotten by history. Is the debate between – and the equation of – Hegel and Bardili, the tragic or the comic? The all-inclusive, profoundly influential thinker and the irrelevant minor figure, sidelined and unimportant: a footnote to the history of philosophy. But *is* Bardili an irrelevance? Is the conjunction meaningful? Is it deliberately whimsical, nonsensical? Could we get at Teufelsdröckh's intentions? Are Carlyle and

Teufelsdröckh identical here? Is Carlyle making a definite point about Hegel or not? The conjunction of Hegel and Bardili mirrors our inability to know Carlyle – it produces questions about sincerity, of the origins of a voice, while refusing to resolve them. This is, of course, the actual 'ban' set up against Hegel. Unlike Hegel and Marx, Carlyle is not identified with his text – he cannot be known as a theory, only as an *identity*. In a sense, it doesn't matter who Hegel and Marx *are*. What matters is their text – that, at least, is their claim. As we have seen, the biographical structure of *Sartor*, its insistence on knowing Teufelsdröckh rather than his theory, is an assault on the integrity of the text, generating its moments of forgetfulness. Carlyle's refusal of authorship marks the position of authorship itself: the failure to know history.

For Carlyle, then, leering on the margins of *Work*, the tension between writing and doing is unresolvable. While the labourers are immersed in activity, Carlyle is absorbed by the grotesque. But this form of absorption is necessary for Carlyle in order to disrupt and disorder the claims of theory – to generate eruptions of activity (of 'work') within its mechanical body. For liberals such as Stephen this is the fundamental problem with Carlyle. If the intellectual is forced to write over his own claims, how is critical or ethical judgement possible? Stephen himself seeks a subjectivity-free 'scientific' discourse comparable to Marx's. But the claim to speak with the 'voice of reason' is fraught with difficulties, as Carlyle himself shows. For Carlyle, the grotesque circumvents the failure of reason to comprehend the multiple, contradictory bodies of history and identity. It is simultaneously dynamic and ironic, both engendering transformative energies and alienating itself from them. It sees unresolved and active bodies of thought and culture.

Notes

Unless otherwise stated, references are to Carlyle, T., *Works*, ed. H.D. Trail, 30 vols, London: Chapman and Hall, 1896–1901.

1. The picture depicts navvies breaking up the surface of a road in order to lay new drains. Carlyle, with F. D. Maurice, watches the proceedings from the side of the street. Bobus, the politician and sausage-maker from *Latter Day Pamphlets*, is referred to in the background of the painting. See 'Hudson's Statue', Carlyle, vol. 20. Figures of passers-by may refer to the ironic contrast of the Dandiacal and Poor Slave sects discussed in *Sartor Resartus*. Carlyle's expression recalls his own contrast of devotion with irony in *Latter Day Pamphlets*, where he claims that the nation is 'smirking, grimacing, cutting jokes about all things, and has not been bent in dreadful earnestness on anything at all'. See 'Parliaments', Carlyle, vol. 20, p. 226. Holman Hunt attacked Brown's depiction of Carlyle, claiming that the missing tooth was a wholly invented 'defect' and that Carlyle's expression was indecorous (Hunt, W.H., *Pre-Raphaelitism and the Pre-Raphaelite Brotherhood*, 2 vols, London: Macmillan, 1905, vol. 2, p. 157). The significance of Carlyle's expression in relation to the tension between absorption and discursivity is discussed in authoritative detail by Colin Trodd (Trodd, C., 'The Laboured Vision and the Realm of Value: Articulations of Identity in Ford Madox Brown's *Work*', in Harding, E. (ed.), *Reframing the Pre-Raphaelites*, Aldershot: Scolar Press, 1996).

2. Brown's own early *Seeds and Fruits of English Poetry* had taken the structure of Gothic decorative illumination as its model. The popularity of the grotesque in early Victorian illustration derived from

54 VICTORIAN CULTURE AND THE IDEA OF THE GROTESQUE

revivals of Gothic marginalia precipitated by the publication of the *Prayerbook of Emperor Maximilian*, with marginalia by Dürer, Cranach and others. S. C. Hall's *Book of British Ballads* (London: J. How, 1843) had included much grotesque imagery derived from recent German ballad illustrations. *Work* subtly deploys Gothic structure without pastiche of medieval illumination, reconstituting it for the proto-sociological gaze of modern social criticism. In this procedure Brown also revises Carlyle's literary devices for pictorial purposes, drawing on *Past and Present*.

3. The relation of the grotesque to realism in Brown's aesthetic is of interest here, especially as the classical body of the labourer and the grotesque body of Carlyle are encompassed by a Hogarthian conception of beauty constructed in the relation of 'Character' to 'Caricature'. Brown's model here is Hogarth's print of the Country Dance in *The Analysis of Beauty* (1753).

4. Fielding, K.J., Introduction to Carlyle, T., *The French Revolution*, Oxford: O.U.P, 1989, p. ix.

5. Seigel, J.P., *Thomas Carlyle: the Critical Heritage*, London: Routledge, 1971, p. 69. Such tendencies continue. Both of these criticisms are quoted by K.J. Fielding in his admirable introduction to *The French Revolution* (*op. cit.* at note 4). Speaking in his own voice, Fielding complains that Carlyle is 'curiously "vulgar" at times, including the grotesque Anglicising of French and clumsy French intrusions' (p. xi).

6. Carlyle's own comments on his writing are full of expressions which emphasize the relationship between writing and excrement. When joking about finding a publisher for *Sartor Resartus*, Carlyle spoke of his problems getting his 'dreck' out. See Colin Trodd's subtly inflected account in Chapter 3 of Carlyle's similar play with constipation and diarrhoea when describing his struggles with his biography of Cromwell. The association between constipation and melancholia in early modern thinking may also be relevant here. See Smith, P.J., 'Ajax by Any Other Name Would Smell as Sweet' (in Lascombe, A. (ed.), *Tudor Theatre: Emotion in the Theatre*, Bern: Peter Lang, 1996), for a discussion of the imagery of constipation in Shakespeare.

7. Alexander, P.P., *Carlyle Redivivus, being an Occasional Discourse on Sauerteig by Smelfungus*, Glasgow: Maclehose, 1881, p. 50. This was the reprinted appendix to Alexander's earlier *Mill and Carlyle*, a critical analysis of Mill's theory of causation in relation to ethical choice. The title refers to Carlyle's notorious pamphlet, *An Occasional Discourse on the Nigger Question*, in which he comes close to advocating the return of slavery. Sauerteig is one of Carlyle's personas, notably in *Past and Present*. Alexander's conjunction of Mill and Carlyle is repeated by Edward Jenks in his *Thomas Carlyle and John Stuart Mill* (Orpington: George Allen, 1888). Jenks takes a very different view from Alexander's. For Jenks, Mill is fatally constricted by his Utilitarian aspiration to functional academic discourse, while Carlyle successfully creates a mode of writing which generates a dynamic of moral and intellectual engagement operating to counter the atomizing specialization of modern culture.

8. Simon Heffer deftly summarizes the anxious commentary on Carlyle during the twentieth century, concentrating on the accusations of proto-fascism (Heffer, S., *Moral Desperado: A Life of Thomas Carlyle*, London: Weidenfeld and Nicolson, 1995, pp. 1–26). The claim that Carlyle turns analytical powers into failure and aberrance is also articulated by Raymond Williams in *Culture and Society*. Perhaps most interesting is the use of Carlyle in Armstrong's recent *Victorian Poetry*. Referring to 'Marxists, feminists and deconstruction' as agents of an implicitly pan-historical 'theory' brought to bear on history, she constitutes Carlyle as the bearer of theory which cannot escape historicity. Oscillating between accounts of Carlyle as an intelligible theorist and as a figure whose 'pathology' traps him in contradiction, she offers his work as a means to speak of the politically embedded projects of the fully 'literary' writers who form the subject of her analysis (Armstrong, I., *Victorian Poetry: Poetry, Poetics and Politics*, London: Routledge, 1993, pp. 3–8). Thus Carlyle becomes emblematic of thinking caught between a legitimate claim to academic attention as applicable theory and becoming an object of that attention as historical symptom. Interestingly, Armstrong makes extensive use of the concept of the grotesque, construing it as a radical aesthetic which refuses to announce itself as such.

9. Postmodern thinking often works to fetishize the *act* of theorization. Theory is offered both as transcendent knowledge and as its substitute. Euphoric accounts of the implosion of logic and the baroque profusion of self-generating theory are to be found in the writings of the Krokers, in which Postmodern grotesque takes its most hysterical form. The conscious 'absurdity' of these sub-Baudrillardian texts is an interesting comparison with Carlyle's 'preposterous' tendencies. See Kroker, A., Kroker, M., and Cook, D. (eds), *Panic Encyclopedia: The Definitive Guide to the Postmodern Scene*, Basingstoke: Macmillan, 1989.

10. The term 'formulas' is used throughout *The French Revolution*. The famous contrast of 'mechanism' and 'dynamism' occurs in *Signs of the Times*. See Carlyle, vol. 27, pp. 56–82.

11. Carlyle, vol. 28, p. 168. The phrase comes from 'On History Again', in which an unnamed Carlylean persona advocates the imaginative compression of history into dramatic narratives. The text itself is presented as a fragment, the surviving part of a full document recently discovered in archives. Its fragmentary form signals the inevitably incomplete nature of historical writing.

12. Carlyle, vol. 1, p. 31.
13. The subtitle of *Sartor Resartus* is 'The Life and Opinions of Herr Teufelsdröckh', echoing the full title of *Tristram Shandy*: 'The Life and Opinions of Tristram Shandy, Gent.' The complex structure of *Shandy*, as communication is complicated to the point of impossibility and the proliferation of subplots threatens to overwhelm the progress of the narrative, is derived from the proto-modern art and literature of Melancholia, epitomized by Shakespeare's *Hamlet*. As an enlightened proponent of Augustan culture, Tristram's father Walter hates the name 'Tristram' (meaning 'Melancholic'), which epitomizes this archaic mystificatory, pessimistic aesthetic. Rational control of the future fails, however, as accident leads his son to be christened with the hated name. In *Shandy* the Melancholic tradition is inverted, as the paralysed, obsessive Hamlet is replaced by the revived, endlessly disruptive figure of Yorick, the court jester as priest. Tragedy repeats itself as comedy.
14. Cameron's comments on Carlyle's position as a proto-existentialist writer are relevant here (Cameron, C., *Thomas Carlyle: The Father of Existentialism?*, MA Dissertation, University of Northumbria, 1994). Likewise, Sartre's *Nausea* dramatizes the analysis of 'engagement' and of the bad faith implicit in the search for 'perfect moments'. Both these concerns are evident in *Sartor*.
15. Carlyle, vol. 1, p. 17.
16. Armstrong, *op. cit.* at note 8, pp. 7, 491–92.
17. Carlyle, vol. 1, p. 118.
18. The reference is to such figures as The Woman Clothed with the Sun (*Revelations* 12, 1). The impossible beings described in *Revelations* were regularly identified as instances of the Sublime by Burke and other theorists.
19. Cameron, *op. cit.* at note 18.
20. Marx, K., *Selected Writings*, ed. D. McLellan, Oxford: O.U.P, 1977, p. 435.
21. Šteig, M., 'George Cruikshank and the Grotesque: A Psychodynamic Approach', in Patten, R. (ed.), *George Cruikshank: A Revaluation*, Princeton: Princeton University Press, 1974, pp. 189ff. Notable instances in Cruikshank include the caricature of urban expansion. *London Going out of Town* (1828), in which houses are seen walking into the countryside, and *The Radical Reformer* (1819), in which a guillotine takes on a life of its own as it chases fleeing representatives of 'the Establishment'. Likewise, cartoons in *Punch* often depict paintings 'coming alive', feet emerging from their frames.
22. Hindson, P., and Gray, T., *Burke's Dramatic Theory of Politics*, Aldershot: Avebury, 1988, pp. 131–42.
23. Burke draws on Hume's theory of causation, according to which causal relations cannot be known, but correlations of events can be experienced, consistent correlations being mistermed 'causal'. Hume's own conservative *History of England*, in which Cromwell is attacked as a radical ideologue, dismissive of social experience, influenced Burke. Thackeray's review of *The French Revolution* contrasts Carlyle with the 'graceful' Hume, whose very prose rejects radical disturbance.
24. Carlyle, vol. 2, p. 2.
25. The most complex of Carlyle's engagements with *Ivanhoe* occurs in *Past and Present*, which introduces several characters from the novel while addressing the documented material on the life of Abbot Samson. Much of the medieval section of *Past and Present* constitutes an implicit examination of *Ivanhoe*'s representation of the feudal.
26. The original 'Eighteenth Brumaire' was Napoleon's coup d'état, the final defeat of the Revolution and the return of a form of monarchy. Hence, for Marx, it is a tragic moment. The revolutionary calendar with its 'natural' names for months (Brumaire = 'misty') had long since been replaced by the traditional calendar when Napoleon III staged his own coup: 'time is out of joint'.
27. Of course, Marx claims scientific status for his account of history. The complexities of his problematic attempt to resolve the relation between the scientific, the philosophical and the polemic in his text has been endlessly discussed. The problem of the subjectless voice is theorized by Louis Althusser (Althusser, L., *For Marx*, trans. B. Brewster, London: Verso, 1990). The Marxist aspiration towards this comprehensive structure may be compared to Carlyle's conflated mode. The term 'instance' is used by Engels in his famous formulation that historical process is determined 'in the last instance' by forces of production.

Appendix

The illustrations of E. J. Sullivan

Edmund Joseph Sullivan (1869–1933) links Carlyle's pioneering formulations of Victorian grotesque with the fin-de-siècle grotesque of Beardsley and Wilde. Like Beardsley, by whom he was influenced, Sullivan illustrated the archetypal 'Decadent' periodical *The Yellow Book*. It was, however, his designs for *Sartor Resartus* (1898) and *The French Revolution* (1910) which were most influential. Both draw on Dürer and on Holbein's *Dance of Death* to find a visual equivalent to the 'German accent', as Sullivan called it, of Carlyle's prose. Sullivan transforms *Sartor* into a modern Emblem Book, as each illustration carries allegorical import, depicting Teufelsdröckh's journey as an encounter with a world caught between caricature and symbol (Figure 2.1). Sullivan's bold, Beardsleyesque use of blank, flat space and odd, florid, decorative arabesques plays on Carlyle's own 'dandiacal' artifice, visualizing his conception of bodies dissolved by clothing into unpredictable patterns of proliferating signs.

In Sullivan's illustrations to *The French Revolution*, the political struggle is envisaged as an invasion of the French Rococo by the Germanic grotesque. The *ancien régime* appears as an abnormal, fantastical world of Watteau-like putti and pierrots. Marat peers up Marie Antionette's dress like the lover in Fragonard's painting *The Swing*, but the ground he lies on is a dung-heap presided over by a toad on a skull (Figure 2.2). Like the celebratory symbolism of royal 'surnames of honour', the corrupted visual language of the Rococo is violated by alien images. Skeletons and demonic apes assault appalled putti, mischievously inverting their world; the profuse drapery above a throne is pulled back to reveal a guillotine: the mechanics of Rococo artifice transformed into a machinery of death (Figure 2.3). The uncontrollable energy of the dance of death is unleashed as competing myths encounter one another, imposing themselves on reality. Cupids and aristocrats alike are decapitated by giant satyrs, and the hydra-headed beast 'Democracy' squashes the royal couple beneath its feet. This Dantesque vision is probably influenced by Doré's prints, but also looks back to the anti-Jacobin engravings of Gillray and Cruikshank, a source of Carlyle's own imagery. Sullivan's preoccupation with the grotesque resurfaces in his illustrations to *The Rubáiyát of Omar Khayyám* (1913). The *Rubáiyát*, a favourite among the Decadents, becomes, for Sullivan, another Emblem Book, each illustration encapsulating a quatrain, where moments of sensuality are haunted by death and the failures of learning. As in *The French Revolution* skeletal figures suddenly erupt into Romantic scenes. Sullivan's illustrations to the late quatrains, in which Omar hears the anguished voices of animated pots, trapped in their drying and crumbling clay, suggest the influence of late Victorian grotesque design, such as the face-jugs made by the Martin brothers (discussed in Chapter 7 of the present book by Shelagh Wilson) (Figure 7.13).

Sullivan's last major deployment of the grotesque was in *The Kaiser's Garland* (1915), a wartime collection of anti-German caricatures in which the Kaiser appears as an absurd, shape-shifting monster in a deranged world. These designs link the Victorian to the Modernist grotesque of Grosz, Dix and Ernst.

2.1 E.J. Sullivan, 'Teufelsdröckh in Monmouth Street', 1898, illustration to Carlyle's *Sartor Resartus*

2.2 E.J. Sullivan, 'The Flourishing of the Fleur de Lis (Marie and Marat)', 1910, illustration to Carlyle's *The French Revolution*

2.3 E. J. Sullivan, 'The Sword of Damocles', 1910, illustration to Carlyle's *The French Revolution*

3

Culture and energy: Ford Madox Brown, Thomas Carlyle and the Cromwellian grotesque

Colin Trodd

Writing to his brother in September 1842, Carlyle, who had been researching in St Ives, states:

Some hundreds of times I have felt, and scores of times I have said and written that Oliver is an impossibility; yet I am still found at it, without any visible results at all. Remorse, too, for my sinful disgraceful sloth accompanies me, as it well may. I am, as it were, without a language. Tons of books have I read on this matter, and it is still only looming as through thick mists on my eye. There looming, or flaming visible – did it ever flame, which it has never yet been made to do – in what terms am I to set it forth. I wish often I could write rhyme. A new form from centre to surface, unlike what I find anywhere in myself or others, would alone be appropriate from the indescribable chiaroscuro and waste bewilderment of this subject.[1]

In December of the same year he records in his journal:

The Preadamite powers of Chaos are in me, and my soul with excess of stupidity, pusillanimity, tailor melancholy, and approaches to mere desperation and dog-madness, is as if blotted out. Strange to reflect, during a three days' rain, when all is mud and misery here below, that a few miles up there *is* everlasting azure, and the sun shining as formerly. No Cromwell will ever come out of me in this world. I dare not even try Cromwell.[2]

Impossible though it is to summarize such pregnant and self-mutilating statements, we might note that a central anxiety running through these passages is the relationship between historical energy and exegetical force. Carlyle demands from Cromwell an expressivity that, transcending the power of rhetoric, enables the commentator to see the lineaments of an authentic historical identity that escapes the picturesque or authoritarian aspects of biography. Carlyle wants to write Cromwell *seeing*. However, this demand that authenticity *be* energy renders Carlyle unsure of the nature of his own desire to see Cromwell. Vision, as paradoxical fusion of the empirical and the metaphysical, becomes self-lacerating: the constant desire to see Cromwell as energy results in the perpetual mutation and metamorphosis of the project of figuring Cromwell. Cromwell is both that which would free Carlyle from the confusion between matter and spirit and that which is hidden in or buried by both. Cromwell's energy, as we shall see, forces the author to direct its powers against himself.

Cromwell is disturbing for another reason. In him, or in writing about him, Carlyle finds the fusion of the grotesque and the uncanny.[3] The process of revealing Cromwell is uncanny in that it involves a form of surrender to buried matters and hidden matter: in articulating Cromwell the disinterred hero becomes the Consciousness through which the author speaks. In order to *see* Cromwell Carlyle fears being 'sunk deep, fifty miles deep, below the region of articulation'.[4] Realization is always estrangement and loss; the hero will give the author life by robbing him of his identity. Moreover, the process of excavating history is a form of descent into the grotesque:

These authentic utterances of the man Oliver himself – I have gathered them from far and near; fished them up from the foul Lethean quagmires where they lay buried; I have washed, or endeavoured to wash them clean from foreign stupidities; and the world shall now see them in their own shape.[5]

Visiting Hungerford Castle, Carlyle informs us that he discovers two forgotten Cromwell letters hidden under 'masses of damp dust; unclean accumulation of beetle-and-spider exuviae'.[6] Aware that in searching the graveyards of the Cromwell archive he will become entangled within a world in which the familiar returns as the strange, Carlyle associates burial with life. Since Cromwell makes life 'spectral' the process of writing him makes presence alienating.

The sense of being subsumed by the uncontrollable forces buried by history determines the way in which Carlyle writes about the experience of being in his narrative. Writing to Emerson in 1844 he notes 'my thrice unfortunate Book on Cromwell is a real descent to Hades, to Golgotha and Chaos! I feel oftenest as if it were possible to die oneself than to bring into life.'[7] Here the grotesque is the experience of being entangled within the language of typology, but never articulating its content. This sense of fusion without resolution is important to our understanding of the Carlylean or Cromwellian grotesque. What Cromwell seems to offer the author is inexhaustible vitality, but this he must turn against himself. Writing becomes the illumination of life that will obscure the author.[8] Cromwell combines the uncanny and the grotesque: the process of understanding him involves the attempt to retrieve something lost or suppressed; the act of revealing Cromwell results in the burial of the self. Writing *Cromwell* is to be lost in a process of endless revelation and despair; and this exile from the self is the only illumination available to the author.[9] Writing, then, is a violation of the idea of the homely: in working on Cromwell Carlyle wants to divine in history the hidden family of truths; in writing *Cromwell* he finds in the historical process endless mutation and fragmentation. To 'commune' with Cromwell the author is obliged to realize that, for his hero, history is the unhomely; that his dwelling is a form of banishment from human pleasure: 'What a rage, wide-sweeping, inexorable as Death, dwells in that heart; – close neighbour to pity, to trembling affection, and soft tears.'[10]

Carlyle's conflation of Cromwell and the grotesque provides the critical framework for this essay.[11] Although art historians have noticed the influence of Carlyle's account of Cromwell on Victorian representations of Civil War and Interregnum subjects, no detailed readings have been made of the relationship between these textual and visual formulations.[12] As the main aim of this chapter is to demonstrate the importance of Carlyle to Ford Madox Brown's representation of Cromwell, it is necessary to review two sets of material at this stage. Firstly I want to mention a couple of early nineteenth-century readings of Cromwell, after which I will go on to address some of the key nineteenth-century articulations of the grotesque.

When Froude claims that Carlyle rescues Cromwell from falsehood, he alludes to specific styles and methods of historical writing. Where the Whig school of Hume and Macaulay defines the Interregnum as the defence of ancient liberties in the face of the neo-feudalism of the Stuarts, Tory writers, such as Scott, see the deracination of Stuart culture in terms of the eviction of ideas like sentiment, domesticity, intimacy and locality from political life. In *Woodstock* Scott provides this image of Cromwell:

> He was ... coarsely made, with harsh and severe features. His manner of speaking ... was energetic and forcible, though neither graceful nor eloquent [and although] he was born of good family ... the fanatic democratic ruler could never acquire, or else disdained to practise, the courtesies usually exercised among the higher classes in their intercourse with each other.[13]

In this Tory Romantic literature Cromwell is defined as a wild aberration of historical truth: he is a violence that gets in the way of national history, custom and order; he is an unlawful force that would destroy the naturalness of those social institutions that constitute the historical process itself. Not belonging to proper history, Cromwell's move from the margins to the centre of political life is plotted in terms of the grotesque suppression of public culture and its traditions.[14] For instance, Dibdin follows a well-established convention when he presents Cromwell as a violator of the national home. His 'campaign of devastation and bloodshed' produces the conditions in which churches and cathedrals are emptied of their treasures or destroyed.[15] Clearly this association of Cromwell with vandalism is an attempt to register his unhomeliness within British history; but when I associate Cromwell with the idea of the unhomely I do so in order to indicate how he could become a proto-

Romantic, that is to say, oxymoronic hero, or sign of modern consciousness itself. This is very much the view of Carlyle and Brown, both of whom are drawn to his 'chaotic' nature, both of whom see in him the dwelling of a force that eradicates the idea of the homely forms of social life. Identifying Cromwell as a matrix of energies and potentialities that cannot be at home in the world, they perceive a being who must, as Chesterton writes, 'outlive a hundred incarnations and always reject the last'.[16] Both Carlyle and Brown associate Cromwell with the unhomely because they see in him a power that operates in the space between historical event and sacramental fact; a truth that alienates the idea that biographical or pictorial representation depict the 'home' of the subject; a force buried deep within a body that is continually at war with itself; a spectral process that would connect void and substance. Cromwell is strange because he is a stranger to himself: in him is a force that registers the unhomeliness of life itself; and if he is that which invades the homeliness of history, his is an invasion that both Carlyle and Brown welcomed.

Before I examine Brown's representations of Cromwell in some detail, I want to acknowledge those articulations of the grotesque that are germane to my main subject of study. A key source for Romantic and Victorian writers on the grotesque is Hugo's 1827 Preface to *Cromwell*, where he asserts that the contradictory or antithetical nature of the grotesque is sanctioned by the Christian doctrine of the Incarnation. Thus in the realm of art the grotesque must break with classical culture in order to immerse itself in nature, 'to mingle in its creations'. As 'one detail of a great whole', it 'passes our comprehension' because it is in 'perfect harmony, not with man, but with all creation'.[17] By associating the grotesque with the nature of human experience and the forms of nature, Hugo breaks with conventional mimetic theory that held that the grotesque, being 'unnatural', is conceptually useless.

Hugo's reading of the progression of art – dividing human culture into the age of the ode (the primitive), the age of the epic (the classical) and the age of drama (the modern-Romantic), the last of which synthesizes the spiritual and the material – is drawn from Hegel's writings on this subject. In his *Lectures on Aesthetics*, Hegel makes a number of interesting points about the nature of modern art by analysing both the sublime and the grotesque. As is well known, he characterizes sublime art as 'the attempt to express the infinite without finding in the realm of phenomena any object which proves itself fitting for this representation'.[18] However, the sublime is also identified by its self-conscious recognition of the futility and impossibility of this project. In contradistinction, the grotesque is a mode of ornamentation and decoration that believes in its power to capture the unrepresentable. The grotesque displaces the sublime by the physicality of display, which as pure animation illustrates the failure of its own quasi-organic features to embody the spiritual. He writes: 'It exaggerate[s] the natural shapes ... of reality ... to intoxicate itself in them ... to do violence to them, to distort and explode them ...'.[19] The grotesque digs deep into the surface of itself to reveal its status as sheer blockage. Seeking transcendence, it mutilates matter by generating the sort of aberrant energy that unlawfully fuses different realms of being.[20] It is unnatural or illegitimate in its commitment to the belief that it can articulate itself in concrete form.

Where both Hugo and Hegel identify the grotesque with the search for the numinous, the British Tory-Romantic discourse presents the grotesque as a form of pseudo-cornucopia: it is the detritus of artistic experience after the consumption of value. Scott, for example, sees in the grotesque the impossible desire for the fusion of things that obtains when the artist fails to associate comprehension with judgement; and for Bagehot it is the ineluctable ruination of art when its subject is absorbed by the processes of articulation. Either way the grotesque is the infection of art by matter. Scott, in his critical essay on E.T.A. Hoffmann, refers to the dangers of 'the unbounded fertility of the author's imagination', which convinces itself that 'the rich contrast of all the varieties of shape and colouring' can 'satisfy the understanding or inform the judgement'.[21] He goes on to allege that in this alien art

all species of combination, however ludicrous, or however shocking, are attempted and executed without scruple. In the other modes of treating the supernatural, even that mystic region is subjected to some laws, however slight; and fancy, in wandering through it, is regulated by some probabilities in the wildest flight.[22]

Where Scott assimilates the grotesque into the rhetoric of lawlessness, Bagehot associates the grotesque with the agitation of the aesthetic process itself. Bagehot sees in the grotesque the endless transformation of common nature, the endless waste of energy. Unlike Scott, for whom the grotesque is an alien anarchic force invading the spaces of national culture, Bagehot aligns the grotesque with the popular, demotic tradition of Hogarth and Dickens.[23] With the grotesque things are out of place: the mind may have been so active that it searches for the 'irregular' and the 'abnormally developed' forms of nature, but there is nothing wild or frenzied about this activity, he claims in his 1858 essay on Dickens.[24] Again unlike Scott, for whom the grotesque is both alien and unhomely, Bagehot finds in Dickens the image of a homely, bourgeois grotesque, a picturesque grotesque.[25] The flawed irregularity of the novelist's mind is redeemed by the charming 'incoherency of incident and aberration of character' that his narratives provide.[26] Although Bagehot sees signs of 'sentimental radicalism' in the novels, Dickens's 'grotesqueness' can be countenanced because it is entwined with a sense of the domestic and the feminine.[27] In 'Wordsworth, Tennyson and Browning; or, Pure, Ornate and Grotesque Art' (1864), a less sanguine account of the grotesque, the only example of its legitimacy is when Browning renders it 'homely, comic, true; reminding us of what *bourgeois* nature really is'.[28]

One of the central themes running through the articulations of the grotesque we have examined is that presence is made alienating, or absurd. The grotesque is that which is aberrant in matter; that which is disordering; that which causes temporal and spatial agitation; that which is deformed or deforming.[29] Brown's attitude to the grotesque is somewhat different. Like Ruskin, for whom Venice is disfigured by 'the pestilence that came and breathed upon her beauty',[30] Brown's initial approach to the grotesque is through what he sees as a monstrous conflation of life and disease.[31] Thus in July 1856 he ventures to Huntingdon to see 'the Cromwell localities'.[32] Like his mentor, Carlyle, Brown finds in Cromwell an irresistible, enigmatic power.[33] 'Cromwell's virile personality', Hueffer informs us in his biography of his grandfather, 'exercised a strong influence' on the painter's mind.[34] Indeed, his favourite son, Oliver, was named after the Lord Protector. Here is Brown's description of the journey into this Cromwellian landscape:

> I went to the farm but the gent was away & the stupid servant knew nothing but sent me to a woman in the next house who took [me] through the dung yard to find her husband and after bawling for him in vain left me to wait for him. As nothing of him appeared except some inarticulate human grunting from an outhouse outside of which two old sows were running about in a terribly perturbed state uttering fearful squalls, responded to by unutterable squeaking from within, I made bold to ope[n] the door, when out rushed furious as an old boar my man, a most hideous looking fellow all boils like Job & very bloody with a knife in his mouth, he was it would seem gelding young pigs & I had disturbed him at his art for which he was it would appear to be an enthusiast.[35]

Brown's first experience of the Cromwellian environment is framed as an expression of caricature; this is a landscape that seems to parody the heroic or tragic grotesque of his master, Carlyle. Visiting the flat landscape of St Ives, hoping to discover the origin of his fascination with Cromwell in the body of history, the artist finds that the inscriptions of history – the legible traces of the past – have been replaced by the sheer profusion of disconnected things. In such writing the body becomes a viscous presence that eradicates the communal web of signs associated with historical understanding. Instead of history, vision registers the grotesque as the endless conflation of animation and infection. If Brown records that matter has made a home where history should be seen, then he finds no value in a material landscape that seems to parody the idea of meaning as dwelling. In place of the image of home we find that the inherent violence of matter violates historical remembrance by blocking the richness of experience.

This trip was part of a research exercise for his *St. Ives. AD 1630. Cromwell on his Farm* (Figure 3.1), which he finally completed in 1874. Hueffer provides us with the following report:

On a white horse, which grazes leisurely by the roadside before us, sits a stalwart man of saturnine visage, in the prime of lusty manhood. He is attired in the sober costume worn by thoughtful men in the early part of Charles I's reign. ... Before him burns a weep of weeds and stubble, which those two labourers have grubbed from the hedges they have been trimming, and it is the flames thereof that have arrested the attention of their master, and on which he now gazes so earnestly yet so absently.

In vain may the buxom wench ... raise her voice ... to tell the master that dinner waits. He hears, and heeds her no more than the little lamb does that nibbles contentedly the herbage by the horse's nose, or than the pig that fancies something good is going on in her neighbourhood.

... that which fixes him is no fairy dance, no pleasing phantasy, but the soul-sobering vision of the prophet or seer. Oliver Cromwell, as we see him here, is supposed by the artist to be returning from a neighbourly visit, and, on his homeward road, to have opened his Bible at these passages:

'Lord, how long? Wilt thou hide Thyself for ever? 'And shall Thy wrath burn like a fire?'

Pondering on the texts, he comes all at once on the burning stubble, and the concrete fact, so palpable to his outward eyes, answers readily to the vision within, and the man lapses in the saddle where he sits, into a religious trance.[36]

Here Cromwell is identified at the end of a passage that has secured the symbolic order of the image. He is given meaning by a significance that shapes him. This reading, derived from Brown's account of the work, clothes both the image and Cromwell within a typological system where material things and events are the illumination of transcendental truths. Here all living things are elements of a mirroring process that records the ordered and structured nature of the universe. Cromwell's home is the home of a history that is already and always there; his movement back to the family residence is his entry into the home of religious truth.[37]

Cromwell, Protector of the Vaudois (Figure 3.2), completed in 1877, depicts the Lord Protector in his role as the defender of European Protestantism. Brown seems to conflate two moments: the composition of the official protest at the massacre of the Vaudois in 1655 by troops acting on behalf of the Duke of Savoy; the production of the letter in 1658 to Louis XIV citing further persecutions of these Protestants of Piedmont.[38] Cromwell, turning to engage the blind Milton, holds the fragment of paper upon which he has scribbled his notes. Milton composes these notes into Latin; Marvell, on the right, will transcribe these words. Cromwell is placed between the map and the declaration of a Day of Humiliation in honour of the Swiss sect.

We can extend and develop our reading of these two paintings. *St. Ives, AD 1630: Cromwell on his Farm* bears witness to the truth of Christianity as the structuring agency of time. Here Cromwell ponders on the threshold of vision and interpretation in a space that fuses the material and the spiritual. By returning home Cromwell is about to be born into history. *Cromwell, Protector of the Vaudois* dramatizes the gap between a typological reading of history and the spaces of historical action. If the symbolism of the sacred retreats to the map, this is because in place of the Book of God we have the world as map. The image, no longer sustaining the authority of typology nor affirming the teleological nature of time itself, reduces Cromwell to the display of power in the body. Beyond St Ives Cromwell is homeless: his entry into political history is not a continuation or revelation of typological form. Such unhomeliness both makes and erases him: giving him an unrepresentable power and strength; burying him deep in forces that he cannot shape or control.

St. Ives, AD 1630: Cromwell on his Farm presents us with the pre-Cromwellian Cromwell absorbed by a subject that he is in the process of recognizing. He is confronted by his own becoming in a narrative that, in confronting him, loses him in the signs and forms of Christian Hermeneutics. Pregnant with the details of a typological system in which the near and the far, the old and the new, the sacred and the mundane are elements of a continuous narrative chain, the painting echoes the iconography of the conversion of St Paul. Cromwell, whose image in this painting Brown claimed is 'aucward & beastly [sic]',[39] is about to become conscious of this revelation that is waiting for him in the dense matter from which the image is made. He is about to be claimed by a typological schema that will make him who he is. If we are confronted with a body marked by the evidence of its origin and destiny, the function of typology must be to acknowledge yet transcend the corporeal form in which Cromwell appears in this pre-Cromwellian moment.[40]

It may well be the case that Brown's interest in Cromwell was political rather than religious, but the later image is not as coherent as the 'Biblical' Cromwell of the St Ives painting. In *Cromwell, Protector of the Vaudois*, it can be seen that the promise of the earlier painting – that the truth of analogy is the identity of history – has been erased in a rather different reading of the nature of agency. As Lord Protector Cromwell may dwarf the map, and he may scrutinize his actions by examining Scripture, but his 'protection' of the Vaudois must take the form of a protest against their massacre. The would-be Protector of the Protestant nations is assimilated by the forms, processes and necessities of international relations; and if his body projects an energy that his discourse cannot embody this is because he seems to be the chaotic, inarticulate power that Carlyle sees in him. Cromwell is deflated by the rhetoric which clothes his proclamation and dispossessed by the authority that the composition registers.[41]

There is, then, no clear continuity between these two representations of Cromwell. Defending the Vaudois is not a process of unveiling spiritual truth or Divine purposefulness: instead of offering the viewer the prospect of engaging with typological exegesis, the composition provides no evidence to suggest that historical facts reveal the providential nature of the universe. If Cromwell's defence of the Vaudois is a type of 'performance', his rhetorical pose is no longer accompanied by a dense web of signs that suggest the universal symbiosis of the secular and the sacred. Here Cromwell may be dressed as a Christian Soldier, but he seems to be at war with the image itself: dislocating the narrative by growing out of the composition, he is forcing himself into a space that he fragments by his presence. Cromwell is grotesque because he is simultaneously engagement with and estrangement from being: his dwelling is a form of perpetual agitation before a typological system he knows but cannot enact. The introspective serenity of St Ives, where the homely Cromwell was a continuation of the spiritual presence that visited him, has vanished: now Cromwell confirms that consciousness is a form of alienation; his swaggering body, cutting into the composition, echoes the brutality that it reacts to.

If Cromwell would draw the action into himself, both Milton and Marvell are isolated from him; and communication is lost in this blind narrative. With Cromwell, whose face, Hueffer informs us, is full of violent emotion,[42] looking becomes the scene of a primal violence or energy that breaks or blocks verbal discourse. It should come as no surprise, therefore, that this division between seeing and speaking is a marked feature of the critical sources that Brown drew upon for his work: Carlyle's *Oliver Cromwell's Letters and Speeches* and *On Heroes, Hero-Worship and the Heroic in History*. In Carlyle's account of Cromwell authentic vision is not observation or contemplation, but a form of action in its own right.[43] And if seeing is an originating power, its authenticity precedes the activity of language. This suspicion of the elegance of language could be traced back to Cromwell himself. During his speech at the opening of Parliament on 17 September 1656, he asserted: 'Rhetoricians, to whom I do not pretend, neither to them nor to the things they use to speak, speak words. Truly our business is to speak things.'[44]

This association of language and action is dealt with in *Cromwell, Protector of the Vaudois*, which captures a moment when the power of the Lord Protector's body cannot be seen and read by Milton, to whom he turns. Although Hueffer refers to the 'almost colossal' proportions of Cromwell's body in this painting,[45] vision cannot join bodies and spaces to form a continuous narrative web. Cromwell – whose writings are known to us largely in fragments, whose speeches are not accompanied by any reliable original transcripts and whose discourse has been characterized by his contemporaries and modern historians as 'opaque' or 'incoherent' – is the source of a transfiguring and violating blindness that forms the contradictory centre of the image.[46] Milton, whose poem *On the Late Massacre in Piedmont* places the Vaudois within a typological frame, faces Cromwell, whose convoluted foreign policy involves him in an alliance with the sworn enemies of Milton's 'slaughtered saints'.[47]

Brown follows Carlyle, for whom Cromwell is an 'irreducible chaotic mass'.[48] Cromwell is the paradoxical nature of an identity formed in the perpetual will to incarnate truth in being. Yet the materialization of truth as being, as revelation of the sacred, is deferred by the processes of corporeal life. Cromwell, who aspires to the condition of purity in which the Word will reveal itself through him, is also the agency for the magnification of the grotesque.[49] He is the writing of the grotesque as confusion in interpretation; the physical gap between pure knowledge and total experience; the living life of a perennial loss that marks the nature and the scandal of being. His power, force and energy cannot grasp the whole that he believes moves through his life, forming his destiny. To paraphrase Carlyle: Cromwell searches for a space in which he can finally flee from his own shadow; his is a form of thinking that thinks against itself in its desire to unite experience, being and knowledge as pure revelation.

Although I have suggested that there is no real contact between these two paintings, this is, of course, not entirely true, because both works deal with the nature of vision. If in the first painting contemplation blocks out perception of the tangible environment, in the second vision is itself occluded. Here Cromwell's vision has no depth. This failure of vision continues to register the grotesque, for Cromwell announces an energy he cannot contain. Incoherence is articulated visually as the misty, irregular, cloudy shape that hovers in front of him. In opposition, above Milton's head, we see in the circular shape of the laurel crown the perfect conflation of form, content, space and object. In contrast to Milton's association with primal totality or plenitude, Cromwell's eyes seem lacerated by the light that hovers in front of him. His view is occluded by this presence, energy or force. There seems to be some sort of tension between the subject and his space, as if the act of seeing were itself a kind of violence or antagonism in and of the body. Likewise, in writing Cromwell Carlyle presents us with an image of the constant mobility of thought itself. Although he has 'more light in the head of him than other men',[50] Cromwell is not so much a personality as the proliferation of life itself; and yet, as a consequence of this intensity, he hovers in a space between the sacred and the physical. In an extraordinary passage from Carlyle's *On Heroes, Hero-Worship and the Heroic in History*, we read:

Poor Cromwell, – great Cromwell! The inarticulate Prophet: Prophet who could not speak. Rude, confused, struggling to utter himself, with his savage depth, with his wild sincerity; and he looked so strange, among the elegant Euphemisms, dainty little Falklands, didactic Chillingworths, diplomatic Clarendons! Consider him. An outer hull of chaotic confusion, visions of the Devil, nervous dreams, almost semi-madness; and yet such a clear determinate man's energy working in the heart of that. A kind of chaotic man. The ray as of pure starlight and fire, working in such an element of boundless hypochondria, *un*formed blackness of darkness! And yet withal this hypochondria, what was it but the very greatness of the man? The depth and tenderness of his wild affections: the quantity of *sympathy* he had with things, – the quantity of insight he would yet get into the heart of things, the mastery he would get over things: this was his hypochondria. The man's misery, as man's misery always does, came of his greatness... It is the character of a prophetic man; a man with his whole soul *seeing*, and struggling to see.[51]

This vision of Cromwell is one that Hugo would describe as 'fleshly' – where the will to incarnate the form of the spiritual in the material realm is perpetually frustrated by the nature of human identity.[52] Carlyle insists that no single image can conjure the character of Cromwell because he is at once the most physical and spiritual of beings. If Cromwell is a 'prophet who cannot speak' he cannot enter the language of types. Involved in the generation of a typological interpretation of history, he blocks all revelation of its truth: 'all his life lay begirt as in a sea of nameless thoughts, which no speech of a mortal could name'.[53] Caught in the 'shapeless' and 'chaotic' nature of his discourse, he cannot assimilate or reveal the significance of things as signs.[54] If the violent profusion of Cromwell's being arises from a self-conscious recognition of the inadequacy of its powers, then its physicality separates him from the numinous forms it would announce. Cromwell is the entrapment of being in pure physicality. In place of the purification of vision, Cromwell is left with the intensification of sight.

It is because Carlyle presents Cromwell as demanding and yet resisting interpretation – hovering in the realm between fact and symbol – that he wants to see Cromwell seeing, thus to reach out and be absorbed by the fusion of the material and the spiritual. A matrix of impulses rather than a network of characteristics, Cromwell cannot be mirrored. Pure energy in search of spiritual purity, he is saved by and lost in a body which has 'too much life'.[55] Cromwell's being is movement. Like Carlyle, Brown presents the Cromwellian body as self-antagonizing. In *Cromwell, Protector of the Vaudois*, movement fragments space: the centre of the composition collapses into the peripheral figure of Marvell, semi-hidden by Cromwell's right arm; his fingers, in holding his script, echo Cromwell's aggressive fingering of the map; his access to writing is caught within the convulsive energy that is Cromwell's body.

We can conclude this study by examining another way in which Cromwell was pictured in Victorian culture. The radical nature of the Carlylean image, which Brown develops with such skill in *Cromwell, Protector of the Vaudois*, is confirmed when we compare the painting with two 1841 paintings by George Cattermole, the antiquarian illustrator and painter.[56] Cattermole, producing an uneasy conflation of the historical style of Delaroche and the intimate style of Stothard, does not know how to treat or place Cromwell.[57] *Cromwell Viewing the Body of Charles I* (Figure 3.3) provides us with a vision of the impossibility of reconciling Cromwell with the idea of historical power. Cromwell is seen from a space over which he has no control: we see the 'domestic' portrait of Charles looking at Cromwell viewing his own corpse; we realize that Cromwell is intimidated by the 'intimacy' that this environment evokes. *Cromwell*

Consulting the Lawyers (Figure 3.4) is even more interesting because of its incoherence. Cromwell seems to have dropped in from a Dutch genre painting, and although his body is as awkward as the representation in Brown's painting, it is absurdly inconsequential. Cattermole wants to look back to Bonington's modification of *style troubadour*, but he cannot find a way of placing the unhomely Cromwell within this intimate Romantic genre, which is, of course, the visual equivalent of Scott's presentation of history as domestic romance.[58] There is real dissonance between the quasi-familial subject-matter and the uneasy compositional structure. Even the title, which provides no specific historical information, renders Cromwell anonymous and abstract; and if he cannot enact the fusion of domestic and public life, his contribution to the 'family' history of the nation will be marginal.[59] It is as if there can be no independent Cromwellian iconography in the tradition to which Cattermole alludes; and that by placing him in a social space from which Charles has been banished he must himself disappear. Cromwell is allowed to play a role in this historical tragedy, but there is no real material depth to his being.[60]

Where Cattermole produces a Romantic and homely antiquarianism – in which history is the drama of colour, texture, custom – such picturesque details are absent in the Cromwellian grotesque. At the end of his 25-page preface to *Cromwell*, which maps out his theory of the grotesque, Hugo describes his ostensible subject in the following passage:

He was a complex, many-sided being, a combination of contrary elements, of many evil mingled with many good qualities, a miracle of genius and narrow-mindedness ... tyrant of Europe and plaything of his family ... a dull, diffuse, obscene orator, but very clear in speaking ... a hypocrite and fanatic, a visionary, governed by the phantoms of his childhood.[61]

Cromwell is dynamic, fertile, active, but he cannot understand or judge. Cromwell is grotesque because with him action is a form of infection, and, as a consequence, his life is a pollution of the Word. In mutilating truth he traduces typology: he blocks the coming into history of the universal, the beautiful, the true. In place of Hugo's atavistic force, both Carlyle and Brown recognize a primal energy that strives to but never does enact the fusion of the corporeal and the numinous. Where Hugo presents the grotesque as the infected form or space in which modern life must conduct itself, Carlyle and Brown present the grotesque as the limit of consciousness. Where Hugo sees Cromwell's rhetoric as a parody of the power of the Word, Carlyle and Brown see in Cromwell a pure physicality hovering between body and language. For Hugo Cromwell is monstrous; for Carlyle and Brown he is impossible.

Notes

1. Froude, J.A., *Thomas Carlyle, a History of his Life in London*, 2 vols, London: Longmans, Green and Co., 1884, vol. 1, p. 279.
2. *Ibid.*, p. 280.
3. In using the term 'grotesque' Carlyle acknowledges the significance of 'phantasmagoria' and 'confusion' at the same time as he criticizes art, its conventions and the formal discourse it generates. See his comments on Tieck in the 'Preface and Introduction to the Book called German Romance', *Critical and Miscellaneous Essays* (3 vols, London: Chapman and Hall, 1869), vol. 1, p. 587. For the standard modern account of the uncanny as primal repression, see Freud, S., 'The Uncanny', in *The Complete Psychological Works*, 24 vols, London: Hogarth Press, 1919, vol. 17, pp. 217–52. A review of the material on the uncanny with which Carlyle was familiar is provided by Jennings, L.B., *The Ludicrous Demon: Aspects of the Grotesque in German Post-Romantic Prose*, Berkeley: University of California Press, 1963.
4. Froude, *op. cit.* at note 1, vol. 1, p. 238.
5. Carlyle, T., *Works*, ed. H.D. Trail, 30 vols, London: Chapman and Hall, 1896–1901, vol. 6, p. 13.
6. *Ibid.*, vol. 8, p. 20.
7. Slater, J. (ed.), *The Correspondence of Emerson and Carlyle*, New York: Columbia University Press, 1964, p. 357.
8. In his fine study of Carlyle's major works, Rosenberg states that 'the fear of being buried alive while trying to rescue Cromwell from two centuries of obloquy is the unstated subject of *Cromwell*' (Rosenberg, J.D., *Carlyle and the Burden of History*, Cambridge, Mass.: Harvard University Press, 1985, p. 137.)
9. Rosenberg's comments are apposite (*ibid.*, p. 142):

    Carlyle's editorial *Elucidations* are thus much more than mere annotation: they are meant to be lesser mirrorings of the divine *fiat-lux*, sudden illuminations of what had long lain formless and dark. That Carlyle sees his editorial function as sacred and life-giving is everywhere evident in the imagery of *Cromwell*, from the Orphic journey of the opening to the luminous death-scene at the end.

    The ambiguity Carlyle sees in and of vision is demonstrated in his paradoxical claim in the introduction that by reading Cromwell's words we 'may first obtain some dim glimpse of the actual Cromwell, and see him darkly face to face' (Carlyle, *op. cit.* at note 5, vol. 6, p. 19). Here Carlyle seems to indicate that Cromwell is the impossible fusion of the material and the spiritual; the chaotic contact of opposites rather than the vision of the sacred from the place of the temporal that Rosenberg claims. (*op. cit.* at note 8, p. 143).

10. Carlyle, *op. cit.* at note 5, vol. 7, p. 54.
11. It was common for critics to identify Carlyle with the process and practice of the grotesque. Samuel Davey wrote in 1875:

    His ideas are expressed in language wild, grotesque, and sometimes terrible ... in fact, our language does not give full play to the singular freaks of his wild fancy ... he breaks through into sentences half German, half English, mingled with slang, street cries, and words which cannot be found in either ancient or modern lexicons ... Carlyle's style is certainly a stumbling-block to critics, and many a thoughtful reader is repelled from the study of his writings by language which often transcends the bounds of intelligibleness, and which brings nothing but confusion and contradiction to his mind ... His humour has in it a wild, grim fancy, with something of the fierce, grotesque, and fiery earnestness of Hogarth, with the free, daring caricature of Cruikshank.

    (See Davey, S., *Darwin, Carlyle and Dickens*, New York: Haskell House, 1971, (reprint of 1875 edition), pp. 45, 47, 54.)

12. The most authoritative account of Carlyle's interventions into visual culture is provided by Paul Barlow (Barlow, P., 'The Imagined Hero as Incarnate Sign: Thomas Carlyle and the Mythology of the National Portrait in Victorian Britain', *Art History* 17 (4), December 1994). In addition to explaining Carlyle's attitude to portraiture, this article also contains valuable material on the relationship between Victorian historiography and British history painting.
13. Scott, W., *Collected Novels*, 26 vols, London and Edinburgh: Adam and Charles Black, 1895, vol. 21, p. 85.
14. Carlyle seeks to counter the dominant view that Cromwell deforms and betrays the constitutional liberties defended by Pym, Hampden and Eliot. See Carlyle, *op. cit.* at note 5, vol. 5, pp. 208–11.

15. Dibdin, T.F., *A Bibliographical, Antiquarian and Picturesque Tour in the Northern Counties of England and in Scotland*, 2 vols, London: James Bohn, 1838, vol. 1, p. 123.
16. Chesterton, G.K., *Thomas Carlyle*, London: Hodder and Stoughton, 1902, p. 17.
17. Hugo, V., 'Preface to *Cromwell*', in *The Dramas of Victor Hugo*, trans. B. Lelior et al., 8 vols, London: H.S. Nicols, 1896, vol. 8, pp. 13, 16.
18. Bosanqust, B. (ed.), *The Introduction to Hegel's Philosophy of Fine Art*, London: Kegan Paul and Tench, 1886, p. 146.
19. *Ibid.*
20. See Ruskin, J., *Works*, ed. E.T. Cook and A. Wedderburn, 39 vols, London: George Allen, 1903–1912, vol. 11, p. 145. Here Ruskin echoes Hegel in his identification of Indian art as the nadir of the grotesque.
21. Scott, W., *The Miscellaneous Works of Scott*, Edinburgh: Whittaker and Co., 1834–1836, vol. 18, p. 290. By contrast, Carlyle, who associates Hoffmann with the grotesque tradition of Rabelais and Callot, is drawn to what he sees as the unhomeliness of his art and life:

    the wages of daily labour, the solace of his five senses, and the intercourse of social or gregarious life, were far from completing his ideal of enjoyment: his better soul languished in these barren scenes, and longed for some worthier soul. This home, unhappily, he was not destined to find ... Moody, sensitive and fantastic, he wandered through the world like a foreign presence, subject to influences of which common natures have happily no glimpse.

    (Carlyle *op. cit.* at note 3, vol. 1, pp. 600–602.)
22. Scott, *op. cit.* at note 21, pp. 290–92.
23. Bagehot praises Scott for his capacity to capture human character without producing a 'thesis' about social life. Therefore he sees in the *Waverley* novels the supreme vitality of life translated into picturesque detail. And yet Scott's love of variation must not be confused with the delineation of the grotesque: he recognizes that the representation of 'monstrosity is no topic for art'. Scott's 'conservative imagination' protects him from 'fanaticism'. 'Vivid' and 'fragmentary', his histories are real because they are not 'doctrinaire'; and the 'romantic sense' of his writing is an openness to the variations in human sensibility. As his Toryism is defined as the capacity to appreciate and respect social differences, it should come as no surprise that Bagehot sees in Scott's art an organic expression of life transformed into cultural democracy by the novel itself. Paradoxically, then, it is because Scott reads, absorbs and transmutes the quotidian into the experience of a democratic aesthetic that he must resist the idea of political democracy. If crowds make for attractive art, this is because they exist to become unified in the process of cultural articulation. Thus the artist is drawn to the ordinary and the familiar in order to govern its processes at the moment in which such elements are recognized. If Scott's aesthetic conservatism brings him to the crowd, his distrust of radicalism makes him suspicious of the idea of political democracy:

    His imagination was singularly penetrated with the strange varieties and motley composition of human life. The extraordinary multitude and striking contrast of the characters in his novels show this at once. And even more strikingly is the same habit of mind indicated by a tendency never to omit an opportunity of describing those varied crowds and assemblages which concentrate for a moment into a unity the scattered and unlike varieties of mankind ... As in the imagination of Shakespeare, so in that of Scott, the principal form and object were the structure – that is a hard word – the undulation and diversified composition of human society; the picture of this stood in the centre, and everything else was accessory and secondary to it ... His objection to democracy ... was that it would sweep away this entire picture, level prince and peasant in a common *égalité*, substitute a scientific rigidity for the irregular and picturesque growth of centuries, replace an abounding and genial life by a symmetrical but lifeless mechanism.

    (Bagehot, W., *The Collected Works*, 12 vols, ed. N. St.-John Stevas, London: The Economist, 1974, vol. 1, pp. 48–54.)
24. *Ibid.*, pp. 80–81.
25. His friend and biographer John Forster sees Dickens's 'grotesque imaginings' as one source of artistic vulgarity. Dickens's 'leading quality was humour. And all humour has in it ... what ordinary people are apt to call exaggeration; but there is an excess beyond the allowable even here, and to "pet" or magnify out of all proper bounds its sense of what is droll, is to put the merely grotesque in its place'. See Forster, J., *The Life of Charles Dickens*, 2 vols, London: J.M. Dent and Co.: 1872, vol. 2, pp. 272–3.
26. Bagehot, *op. cit.* at note 23, pp. 96–97.
27. *Ibid.*, pp. 100–107.

28. *Ibid.*, p. 361.

29. Other readings of the political and social value of the grotesque were made in this period. Ruskin's comments in *The Stones of Venice* seem to suggest that certain forms of the medieval grotesque, operating in a space beyond official culture, are able to fuse work, art and play (Ruskin, *op. cit.* at note 20, vol. 3, pp. 131–71). Less well known is Thomas Wright's *History of Caricature and Grotesque in Literature and Art* (London: Virtue, 1865), which claims that the development of the grotesque mirrors the shift from feudal to modern society. Associating the grotesque with the English spirit of freedom, he sees in it the perpetual fusion of tradition and innovation (p. 183). For an account of the possibility of generating the grotesque as cultural critique in Victorian poetry, see Armstrong, I., *Victorian Poetry: Poetry, Poetics and Politics*, London: Routledge, 1993, pp. 231–45, 285–91.

30. Ruskin, *op. cit.* at note 20, vol. 3, p. 121.

31. The identification of Brown with the idea of the grotesque is made by at least four late Victorian and Edwardian commentators: Holman Hunt dismissed the cartoon of *The Body of Harold Brought Before William the Conqueror* because it is full of 'grotesque incidents'; D.S. MacColl sees in his 'love of grotesque dramatic incident' the conflation of Hogarthian deformity and Pre-Raphaelite intensity; Henry James makes the claim that Brown's 'sincerity' generates endless 'perversities'; and Helen M. Madox Rossetti claims that the characteristics of his art are 'originality and courage of conception and invention, a deep regard for truth, and an individuality in all his works, so strong and so unfettered that it not infrequently borders on the grotesque'. See Hunt, W.H., *Pre-Raphaelitism and the Pre-Raphaelite Brotherhood*, 2 vols, London: Macmillan, 1905, vol. 1, p. 120; MacColl, D.S., *Nineteenth Century Art*, Glasgow: James Maclehose and Sons, 1902, p. 122; James, H., 'London', *Harper's Weekly*, reprinted in Sweeney, J.L. (ed.), *The Painter's Eye: Notes and Essays on the Pictorial Arts by Henry James*, London: Rupert Hart-Davis, 1956, p. 249; Madox Rossetti, H., *Ford Madox Brown*, London: De La More Press, 1901, p. 14.

32. Surtees, V. (ed.), *The Diary of Ford Madox Brown*, New Haven and London: Yale University Press, 1981, p. 176.

33. For an account of the importance of Carlyle to Brown, see Trodd, C., 'The Laboured Vision and the Realm of Value: Articulations of Identity in Ford Madox Brown's *Work*', in Harding, E. (ed.), *Reframing the Pre-Raphaelites*, Aldershot: Scolar Press, 1996. Valuable material concerning the popularity of Cromwellian and related subjects can be found in Strong, R., *And When did you last see your Father?*, London: Thames and Hudson, 1978, pp. 146–51; and Cromwell's place in nineteenth-century popular culture is explored by T.W. Mason (Mason, T.W., 'Nineteenth-Century Cromwell', *Past and Present* 40, 1968, pp. 187–91).

34. Hueffer, F.M., *Ford Madox Brown, a Record of his Life and Work*, London: Longman, 1896, p. 311.

35. Surtees, *op. cit.* at note 32, p. 177.

36. Hueffer, *op. cit.* at note 34, pp. 290–92.

37. Of the watercolour version, shown at his 1865 exhibition, Brown produced the following catalogue entry:

    At this ... date ... when Cromwell was engaged in cattle farming, the electrical unease of nerves which is felt by nations prior to the bursting of the psychological storm, seems to have produced in him a state of exalted religious fervour mingled with hypochondria, now owing to the 'Letters and Speeches', pretty generally understood. In my composition the farmer is intended to foreshadow the king, and everything is significant or emblematic. (Brown, F.M., *The Exhibition of Work and Other Paintings*, London: McCorquodale and Co., 1865, p. 10.) Such language echoes the typological nature of Christian hermeneutics, as described by Meyer Schapiro: 'the universe – nature and history – is saturated with Christian finality, everything points beyond itself to a formal system evident in the analogical structure of things, due to a divine intention working itself out in time' (Schapiro, M., *Late Antique, Early Christian and Medieval Art*, New York: Braziller, 1979, p. 43). The typological nature of Brown's work is extended to the frame, where we find these inscriptions: (left) 'Lord, how long wilt thou hide thyself – forever? And shall thy wrath burn like fire?'; (right) 'Living neither in any considerable height, nor yet in obscurity, I did endeavour to discharge the duty of an honest man.' The first quotation is taken from Psalm 89, verse 45 of the Book of Common Prayer; the second from a speech made by Cromwell on 12 September 1654, as cited by Carlyle, *op. cit.* at note 5, vol. 3, p. 41. Bennett provides the most comprehensive account of the details surrounding the creation and reception of the painting; and although he does not discuss this work, Sussman offers a detailed reading of the relationship between Pre-Raphaelite iconography and typological expression (see Bennett, M., *Artists of the Pre-Raphaelite Circle*, London: Lund Humphries, 1988; Sussman, H.L., *Fact into Figure*, Columbus: Ohio State University Press, 1979).

38. S.R. Gardiner's *History of the Commonwealth and Protectorate* (4 vols, London: Longmans, Green and Co., 1916) provides a detailed account of the 1655 episode and its place in the foreign policy of the

Protectorate (vol. 4, pp. 177–94). J. Treuherz (*Pre-Raphaelite Paintings from the Manchester City Art Gallery*, London: Lund Humphries, 1980, pp. 98–99), following Hueffer (*op. cit.* at note 34, pp. 311–13), places the subject of the painting in 1658. Brown's image, presenting Cromwell as a primal force fighting within the form of language, seems to echo Carlyle's account of the later episode in the treatment of the relationship between Cromwell and Milton. Carlyle refers to the production of 'an emphatic State-Letter, which Oliver Cromwell meant and John Milton thought and wrote into words' (Carlyle, *op. cit.* at note 5, vol. 4, p. 185).

39. Surtees, *op. cit.* at note 32, p. 175.

40. Rabin infers that Brown's painting seeks to celebrate Cromwell's position within English literature. Elsewhere she makes the equally bizarre claim that the work depicts him 'when he was out of power', seeking the 'answer to the riddle of his interregnum'. See Rabin, L., *Ford Madox Brown and the Pre-Raphaelite History Picture*, New York: Garland, 1978, pp. 242–45.

41. Strong, however, reads this painting as an endorsement of a quasi-Whig reading of British history. He claims that Brown, celebrating the foreign policy and maritime power of the Protectorate, paints a patriotic image of the moment before 'the great age of the British Empire' (*op. cit.* at note 33, p. 150).

42. Hueffer, *op. cit.* at note 34, p. 312.

43. Carlyle, *op. cit.* at note 5, vol. 5, p. 218.

44. Roots, I., *Speeches of Oliver Cromwell*, London: J.M. Dent, 1989, p. 79.

45. Hueffer, *op. cit.* at note 34, p. 312.

46. Roots, *op. cit.* at note 44, pp. x–xxiii.

47. Milton, J., *Poems*, ed. J. Goldberg and S. Orgel, Oxford: O.U.P, 1991, p. 80; Gardiner, *op. cit.* at note 38, vol. 4, pp. 189–94.

48. Carlyle, *op. cit.* at note 5, vol. 5, p. 211.

49. The complexity of Carlyle's approach to Cromwell can be seen when it is compared with the orthodox attitude, here represented by Scott in *Woodstock* (*op. cit.* at note 13, p. 85):

    Cromwell was wont to invest his meaning, or that which seemed to be his meaning, in such a mist of words, surrounding it with so many exclusions and exemptions, and fortifying it with such a labyrinth of parentheses, that though one of the shrewdest men in England, he was, perhaps, the most unintelligible speaker that ever perplexed an audience.

50. Carlyle, *op. cit.* at note 5, vol. 5, p. 213.

51. *Ibid.*, vol. 5, pp. 217–18.

52. Hugo, *op. cit.* at note 17, p. 16.

53. Carlyle, *op. cit.* at note 5, vol. 5, p. 223.

54. *Ibid.*, vol. 5, p. 234.

55. *Ibid.*, vol. 5, p. 223.

56. These images were used as engravings for his brother's account of the 1640s (Cattermole, R., *The Great Civil War of Charles I and the Parliament*, 2 vols, London: Longman and Co., 1841, 1845). Both volumes, focusing on the King's plight, generate narrative structures in which his true identity is revealed in domestic environments, a method which allows for the contrast between monarchical serenity and the ideological machinations of his enemies. The embodiment of the idea of the national family, the Stuarts are evicted from their natural home by 'fanatics', the most appalling of whom was Cromwell, the 'arch deceiver' (vol. 2, pp. 141–201). It should be noted that Richard Cattermole was himself a watercolour artist of some merit. George, like his brother, was a Tory (see Hardie, M., *Water-colour Painting in Britain*, 3 vols, London: B.T. Batsford, 1968, pp. 89–90). Carlyle, of course, wrote his account of Cromwell to oppose writers like Cattermole.

57. Roget claims that Cattermole's figures are 'the living attributes of the past' (Roget, J.L., *A History of the 'Old' Water-Colour Society*, London: Longmans Green and Co., 1891, vol. 2, p. 61). Ruskin, however, associates him with a deformed version of the grotesque in *Modern Painters*, where he writes: 'Cattermole has very grand conceptions of general form, but wild and without substance, and therefore incapable of long maintaining their attractiveness, especially lately, the execution having become in the last degree coarse and affected' (Ruskin, *op. cit.* at note 20, vol. 3, p. 603). Elsewhere, caught by the standard rhetoric of the grotesque, Cattermole is associated with 'exaggeration, childish fantasticism [and] caricature ... substituting for the serious and subdued work of legitimate imagination monster machicolations, and colossal cusps and crockets' (*ibid.*, vol. 3, p. 221). Looking at the same images, the celebrated German art historian Gustav Waagen finds signs of 'masterly' design, compo-

sition and colouring (Waagen, G., *Galleries and Cabinets of Art in Great Britain*, London: John Murray, 1857, p. 204). Cattermole's skills as an illustrator of the antiquarian grotesque were deployed by his friend Dickens, for whom he worked on many projects. Writing to him about a design for *Barnaby Rudge*, Dickens states: 'I think it will make a queer picturesque thing in your hands' (see House, M., and Storey, G. (eds), *The Letters of Charles Dickens*, 4 vols, Oxford: O.U.P, 1965, vol. 1, p. 352). In the same volume (p. 576) he recommends to Cattermole Hood's self-styled essay in the grotesque, *Hood's Own, or Laughter from Year to Year* of 1839. There are over 70 references to Cattermole in the first two volumes.

58. Waagen (*op. cit.* at note 57, p. 102) praises Cattermole's *The Warning* because it demonstrates 'the gloomy chivalrous feeling so often conspicuous in Walter Scott's novels'.

59. The images were reproduced in volume iv of *The Family History of England* (1871), edited by J. Taylor.

60. The Tory Victorian approach to Cromwell is to compare his cruelty and tyranny to the nobility and serenity of Charles I. Daniel Maclise's *An Interview between Charles I and Oliver Cromwell* contrasts the warmth of domestic virtue (Charles) with the austerity of state power (Cromwell). The dichotomy between liberty and authority could be played out according to political affiliation. In the theatre, for instance, the home became the battlefield for warring articulations of Charles I and Cromwell. The Tory Romanticism of W.G. Wills's *Charles the First, an Historical Tragedy* (Edinburgh and London: William Blackwood, 1873) presents Cromwell's obsessive pursuit of power as that which exiles him from any understanding of domesticity and national culture. Cromwell, we are informed, has 'no reverence for the marble pile of England's past ... [he will] deface the fairest monuments of history, inscribing with coarse sacrilege their names on its most sacred tablets; scarring beauty that it took centuries to make, and but an hour to mar' (p. 46).

In opposition, Alfred Bate Richards's *Oliver Cromwell: an Historical Tragedy* (London: Effingham Wilson, 1873) insists on the 'private' dimension to Cromwell's character by underlining his commitment to family life and by asserting his allegiance to inherited custom and the idea of locality. The renunciation of this domestic bliss is made in order to defend 'the rights of property' (p. 16); the tragedy is that the execution of the king destroys Cromwell's household because his favourite daughter, Elizabeth, is a Royalist, whose death leads to Cromwell's own demise. In both plays the 'enemy' is the same: alienating, centralizing power that denies the organic nature of authentic authority.

61. Hugo, *op. cit.* at note 17, p. 34.

3.1 Ford Madox Brown, *St. Ives AD 1631: Cromwell on his Farm*, 1874, 141 × 105.5 cm

3.2 Ford Madox Brown, *Cromwell, Protector of the Vaudois*, 1877, 86 ×107 cm

3.3 George Cattermole, *Cromwell Viewing the Body of Charles I*, 1841

3.4 George Cattermole, *Cromwell Consulting the Lawyers*, 1841

4

'Griffinism, grace and all': the riddle of the grotesque in John Ruskin's *Modern Painters*

Lucy Hartley

I

In an evocative passage from *The Stones of Venice*, John Ruskin directs his readers through 'the heavy door whose bronze network closes the place of his rest' and into the church of St Mark's:

It is lost in the still deeper twilight to which the eye must be accustomed for some moments before the form of the building can be traced; and then there opens before us a vast cave, hewn out into the form of a Cross, and divided into shadowy aisles by many pillars. Round the domes of its roofs the light enters only through narrow apertures like large stars; and here and there a ray or two from some far-away casement wanders into the darkness, and casts a narrow phosphoric stream upon the waves of marble that heave and fall in a thousand colours along the floor.[1]

The formlessness which perplexes the eye threatens to submerge the viewer in darkness, but as the eye adjusts to the lack of light, St Mark's is constructed before the eye, literally (and hastily) transformed from amorphous space to visual objects to unified whole through a process of contingent construction. The dark space named St Mark's is given a frame in the shape of a Cross, depth through aisles, pillars, domes, and then colour with the few rays of light which flash from a distant casement across the marble floor. This shadowy abyss that opens out before the eyes is broken up by a series of objects – cave, cross, pillars – which qualify the formlessness of the initial impression and produce in its place a three-dimensional form which appears to license another set of impressions. Thus, the Cross fixes and extends the vision, at once controlling the movement of the eye in identifying the disparate objects and enabling the eye to roam around the darkened interior:

Under foot and over head, a continual succession of crowded imagery, one picture passing into another, as in a dream; forms beautiful and terrible mixed together; dragons and serpents, and ravening beasts of prey, and graceful birds that in the midst of them drink from running fountains and feed from vases of crystal; the passions and the pleasures of human life symbolized together, and the mystery of redemption; for the mazes of interwoven lines and changeful pictures lead always at last to the Cross, lifted and carved in every place and upon every stone; sometimes with the serpent of eternity wrapt round it, sometimes with doves beneath its arms, and sweet herbage growing forth from its feet; but conspicuous most of all on the great rood that crosses the church before the altar, raised in bright blazonry against the shadow of the apse.[2]

This can be (re)written as follows: an initial impression is reported, objectified, qualified, replaced by multiple impressions, symbolized, and then mystically resurrected in order to ensure that the Cross is the point of convergence for the action of the eye and the associations of the mind. The perceptual sequence now reads as a shift from material form to mental expression to metaphysical understanding; and it is this shift that Ruskin attempts to demonstrate in quantitative terms by labouring through the rise and fall of Venice from Byzantine through Gothic to Renaissance times. In the Apocalyptic (and almost certainly Miltonic) vision of St Mark's, then, the form of the Cross is relied on for its ability to attract attention through the maze of images, magnetically drawing the eye through 'forms beautiful and terrible' – dragon and 'graceful bird', line and picture, serpent and dove, shadow and light – until this visual experience can be consummated in a union of form with symbol and concept.

The convergence of form, symbol and concept is crucial here, for it illuminates the way in which Ruskin's visual experience depends on a continuous, controlled link between eye and mind and soul which shapes impressions into nobler forms through the operation of the cognitive faculties. Any gaps between impression(s) and object which appear to break the continuity of this perceptual sequence are cast as distortions, free-associations of a kind that must be quickly subsumed within an ethical frame before they undermine the perception of the object and/or the existence of the object itself. The clue to understanding how these gaps in observation define Ruskin's concept of the grotesque and determine its position in his system of art lies in the second word of a short passage of *Modern Painters*:

A fine grotesque is the expression, in a moment, by a series of symbols thrown together in bold and fearless connection, of truths which it would have taken a long time to express in any verbal way, and of which the connection is left for the beholder to work out for himself; the gaps, left or overleaped by the haste of the imagination forming the grotesque character.[3]

In qualitative terms the grotesque is double-edged: it is fine, noble, true when applied to Gothic art and architecture and yet terrible, ignoble, false when applied to Renaissance art and architecture. To Ruskin, an understanding of the grotesque equals an understanding of the connection between art, ethics and the nation in nineteenth-century culture, for what the grotesque constitutes is a test of judgement whereby the choice is good or evil, truth or lie, and the reward is moral or sensual; it is almost like *The Choice of Hercules* (1727), rewritten by Ruskin for the Victorians so that the dilemma is an ethical rather than a civic one.[4] And what the grotesque promises is a moral education which can teach the difference between the forces of Life and Death that are Ruskin's emblems of Good and Evil. Thus, the fine grotesque represents the path of truth and requires an 'effort of the mind' to ensure that it is distinguished from the terrible grotesque, but the reward at the end of the path is the closing of the gaps in observation and the convergence of form, symbol and concept in an emblem of Life. This mental labour contains the possibility of producing 'the sense ... of there being an infinite power and meaning in the thing seen, beyond all that is apparent therein, giving the highest sublimity even to the most trivial object so presented and so contemplated';[5] it promises to distinguish right from wrong, but the difficulty is in deciding whether the grotesque is a reliable source of such moral judgement.

What is often overlooked in critical work on Ruskin (for example, that of P. Ball, E. K. Helsinger and R. Hewison)[6] is the importance of the grotesque as an act of mental labour that performs this distinction. A notable exception is Lindsay Smith's work on Victorian photography and perception, which recognizes the 'dual function of the grotesque'.[7] Smith argues that Ruskin's grotesque is rhetorically ambiguous because it uses 'optical agency' to produce 'a manifestation of the process of transcendence before the eye by way of a retention of ambiguity through aberration';[8] in other words, the grotesque 'disorients' the subject by concentrating on the mechanism of the eye: it 'formalises the gap between the actual appearance of the sculpture ... and the beholder's expectation of a monumental artefact'.[9] The consequence is that 'like the agency of a riddle whose perplexity is never lost, but returns with each telling, the grotesque reconstitutes its gaps each time it is seen':[10] 'it is ... that which it represents' and therefore, Smith says, this makes the grotesque populist where the sublime is exclusive:

It is for him [Ruskin] opposed to the sublime, and facilitates a critique of it as it crystallises a post-Romantic shift in perceptual habits ... Hence, what is implied in Ruskin's dual function of the grotesque – as a movement from a single figure to a visual method, a shift from noun to verb – represents a fundamental desire to expose a disruption in optical agency and visual discourse which in turn frustrates the dualism of the empirical and the transcendental within Victorian culture.[11]

Herein lies the problem: by using the grotesque as a transfer device to move from an individual to a collective endeavour, a Romantic to a Victorian way of seeing, Smith sets up a binary opposition between the sublime and the grotesque which does not account for the sublime as either a product of the (fine) grotesque – 'the sense ... of there being an infinite power and meaning in the thing seen, beyond all that is apparent therein, giving the highest sublimity even to the most trivial object so presented and so contemplated'[12] – or a dialectical counter to the excesses of the (terrible) grotesque: 'now, so far as the truth is seen by the imagination in its wholeness and quietness, the vision is sublime; but so far as it is narrowed and broken by the inconsistencies of the human capacity, it becomes grotesque.'[13] Mikhail Bakhtin reminds us of this unreliability, which is fundamental to the grotesque form, even though he gives the grotesque a rather different provenance as shorthand for exaggeration, hyperbole, and excess. In fact, Bakhtin claims that the grotesque body 'is a body in the act of becoming. It is never finished, never completed; it is continually built, created, and builds and creates another body':[14]

The artistic logic of the grotesque image ignores the closed, smooth, and impenetrable surface of the body and retains only its excrescences (sprouts and buds) and orifices, only that which leads beyond the body's limited space or into the body's depths. Mountains and abysses, such is the relief of the grotesque body; or speaking in architectural terms, towers and subterranean passages.[15]

At first glance this may seem far removed from Ruskin's definition of the grotesque, yet the continuous surfaces and discontinuous depths that represent 'a body in the act of becoming' echo the use Ruskin makes of the Cross in St Mark's to distinguish between formlessness and form by acting as an emblem of Life.

What I want to do in this chapter, then, is to examine the way in which the grotesque constitutes a test of judgement that functions without determined rules but involves a value-laden choice between good and evil. Why is its very particular visual experience made to involve an ethical choice between different forms of art? What are the conditions under which the choice is made? And how does it help to answer the claims of art in the nineteenth century? It may well be that this casting of the grotesque as a test of judgement is indicative of a stark form of aesthetic idealism on Ruskin's part; yet to answer these questions it is essential to recognize two influences that impact significantly on this theory of art. First, Plato and a system of knowledge wherein the beautiful resides in the realm of ideas and the grotesque is a corrupting form of imitation; and second, Kant and a theory of art predicated on the conditions of aesthetic judgement. Once recognized, it will become clear that the grotesque acts metonymically for these strands of influence, and that the riddle of the grotesque lies in disentangling the peculiarity of the choice offered by each influence.

II

The very essence of Ruskin's position can be grasped in three points which I want to outline in a different order to the one adopted in *Modern Painters* and

The Stones of Venice. The first concerns Ruskin's historiography of Venice and the use to which it is put. With the publication of the third volume of *Modern Painters*, Ruskin identified three kinds of true ideal, purist, naturalist and grotesque, which would play fundamental roles in his theory of art. These three kinds of true ideal shape Ruskin's Venice; they map its rise and fall from Byzantine through Gothic to Renaissance times and are to be found in the architectural development of St Mark's from its Byzantine 'foundations', through its Gothic 'sea-stories', to its Renaissance 'fall'.[16] Indeed, as Figure 4.1 illustrates, Ruskin's theory of art has two planes, one representing the chronological development of architectural forms through time (the horizontal axis) and the other representing the classification of these forms according to a type of judgement (the vertical axis). The point is that in completing a move from the purism of Byzantine 'foundations' to the naturalism of Gothic 'sea-stories' and the sensualism of the Renaissance 'fall', Ruskin struggles to uphold both a Platonic theory of forms and a Kantian conception of aesthetic judgement. The former positions the beautiful before the (terrible) grotesque on a sliding scale from truth to falsity, nobility to ignobility, whilst the latter provides a distinction between form and quality which ensures that the very existence of a (terrible) grotesque which lacks the intrinsic moral worth of the (fine) grotesque is the condition for any possibility of aesthetic judgement.[17] Now, it seems to me that these two planes co-exist in Ruskin's theory of art as essential arbiters of an uneasy but necessary tension between idealism and phenomenalism, where the former marks the conceptual and the latter the perceptual tendencies of Ruskin's thought. Ruskin's division of aesthetic from theoretic articulates this dualism:

4.1 Ruskin's theory of art

concept	THEORETIC	IMAGINATIVE	AESTHETIC
form	BEAUTIFUL	ORGANIC	GROTESQUE
classification			
quality	MORAL	INTELLECTUAL	SENSUAL
quantity	BYZANTINE 'foundations' purist	GOTHIC 'sea-stories' naturalist	RENAISSANCE 'fall' sensualist

chronology

Now the term 'aesthesis' properly signifies mere sensual perception of the outward qualities and necessary effects of bodies; in which sense only, if we would arrive at any accurate conclusions on this difficult subject, it should always be used. But I wholly deny that the impressions of beauty are in any way sensual; they are neither sensual nor intellectual, but moral: and for the faculty receiving them, whose difference from mere perception I shallimmediately endeavour to explain, no term can be more accurate or convenient than that employed by the Greeks, 'Theoretic', which I pray permission, therefore, always to use, and to call the operation of the faculty itself, Theoria.[18]

This dualism of aesthetic and theoretic, phenomenalism and idealism, is pivotal to Ruskin's art theorizing for the nineteenth century, and so to characterize this project in terms of an opposition between the sublime and the grotesque, as do Smith and Sprinker,[19] is misleading. Indeed, the opposition should be between the fine and the terrible forms of grotesque, which function dialectically and, under certain conditions, contain the possibility of producing a third term, the beautiful. For in removing the idea of the beautiful from a sensual, aesthetic sphere to a moral, theoretical one, Ruskin separates the aesthetic from the true and the good in a defiant gesture which seeks to ensure that the ideological justification for his theory of art remains beyond the idiosyncrasies of 'mere sensual perception'. The irony is that the pleasures of the senses which apparently push the aesthetic apart from the theoretic cannot be removed from or discredited within the system because they are entirely necessary to the identification of intrinsic moral worth in the theoretic. The aesthetic cannot involve the beautiful, the argument goes, as it contains the false and the bad perceptions of the material world where the theoretic contains the true and the good ones. Without the naming of sensuous impressions as aesthetic, however, there would be no possibility of identifying the impressions of beauty as theoretic, because the aesthetic provides the conditions under which a judgement of difference which produces the theoretic can occur.

The second point helps to clarify this. The Gothic or naturalist kind of true ideal is the paradigm for these conditions because, according to Ruskin, the production of this form occurred at a time when work and art found a connection in Gothic architecture through a unity of mental expression and material form. Savageness, changefulness, naturalism, grotesqueness, rigidity and redundance are the six characters which make up Gothic building and which, in turn, express the rudeness, love of change, love of nature, disturbed imagination, obstinacy and generosity characteristic of the builder's mind.[20] The Gothic is historically specific; and yet Ruskin is unbending in his belief that its very particular visual experience can help to answer the claims of art in the nineteenth century. For the attraction of the Gothic lies with the labour of its construction, which Ruskin believed provided the worker with an essential understanding of his position in society and an opportunity for creation within these societal bounds: 'I shall show that the greatest distinctive character of Gothic is on the workman's heart and mind',[21] the workman, that is, as builder and artist. Isobel Armstrong claims that 'the Gothic may be a reflection of ... freedom but it is also an art of *resistance* to bondage, of the religious principle and "revolutionary ornament", a moment when the individual consciousness gave material form to art within a corporate social organisation and found a way of representing certain attributes of freedom'.[22] Put like this, the translation of work into art sounds suspiciously like a justification for Ruskin's own project in presenting a theory of art. Nonetheless, as Armstrong points out, it is the grotesque element of Gothic which enables the representation, indeed, the 'self-representation',[23] of the worker otherwise hopelessly bound to society:

> The importance of the theory of the Grotesque is that it is a theory of representation based on a social and not a psychological analysis, seeing psychological experience as determined by cultural conditions ... It is uncompromising in its understanding that the cultural production of a whole society and its consciousness will be formed by the nature of its dominant form of work. It does not see art in terms of progression or cultural continuity or a disinterested ethical tradition to which a way must be found of giving access to the underprivileged ... It is alone at this time in finding an alternative to moral or psychological and individualist theory.[24]

I have quoted from Armstrong at length because it seems to me that by making work determine representation, she lays too heavy a stress on a materialism assumed for Ruskin at the expense of any formalism. There is no doubt of the philanthropic intention which directs Ruskin's interest in art, but to isolate the grotesque as the emblem of this social endeavour is to obscure the (possible) unreliability of the grotesque as a form of aesthetic judgement.

Picking up the argument from *The Stones of Venice*, it becomes clear that Ruskin sees in the instability of the grotesque form the means of a moral education for the English nation. According to Ruskin, 'a delight in the contemplation of bestial vice', 'the expression of low sarcasm' and a 'spirit of idiotic mockery' characterize the last period of the Renaissance, which he has classified 'grotesque';[25] 'this base grotesqueness' must be separated from 'that magnificent condition of fantastic imagination ... for the distinction between the true and false grotesque is one which the present tendencies of the English mind have rendered it practically important to ascertain'.[26] Consider the first illustration Ruskin gives of this distinction (Figure 4.2.): in examining these two grotesques the task, Ruskin says, is to ascertain the nature of the difference which exists between the two' and the means of doing this is to make 'an accurate inquiry into the true essence of the grotesque spirit itself';[27] to decide how the two grotesques differ is to consider the conditions of mind they represent and to judge the purposiveness of the effect. What this presupposes, and what now appears to be presupposed in Ruskin's theory of art, is not only that the grotesque effects the separation of the aesthetic from the theoretic but also that the form of judgement it promises acts as an index of the ethical form of the nation's art. Yet the grotesque appears as a riddle throughout Ruskin's work, and as such functions on the basis of a promise to frame fine rather than terrible forms, tell true from false, Life from Death; but it does not (indeed, cannot) guarantee the stability of its operation because it functions without determined rules. We know that the grotesque is composed of two elements, ludicrous and fearful, and as one or other of these elements dominates, the grotesque becomes sportive (Renaissance) or terrible (Gothic), expressing jest (ignoble grotesque) or fearfulness (noble grotesque). The difficulty is in believing with Ruskin that the moral judgement of the grotesque is a universally shared capacity:

> I would have the reader discern so quickly that, as he passes along a street, he may, by glance of the eye, distinguish the noble from the ignoble work. He can do this, if he permit free play to his natural instincts; and all that I have to do for him is to remove from those instincts the artificial restraints which prevent their action, and to encourage them to an unaffected and unbiassed choice between right and wrong.[28]

This brings us onto the third point, often overlooked in Ruskin criticism, namely the playfulness of the grotesque; for Ruskin located the act of judgement in a natural and instinctive free play, the possession of which determines the ethical purpose of the grotesque form.

To Ruskin, play is not in opposition to but complementary of work, 'springing as it does from ... minds highly comprehensive of truth'.[29] The grotesque depends on this play of the imagination to produce a test of judgement, but the choice which results is determined by an intellectual effort capable of translating visual pleasure into an experience that moves beyond mere sensual enjoyment. Ruskin explains:

> First, then, what are the conditions of playfulness which we fitly express in noble art, or which (for this is the same thing) are consistent with nobleness in humanity? In other words, what is the proper function of play, with respect not to youth merely, but to all mankind?[30]

And answering his own question, he replies:

> It is a much more serious question than may be at first supposed; for a healthy manner of play is necessary in order to a healthy manner of work: and because the choice of our recreation is, in most cases, left to ourselves, while the nature of our work is generally fixed by necessity or authority, it may well be doubted whether more distressful consequences may not have resulted from mistaken choice in play than from mistaken direction in labour.[31]

There is nothing new or surprising in this formulation of play; indeed, as I have mentioned already, it is remarkably similar to Kant's discussion of the beautiful in *The Critique of Judgement*; however, what helps us to understand the grotesque is the alignment of play with choice, and work with direction.[32] The distinction between these terms is slight but significant, because it demonstrates that the difference between terrible grotesque and fine grotesque is not dependent on the playfulness of the imagination but on the labour of the intellect. Play precedes and determines work: it underpins work, hence 'a healthy manner of play is necessary in order to a healthy manner of work'. Play is free whereas work is bound by certain rules, 'necessity or authority'; play involves choice, work requires direction; and so a 'mistaken choice in play' has 'more distressful consequences' than a 'mistaken direction in labour'. It is not so much that without play there would be no work, simply that play plus work produces judgement.

On the basis of these distinctions, Ruskin provides himself with some leverage for viewing his formulation of the grotesque as an index of the greatness of the art produced by the English nation, for we are reminded in *Modern Painters* that the grotesque is composed of two elements but produces three widely different kinds of art:

(A) Art arising from healthful but irrational play of the imagination in times of rest
(B) Art arising from irregular and accidental contemplation of terrible things; or evil in general
(C) Art arising from the confusion of the imagination by the presence of truths which it cannot wholly grasp.[33]

The first, (A), 'as in Shakspere's [sic] Ariel and Titania, and in Scott's White Lady' is, Ruskin says, 'comparatively rare. It is hardly ever free from some slight taint of the inclination to evil; still more rarely is it, when so free, natural to the mind.'[34] The second, (B), 'is the central form of this art, arising from contemplation of evil, which forms the link of connection between it and the sensualist ideals ... the fact being that the imagination, when at play, is curiously like children, and likes to play with fire'.[35] The third, (C), 'is a thoroughly noble one. It is that which arises out of the use or fancy of tangible signs to set forth an otherwise less expressible truth; including nearly the whole range of symbolical and allegorical art and poetry';[36] and, in fact, Ruskin qualifies this third form quickly in what proves to be a crucial definition: 'a fine grotesque ... [as] the expression, in a moment, by a series of symbols thrown together in bold and fearless connection, of truths which it would have taken a long time to express in any verbal way'.[37]

For Ruskin, then, the originality of this approach to art is not just that it differentiates ignoble from noble forms – (B) from (C) – and in so doing separates aesthetic from theoretic. What is specific to Ruskin is the way in which he treats the perceptual sequence that divides the perception of reality (aesthetic) from an understanding of its intention (theoretic). For whilst the latter (C) works hard to forge a connection between material form and mental expression in order to express the unity of the sequence, the former (B) disrupts the relation between external and internal, divorcing perception from intention, and in so doing forces attention on a material form without a mental expression, a surface without substance:

The grotesque which comes to all men in a disturbed dream is the intelligible example of this kind but also the most ignoble. The imagination, in this instance, being entirely deprived of all aid from reason, and incapable of self-government. I believe, however, that the noblest forms of imaginative power are also in some sort ungovernable, and have in them something of the character of dreams; so that the vision, of whatever kind, comes uncalled, and will not submit itself to the seer, but conquers him, and forces him to speak as a prophet, having no power over his words or thoughts.[38]

What is present in this description, and notably absent in the vision of St Mark's,[39] is a recognition that it is not the imaginative faculty but the intellectual faculty which produces the (terrible) grotesque: 'the imagination ... being entirely deprived of all aid from reason, and incapable of self-government'. Ruskin's comparison of the two griffins (Figure 4.3) brings this formulation clearly into focus, for it makes manifest the 'delicately wrought lie' of the classical griffin which 'fails in the presence of the rough truth' of the medieval (Lombard) griffin:[40]

The difference is, that the Lombard workman did really see a griffin in his imagination, and carved it from the life, meaning to declare to all ages that he had verily seen with his immortal eyes such a griffin as that; but the classical workman never saw a griffin at all, nor anything else; but put the whole thing together by line and rule ... So that, taking truth first, the honest imagination gains everything; it has griffinism, and grace, and usefulness, all at once: but the false composer, caring for nothing but himself and his rules, loses everything, – griffinism, grace, and all.[41]

So, it is 'usefulness' combined with rudeness of surface which marks the difference in this best-known example of Ruskin's grotesque. Without usefulness or rudeness, the classical griffin is valueless; it is a material form without mental expression, simply surface without substance, play without work.

III

The criticism of the visual arts in this period involves the encounter of two determinations: on the one hand, the reconfiguration of the eighteenth-century notion of the sublime and, on the other, the inauguration of a distinctively modern economy of art. Ruskin's definition of the grotesque is, I think, an attempt to balance these two claims by introducing a system of art which pretends to separate aesthetic from theoretic in order to define the frames and thus the formal properties of this system. This formalism is presented as a refusal to accept that art simply imitates the material world; instead, what art does (or should do) is to provide a test of judgement, an ethical choice, which is made manifest through the nature of the difference between the aesthetic and theoretic frames:

> The faculty for art is not one which we can separately cultivate, still less, in the exercise of it, a gift which can be learned by imitation or direction, but that in this faculty we are to hail a visible sign of national virtue; it springs from such virtue without fail or stint, and no artificial stimulus can produce anything but a semblance and mockery.[42]

For the most part, Ruskin's argument moves so as to sustain the difference between these frames and to ensure that the independence of the theoretic from the aesthetic guarantees the autonomy of judgement from the interests of the senses or the intellect. It does not follow from this, though, that the theoretic can be kept independent of the aesthetic nor judgement alienated from senses or intellect. Thus, this formalism demands that the focus is the mechanism of the work of art; the rhetoric of the image within the frame and its prevailing metaphor is that of an organism, a harmonious system:

> The art of a nation much resembles the corolla of a flower; its brightness of colour is dependent on the general health of the plant, and you can only command the hue, or modify the form of the blossom, by medicine or nourishment applied patiently to the root, not by manipulation of the petals.[43]

What is more, this formalism espouses a social relativism that sounds, at times, very utilitarian, and yet constructs a natural order based on divine laws:

> This, then, I take for an ideal of an Ethical perfectness – a harmony, namely, of the virtues on which I need not severally dwell, being by all men recognized – this balanced harmony being energized under a true and reasonable acknowledgement of the place in which we stand, of the circumstances over which we may have control, of the relation of our powers to these and to other beings than ourselves, and of the divine laws which directly govern both us and them.[44]

It is clear that this is close to the organic naturalism of the Gothic (see Figure 4.1), and it is also clear that Ruskin's praise of Turner and support for the Pre-Raphaelite Brotherhood derived from exactly this kind of belief in the connection between the form of art and the greatness of the nation in the period. The question Ruskin asks most frequently concerns the object of art and the answer he gives most persistently lies with judgement.

If the grotesque constitutes a test of judgement, then its very particular visual experience involves an ethical choice not only between different forms of art but also between different forms of history. The choice is between the terrible and the fine grotesque, the Renaissance and the Gothic; and the choice determines the frame. According to Ruskin, modern art must work towards a consciousness of these frames through an understanding of its past:

> The worst characters of modern work result from its constant appeal to our desire of change, and pathetic excitement; while the best features of the elder art appealed to the object of contemplation. It would appear to be the object of the truest artists to give

permanence to images such as we should always desire to behold, and might behold without agitation; while the inferior branches of design are concerned with the acuter passions which depend on the turn of a narrative, or the course of an emotion.[45]

To improve the art of England, Ruskin argues that painters should aspire towards the older art 'of contemplation'. Like Veronese they must 'perceive the reality of the act' and like Giotto they must 'understand its intention';[46] only then can a 'new era of art' emerge, a distinctively modern tradition which is represented in the work of Turner, Watts and Rossetti: this is the 'true union of the grotesque with the realistic power'.[47]

Notes

Unless otherwise stated, references are to Ruskin, J., *The Complete Works of John Ruskin*, 39 vols, ed. E.T. Cook and Alexander Wedderburn, London: George Allen, 1903–1912.

1. Ruskin, vol. 10, p. 88.
2. *Ibid.*, pp. 88–89. It is impossible to resist noting that there is a remarkable similarity between a section of Charles Dickens's *Pictures from Italy* (1846) and this dream-like vision of St Mark's. Dickens's narrative may be more directly personal and subjective than Ruskin's (or at least than Ruskin's purports to be), yet its response to the breakdown of narrative structure is articulated in the same fashion:

    I had been travelling for some days, resting very little in the night, and never in the day. The rapid and unbroken succession of novelties that had passed before me, came back like half-formed dreams; and a crowd of objects wandered in the greatest confusion through my mind, as I travelled on, by a solitary road. At intervals, some one among them would stop, as it were, in its restless flitting to and fro, and enable me to look at it, quite steadily, and behold it in full distinctness. After a few moments, it would dissolve, like a view in a magic lantern; and while I saw some part of it quite plainly, and some faintly, and some not at all, would show me another of the many places I had lately seen, lingering behind it and coming through it. This was no sooner visible than, in its turn, it melted into something else.

    (Dickens, C., *Pictures from Italy*, London: Bradbury and Evans, 1849, p. 72.)

3. Ruskin, vol. 5, p. 132.
4. Barrell, J., 'The Dangerous Goddess: Masculinity, Prestige and the Aesthetic in Early Eighteenth-Century Britain', in *The Birth of Pandora and the Division of Knowledge*, Basingstoke: Macmillan, 1992, pp. 63–87: pp. 65–66. In this chapter John Barrell gives an excellent account of the role of the figure of Venus in affirming civic humanism as a fantasy of masculinity in eighteenth-century discourses on the arts. Arguing that the notion of a civic character may not exclude the possibility of aesthetic pleasure, he suggests that 'the claim made by the civic discourse, that it is possible to subtract the sensual from the aesthetic, or to detach the aesthetic from the sensual, and so to enjoy Venus's body on aesthetic terms while remaining unmoved by her sensuality, may have come to serve some new purposes' (p. 83). See also Alex Potts on this theme: Potts, A., *Flesh and the Ideal: Winckelmann and the Origins of Art History*, New Haven: Yale University Press, 1994.
5. Ruskin, vol. 5, p. 133.
6. Ball, P., *The Science of Aspects: The Changing World of Fact in the Work of Coleridge, Ruskin and Hopkins*, London: The Athlone Press, 1971; Helsinger, E.K., *Ruskin and the Art of the Beholder*, Cambridge, Mass.: Harvard University Press, 1982; Hewison, R., *John Ruskin: The Argument of the Eye*, Princeton: Princeton University Press, 1976.
7. Smith, L., *Victorian Photography, Painting and Poetry*, Cambridge: Cambridge University Press, 1995, p. 68.
8. *Ibid.*, p. 52. The use of the term 'aberration' to describe the effect of the grotesque on perception is common in Ruskin criticism; see in particular Armstrong, I., *Victorian Poetry: Poetry, Poetics and Politics*, London: Routledge, 1993; Sprinkler, M., *Imaginary Relations*, London: Verso, 1987. Smith extends the use of 'grotesque' as perceptual aberration by using the developing discourse of photography to (literally) embody its material form:

> Perceptual aberration stands for the suspension of the imagination in the face of 'truths' presented to it in conglomerate form. Like the experience of infinity in the sublime [the grotesque] creates a discontinuity between what can be grasped and what is felt to be meaningful.
>
> (Smith, *op. cit.* at note 7, p. 67.)

9. *Ibid.*, p. 66.
10. *Ibid.*, p. 67.
11. *Ibid.*, p. 68.
12. Ruskin, vol. 5, p. 133.
13. Ruskin, vol. 11, p. 181.
14. Bakhtin, M., *Rabelais and His World*, Bloomington, Indiana: Indiana University Press, 1984, p. 317.
15. *Ibid.*, pp. 317–18.
16. Ruskin, vol. 9, pp. xxxiv, xlv. Ruskin described the reasoning behind such terms in two letters to his father in 1851 and 1853 respectively: 'The second volume is to be called "The Sea-Stories", for what on land we call a ground floor, I always call in speaking of Venetian building the *Sea* Story, and this will give you the kind of double meaning to the title of the second volume that there is in the first'; and 'I almost wish I had thought of Isaiah xxxiv 11 before fixing the title of the third volume. I think "The Stones of Emptiness" would so *precisely* have fitted the Renaissance architecture' (Ruskin, vol. 10, p. xliv).
17. For a more detailed explanation of the Kantian attempt to secure an autonomous domain for the aesthetic apart from the true and the good, see in particular Bernstein, J.M., *The Fate of Art: Aesthetic Alienation from Kant to Derrida and Adorno*, Cambridge: Polity, 1992, pp. 17–65; Crowther, P., *Critical Aesthetics and Postmodernism*, Oxford: Clarendon Press, 1993, pp. 56–71; Eagleton, T., *The Ideology of the Aesthetic*, Oxford: Blackwell, 1990, pp. 71–101.
18. Ruskin, vol. 4, p. 42.
19. Smith, *op. cit.* at note 7, p. 68; Sprinkler, *op. cit.* at note 8, p. 22.
20. Ruskin, vol. 10, p. 184.
21. *Ibid.*, p. 180.
22. Armstrong, *op. cit.* at note 8, p. 237.
23. *Ibid.*, p. 237.
24. *Ibid.*, p. 240.
25. Ruskin, vol. 11, p. 145.
26. *Ibid.*, pp. 145–46.
27. *Ibid.*, p. 151.
28. Ruskin, vol. 9, p. 62.
29. Ruskin, vol. 5, p. 138.
30. Ruskin, vol. 11, p. 151.
31. *Ibid.*, pp. 151–52.
32. The O.E.D defines play as an occupation, an amusement, a performance, an exercise; it is gambling, a dramatic piece, participation in a game, freedom of movement and fitful movement. However, it is the last of these (play as fitful movement) that seems to be the most apt sense in which Ruskin uses the term to describe the actions of the grotesque.
33. Ruskin, vol. 5, p. 130.
34. *Ibid.*, p. 131.
35. *Ibid.*
36. *Ibid.*, p. 132.
37. *Ibid.*
38. Ruskin, vol. 11, p. 178.
39. Ruskin, vol. 10, pp. 88–89.
40. Ruskin, vol. 5, p. 141.

41. *Ibid.*, pp. 141, 146–47.
42. Ruskin, vol. 19, p. 164.
43. *Ibid.*, p. 198.
44. *Ibid.*, p. 171.
45. Ruskin, vol. 24, p. 109.
46. *Ibid.*, p. 101.
47. Ruskin, vol. 5, p. 137.

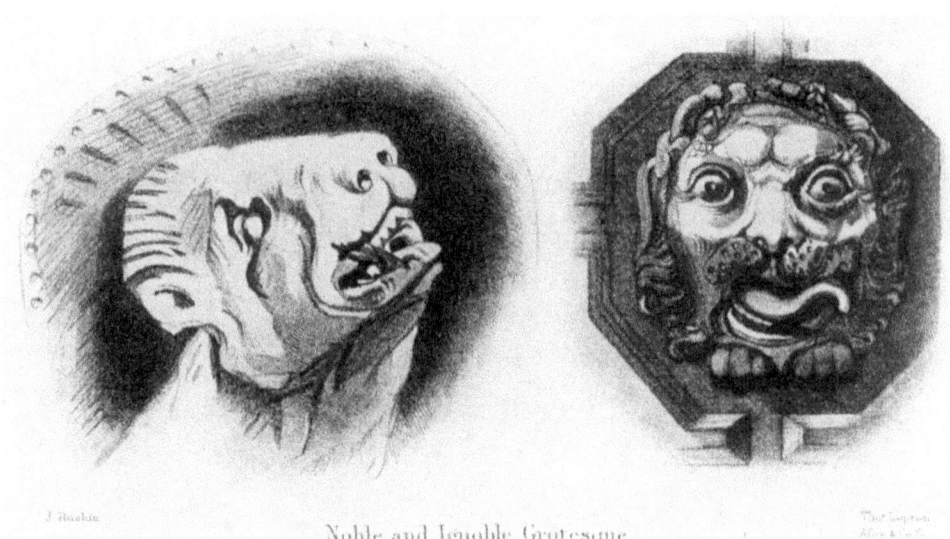

4.2   John Ruskin, 'Noble and Ignoble Grotesque', from *The Stones of Venice*, 1851–1853
4.3   John Ruskin, 'True and False Griffins', from *The Stones of Venice*

5

Grotesque obscenities: Thomas Woolner's *Civilization* and its discontents

Paul Barlow

In 1846 the Pre-Raphaelite sculptor Thomas Woolner made a figure of *Puck* (Figure 5.1). Puck appears as a muscular youth with pointed ears, his foot raised to prod a ruminative toad in danger from an approaching snake. The statue marks a point of instability, dislocation and bodily distortion. Puck is an agent of indisciplined activity, his toe poised to initiate the toad's instant leap, before the snake's sudden lunge. In this respect he is a personification of the violence and vitality of unconstrained nature, of its excess and impropriety. As a supernatural agent of physicality and desire *Puck* modernizes that epitome of the sculptural grotesque, the gargoyle.

Puck pointedly refuses a Neo-classical aesthetic in favour of preoccupations that signal Woolner's alliance with 'Germanic' cultural modernity, in which the concept of the grotesque played a significant part. Certainly, when Woolner sent a cast of the sculpture to Coventry Patmore, Patmore was quick to equate the grotesque with the modern. As he wrote to Woolner,

I was charmed, when the man uncovered your present, to find that it was the product of a grotesque fancy in harmony with the modern mind, instead of being an attempt at that kind of beauty in which it seems to me we can scarcely hope to compare with the Greeks. Being constantly haunted with the idea of Greek sculpture whenever I visit an exhibition of modern art of the same kind, you cannot think what a strange impression of vapidness and impotence I receive on such occasions.[1]

For Patmore, the grotesque is Woolner's act of resistance to a 'haunting', an affirmation of life in the face of impotence and death marked by vapid 'beauty'. Woolner reconstitutes aesthetic pleasure for the modern mind, identifying an act of inversion in which the grotesque takes on the values of the Classical (harmony, charm), while the Classical itself is constituted as grotesque (haunted, strange, aberrant).[2] The modern mind recognizes itself in the grotesque or, as A.W. Schlegel had put it in an influential essay, experiences 'a secret attraction to chaos lying in the very bosom of an ordered universe'.³ As a *mischievous* or irresponsible aesthetic, identified by wilful refusal of orderliness, the grotesque realizes that secret attraction.

If *Puck* deploys the category of the grotesque as a sign of the modern, the opposite is true of a sculpture completed by Woolner twenty years later. In *Civilization* (Figure 5.2, 1856–1866, Wallington Hall, Northumberland) the grotesque is equated with the primitive.⁴ A modern mother is depicted teaching her son to say his prayers. As she firmly places his hands together, she acts as an agent of stability, taming the wayward impulses of the child, who purses his lips for a good-night kiss. The mother's loose, generalized night-gown is the modern equivalent to Classical drapery. It hangs down over a pedestal on which her child stands. On the pedestal are carved scenes of ancient barbarism (Figures 5.3, 5.4, 5.5) – primal conditions from which civilization has evolved: Druids sacrifice victims in a wicker cage; a family gobbles and tears at raw meat; a warrior in a scythed chariot charges at his enemies. Here the raw and disruptive energies celebrated in *Puck* are forced to the margins of a revitalized Neo-classicism equated with the values of civilization itself. The civilizing project is visualized as the suppression of the grotesque, a process of refinement and stabilization in which anarchic impulse is brought under control.

How are we to understand this double deployment of the grotesque in Woolner's work? If *Puck* affirms an avant-garde aesthetic, *Civilization* seems to mark a failure to pursue the promise of modernity; it capitulates to the 'Victorian'. The sculpture seems to endorse those values that mark the Victorian as a problem for the late twentieth century: woman as an agent of purification, the progress of 'civilization', the equation of the primitive with the barbaric. When, towards the end of the century, avant-garde identity came to be constituted in opposition to such values, the inversion of Woolner's aesthetic offered a means to visualize this act. It was Aubrey Beardsley who claimed, 'I am grotesque, or I am nothing'. For Beardsley the grotesque offered a means to negate the domestic virtues proclaimed in works like *Civilization*, to distance himself from Victorian identity.

Seen in this light, Woolner's move from *Puck* to *Civilization* may be said to epitomize the construction of a specifically Victorian position with regard to the grotesque. The view that such a Victorian moment stands as a blockage between the legitimate avant-gardes of Romanticism and Modernism still persists. Like Patmore, twentieth-century commentators have identified sculptures like *Civilization* as an embodiment of 'vapidness and impotence'. However, for Woolner *Civilization* represented his mature meditation on the relationship between the grotesque and the beautiful. As an attempt to visualize the construction of modernity by structuring the relation between conflicting aesthetic categories the sculpture deserves close inspection. This is particularly so because it stands as the centrepiece of a decorative scheme devised with the participation of Ruskin, whose attempts to theorize the grotesque are the most important accounts of the concept within Victorian aesthetics. The Ruskinian account of the 'noble' grotesque is, I will show, implicitly assimilated by Woolner to his own aesthetic. In doing so, he produces a sculpture in which a complex of interrelated articulations of the grotesque is adapted with reference to the Ruskinian model.

Civilization was executed for the central room of Wallington Hall in Northumbria. Sir Walter and Lady Pauline Trevelyan, the owners of the hall, had covered over the open courtyard in the centre of the building to create a large reception room. As a close friend and disciple of Ruskin, Pauline Trevelyan sought his advice for the decoration of the new space. The conditions for which *Civilization* was made were, therefore, explicitly intended as a realization of Ruskinian values. Ruskin himself painted one of the decorative floral borders which intersperse W.B. Scott's mural paintings, the principal feature of the scheme. These illustrate the history of Northumbria from the building of Hadrian's wall through to the industrial development of Tyneside.[5] *Civilization* was to be placed in the centre of the room. It was intended that it should epitomize and symbolize the values defining progressive social development. In this respect it is both ahistorical and a model of the completion of the historical process. In terms of contemporary aesthetics, it is a conflation of the Ideal and the Real, or rather it identifies the *act* of realizing the ideal, of bringing into being civilized values.

The principal scene, therefore, seeks to define a merging of distinct categories, ones which for mid-Victorian artists and critics lay in a problematic relation to one another. The Pre-Raphaelites had defined themselves by their opposition to pictorial practices which elided the complexity both of the act of representation and of its object. 'Nature' was that towards which representation aspired.[6] In part, the visible elaboration or eccentricity of Pre-Raphaelite style marked representation as a project rather than as performance: something inescapably incomplete and therefore uncontained. *Puck* was consistent with these concerns.[7] The accumulation of superimposed, multiple shapes identifies the intrusive potential of nature to force open representational convention. The surface of the sculpture erupts into multiple shapes, just as Puck's own body thickens or sharpens unpredictably. Here, then, beauty is forced to yield to the grotesque by the aspiration to realize complexity and activity. Similar structures are evident in paintings like Ford Madox Brown's *Work*, in which the real is conflated with the grotesque as a sign of the eruption of a productive dynamic which threatens and destabilizes the representation of social relations.

These strategies are antithetical to Woolner's project in *Civilization*. If for Brown modernity is grotesque because of an inadequacy implicit in the aesthetics of representation, for Woolner representation has to be identified as an agency of control.[8] To realize the ideal is to expel the grotesque. In this process is identified the structural logic of *Civilization*. The main scene, then, is concerned with the resolution of the real into the ideal. The grotesque is exiled to the pedestal above which the principal figures stand. As Woolner himself explained,

> The notion of the pedestal is to give the contrast between our primitive habits and the ideal aims of our modern life as shown in the lady's attempt to discipline the child's affections, by making him say his prayers before permitting his caresses. A woman has been chosen in preference to a man because the position of women always marks the degree to which the civilization of a nation has reached.[9]

Woolner's language here is carefully chosen. While he claims 'modern life' to be distinct from the primitive, he also signals a connection. The correlation of the terms 'habits' and 'aims' with the process of separating the primitive from the modern points to an unresolved relation between the two. The mother's discipline is a civilizing act. It is not simply the ancient past, but 'our' present habits which require control. This is the clue to the logic with which Woolner deploys the grotesque in *Civilization*. In *Puck*, the grotesque was realized in the form of the sculpture as a whole – its mischievous refusal of Classical 'discipline'. *Civilization*, by contrast, is defined by the formal relation between control and indiscipline, a theme that runs through the sculpture in a subtle series of variations. Most importantly, the civilizing alienation of the grotesque comes to be defined in terms of the *practice* of sculpture itself. The eruption of activity that characterized *Puck* is replaced by a play on stages in the process of completing the sculpted image, a move from the grotesque reliefs to the fully formed and rounded figures of the mother and child. The tension between the civilized group and the figures on the pedestal is defined as a distinction between complete and incomplete formation.

Woolner's exploration of this distinction is complex. Its significance is evident if we contrast *Civilization* with a sculpture that Woolner would certainly have had in mind as he formed his ideas for his own work in the late 1850s. Auguste-Hyacinthe De Bay's *The First Cradle* (*Le Berceau Primitif*) of 1845 had by the time Woolner started work on *Civilization* become one of the best-known of modern sculptures. It had been shown at the Great Exhibition of 1851 and was engraved in the *Art Journal* in 1856. It depicts Eve cradling in her arms her two baby sons, Cain and Abel. On the pedestal are scenes of the murder of Abel and the sacrifices of the two brothers.[10] The connection with Woolner's own contrast of maternal care with ancient violence and sacrifice is clear. In important respects, however, Woolner reverses the implications of De Bay's work. De Bay depicts the consequences of the Fall, Woolner the process of Redemption. In De Bay's sculpture the primal intimacy of the maternal cradle is the centre of the work. It was the depiction of the cradled babies that had made the work famous. Cain and Abel snuggle together, a single mass of undulating shapes, the contours of their bodies confused. On the pedestal figures turn from one another and motifs are isolated. Woolner, in contrast, is careful to demonstrate the *separateness* of his own mother and child. The boy looks up to his mother, but the fusion of their bodies is denied as she 'disciplines his affections' by refusing her kiss. The tension between proximity and separation, affection and discipline, characterizes Woolner's group. The child's face almost touches that of the mother, but remains distinct. His body twists in *contrapposto*, partly away, partly towards her. This inversion of De Bay's principles is also apparent on the pedestal. Here forms protrude, merge and blur in profuse confusion. The wicker cage in which the Druids kill their victims appears as a carbuncular growth in which massed fragments of faces and bodies are forced together.

Civilization, then, works as a sustained critical inversion of *The First Cradle*. The distortions and dislocations of infant bodies, particularly evident in the *Art Journal*'s 1856 engraving of De Bay's sculpture, are reconstituted as instances of bodily aberrance: scandalous eruptions and monstrous growths. The relation of this to the Rabelaisian tradition of the grotesque, of the Gargantuan body, will, I hope, become evident. Woolner himself signals such a relation in the structure and iconography of the pedestal scenes.

Grotesque barbarism

These scenes represent the barbarian culture of the ancient Celts. As the first known inhabitants of Northumbria, they constitute the earliest form of local identity. In so far as *Civilization* claims universality, however, they are also general instances of the barbaric. The principal scene, on the front of the pedestal, depicts a family group. The mother is physically excessive: broad, fleshy, with large exposed breasts and thick unconstrained hair.[11] Her open, aggressive gesture contrasts with the restraining action of the modern mother. However, the barbaric group as a whole is characterized by a *squashing* or constricting of figures. Each figure rubs up against another, the proximity of flesh to flesh continually emphasized. Bodies are distorted into a series of bulging, fragmentary lumps accumulating over the surface. This is at its most extreme in the top right corner of the image, in which the body is distorted almost to the point of incoherence. A mass of hands contracted into fists accumulates around an unspecified form, while the bewhiskered father appears to be chewing his own hand. Pressed against his knuckles, the mother clutches a bent knife which she points towards her own child. The knife's point ends in a thick, blunt blob.

According to Woolner, this half-unintelligible image depicts a family feeding their young son raw meat on the point of a sword. While the father tears the meat from a bone with his teeth, the mother points the sword towards her son's mouth, 'praying the gods will make him so ferocious he will destroy all his enemies'. For Woolner the scene epitomized barbaric culture, predicated on the celebration of violence. However, the group is also a primal family, and thus the origin of the social and educative impulses that would eventually develop into the full condition of civilization, as realized in the main group. The barbaric family are thus caught in contradiction, their nurturing functions forging an urge for unrelenting destructiveness.

In deploying the grotesque as a means to articulate this contradictory condition, Woolner demonstrates the complexity of the concept as it came to apply to the cultural debates of the mid-century. In particular he refers to Ruskin's important distinction between the noble and ignoble forms of the grotesque, while also drawing on the alternative ideas articulated by the antiquarian Thomas Wright in his *History of Caricature and Grotesque*.[12] Wright and his collaborator William Fairholt had initially published their researches in articles for the *Art Journal* just as Woolner began working on the pedestal reliefs.[13] Both authors illustrate numerous examples of contorted bodies engaged in acts involving the violation of propriety, the negation of restraint, and the eruption of destructive energies. Wright describes a series of Gothic corbels, bosses and misericords depicting faces eaten at by demonic creatures, domesticity generating violence and figures twisting into impossible forms. Several can be related to Woolner's principal relief (Figure 5.6).

Wright's conflation of the grotesque with caricature is important. Woolner's other major sculptural work in the early 1860s was for the new Manchester Assize Courts, designed by Alfred Waterhouse. Waterhouse also employed the O'Shea brothers, stone-carvers who had previously worked on the Natural History Museum at Oxford under the direction of Ruskin. Ruskin had hoped that their independent decorative work would lead a revival of the spirit of Gothic carving, but was eventually disappointed.[14] Woolner had also participated in this experiment.[15] In Manchester, while Woolner made statues of kings and lawgivers, the O'Sheas worked on designs for capitals.[16] Most importantly, it seems likely that they were responsible for the two capitals in the entrance portico of the building, on which were carved scenes from the history of punishment.[17] These are grotesque in Wright's and Fairholt's sense of the term; figures are ridiculed and tortured in caricatured form. A 'scold' wearing a bridle is pointed at by a man holding her by its lead (Figure 5.7); others labelled 'knave' and 'rogue' are exposed in the stocks and pillory. The head of a man about to be guillotined juts out from the block, a projecting knob of stone.

The disrupting of space, form and bodily order evident in these carvings is reminiscent of the 'mischief' in *Puck*. The connection with Woolner's contemporary work for *Civilization* is, however, more complex. The capitals were intended to illustrate archaic forms of punishment, superseded by progressive modern justice.[18] All involve public exposure and humiliation. The idea may have been suggested by Fairholt's essay 'On a Grotesque Mask of Punishment', which illustrates and discusses a scold's bridle. Fairholt argues that ridicule was a transitional form of punishment, replacing earlier 'severity'. Experience of the grotesque was designed to 'produce a feeling of shame'.[19] In this, grotesque punishment reveals both primitive cruelty and a crude intimation of humane intent, foreshadowing the modern enlightened view that the purpose of punishment is moral reform.[20]

The capitals, however, emphasize the victimizing of the guilty: a conjoining of criminality with its abhorrent punishment. They detail violations practised on the bodies and identities of the punished. The scold's bridle literally blocks out the features of the punished woman. *Civilization*, in contrast, specifically seeks to incorporate the grotesque into an aesthetic form which identifies the logic of cultural progress. Woolner's grotesques point up the dominance of civilized values by a tendency towards the absurd. Barbaric attempts to embody the values of the nuclear family are visualized as parodic, sliding towards visual nonsense. Unlike the O'Sheas, however, Woolner limits his use of caricature, which is largely restricted to the figure of the father. In this, he signals his relationship with Ruskin's account of the grotesque. Ruskin had discussed the grotesque in detail in *The Stones of Venice*, later clarifying his position in volume three of *Modern Painters*. The *Art Journal*, reviewing *Modern Painters*, had criticized Ruskin for glossing over the humour of grotesquery by blurring the distinction between the grotesque and the sublime.[21] The work of Wright and Fairholt implicitly supported this criticism by arguing for a continuous line of grotesque satire from medieval gargoyles through to Hogarth and Gillray. Such a trajectory was anathema to Ruskin. For Ruskin, the grotesque at its truest was a sign of a conscious recognition of the failure of the imagination in the contemplation of a world both more terrible and more complex than can be fully understood. Whereas the sublime recognizes the impossibility of symbolization, marking the collapse of legibility, the grotesque generates a disordered, alien iconography.[22] It reveals a confusion: a disconnection of representation from the real. Its relation to comedy lies in the fact that represented conditions tend to be read as absurd in the face of this knowledge of failure. Such an argument implies that the noblest grotesques are the least comic, which is certainly evident in Ruskin's illustrations (see Figure 4.2). He contrasts a 'noble' grotesque head, gazing upwards from its own crudely articulated body, with an 'ignoble' figure, wide-eyed, licking its lips.

This is clearly relevant to Woolner's principal relief, in which the upward gaze of the mother is set against the twisted, downturned face of the father. However, Woolner's image can be directly connected with Ruskin's analysis of another grotesque. Writing of demonic figures carved on Rouen cathedral

(Figure 5.8), Ruskin comments that 'the upper creature on the left is biting something, the form of which is hardly traceable in the defaced stone – but biting he is'. In contrast, the figure at the right is engaged in 'gloomy and angry brooding ... the fellow is vexed and puzzled in his malice'.[23] For Ruskin, the figure is disturbed by its desire to bite and deface, attaining a confused consciousness of its own evil. The connection of Ruskin's 'upper creature' with Woolner's biting father is clear. The deliberately confusing representation of the leg of meat he chews mimics the effects of defacement; its form is 'hardly traceable' in the stone. The figure of the mother, however, corresponds to Ruskin's account of puzzled self-consciousness in malice. In this respect she holds in her figure the Ruskinian correlation of the grotesque and the sublime.

The full complexity of this process is related to the way in which Woolner articulates the sculpture of the reliefs. He retains elements of caricature by exploiting the spatial ambivalence of relief itself. As the figures emerge from the surface of the stone, their bodies move from two- to three-dimensional form. The left foot of the barbaric mother is flat across the plane of the image, while her right protrudes from the surface. The relationship between the rounded figures and the stone from which they emerge creates a series of points of unresolved transition at which the figures twist away from 'nature' towards partially defined spaces which are never fully constituted by perspectival logic. This twisted and distorted account of the figures is clearly an attempt to realize the implication that these individuals are only half evolved as human beings, trapped in a condition between full humanity and an unformed or inchoate materiality. The image is at its most distorted where the father gnaws at the meat, his head squeezing back into the stone from which it is constituted. In one of the other reliefs, worshippers at the shrine of Druidic mass murder are shown with their faces buried in the body of the stone, backs turned to the viewer: effacing their own identity in their submission to a religion devoted to annihilation.

The pedestal, then, works by pulling between visibility and oblivion. It does this in two contrary ways. The Celtic worshippers epitomize the flattening or squashing of the body, a failure of realization, or rather a refusal to move towards the fulfilled civilization represented by the central group. All the figures on the base are only partially realized in this respect. The barbaric mother looks up towards the civilized mother, but remains locked within her own enclosed space. The pagan worshippers hide from the light. But this failure to emerge from the raw materials from which they are constructed is set against a very different act of effacement. This is most evident in the relief at the rear, which depicts a Celtic charioteer attacking an enemy. As he drives forward, pointing his spear ahead, he runs into the dress of the civilized mother, draped across the edge of the space he occupies. The dress is covering over the point at which the act of violence is about to take place, the location of the unseen enemy towards which the charioteer drives. In this respect the dress acts to efface the barbarism represented by the reliefs. It wipes away violence.

In a sense, then, the 'enemy' attacked by the charioteer is the process of civilization itself, represented by the drapery. The charioteer rides into it, fruitlessly attempting to resist its spread by force of arms. Instead, he rides towards oblivion, wiping himself out of the future. By extending from its own space to cover the relief, the civilized woman's dress comes to epitomize the general function of drapery, moving from its specific role in the naturalistic depiction of her figure towards an 'ideal' one, the act of covering indisciplined and exposed nature. The naked body and unconstrained violence of the charioteer indicate his proximity to the primal indiscipline that civilization seeks to tame. Riding into the drapery he becomes both clothed and concealed.

The pose and gesture of the barbaric mother acquires its meaning in relation to these other scenes. As we have seen, Woolner has deliberately generated iconographical confusion, marking the contradictory, 'vexed and puzzled' condition of the barbaric family. These contradictions centre on the mother, the legibility of whose pose fragments into irreconcilable functions. Woolner states that she is appealing to pagan gods for power to destroy. The clutching gesture, however, suggests that she is reaching for the drapery above her. Her fingers stretch just beyond the frame of her own space. She can, therefore, be read as seeking to liberate herself from her own trapped condition, to pull away from materiality. While the grotesque male pushes himself back into the stone and into caricature, the woman attempts to reach beyond it, to become more 'natural'. The apparent grasping for the dress above her can be construed as an attempt to participate in the fully realized femininity of the civilized woman: to clothe herself and to erase her own obtrusive primitivism. In this, she implies a half-formed recognition of her own barbarism and lewd nakedness. Whereas the charioteer attempts to destroy the civilizing/effacing drapery, the barbaric mother aspires to reach it. Her pagan religion of destruction contains the seeds of civilized spirituality and modesty. Though the father is trapped in the grotesque by his own violence and physicality, the mother instances a primal form of the category of the sublime.[24]

Grotesque Renaissance

Woolner, then, has constructed a composition in which Ruskin's account of the grotesque is reconciled with a Classical aesthetic. But this Classicism signals its own claim to the ideal by a suppression of the grotesque: one unknowable to the barbaric figures who are thus locked in a confusion in which iconographical stability and bodily control fail. The structure of the sculpture moves between the contrary processes of realizing the ideal and of reducing the real to the material. This is the meaning of the double effacement. The sculptural formation of the body is itself held between ideal purity and unformed substance. The complexity of lived experience lies between these positions. It is this Pre-Raphaelite conception of the inescapable complexity of the 'natural' that allows Woolner to offer the possibility of modernized Classicism. Throughout the pedestal scenes, Woolner translates the Medieval images discussed by Ruskin and Wright from Gothic to Classical language; in so doing he moves away from Ruskin towards an exploration of the Renaissance sculptural legacy in the light of modern aesthetic and cultural preoccupations.

Woolner's declared aim was to 'bring sculpture to a closer proximity to nature than it is at present'.[25] He prided himself on the 'look of vitality' he could infuse in the sculpted image. In themselves, these statements are little more than Pre-Raphaelite commonplaces. However, they acquire specific significance when we consider Woolner's deployment of Renaissance Classicism. This is most evident in the complex pose of the modern child, which imitates the *contrapposto* of Michelangelo's figures. The motif of incomplete forms striving to emerge from stone itself derives from Michelangelo, whose unfinished works had been discussed in a recent biography of the artist. One figure was described as heroically 'struggling to break forth from the marble block in which it is embedded'.[26] The most important of these unfinished, struggling, figures, the so-called 'Slaves', were directly connected to Renaissance categorizations of the grotesque, since after Michelangelo's death they had been incorporated into the walls of a grotto, along with other half-formed figures.[27] This Renaissance conception of grotesque primitivism – bizarre, rustic, uneven – can be set against Michelangelo's well-known Platonic theory that the sculptural 'idea' is hidden in the stone, only requiring liberation by the sculptor. Woolner was certainly familiar with this view. In his epic poem *Pygmalion*, he describes his sculptor-hero at work,

> bound
> Unto the dimly formed uncertain things
> His active chisel laboured to release
> From their confinement in the marble world.[28]

In *Civilization*, the modern child refers to this account of the sculptural project. If the barbaric figures are still trapped in the pedestal, the child stands on top of it. He has in a sense been 'born' from the stone, freed from partially formed matter into full humanity. Thus, Woolner transforms Michelangelo's static Platonic distinction between the ideal and the material into a dynamic, generative conception. The Michelangelesque figure emerges from grotesque incompletion as a naked new-born child, but in doing so he enters into conditions in which Michelangelo's conception of the ideal, defined by the naked body, is superseded by a more 'civilizing' articulation of ideal aims, defined by the role of drapery. The Michelangelesque body is presented as a moment in the move towards the ideal, rather than its successful completion.[29]

Woolner's position is consistent with that of Michelangelo's Victorian biographer, Hartford. According to Hartford, Michelangelo was enthralled by 'the fanciful theories of Platonism, and wrapped up in its abstractions... But however elevated in themselves such sentiments may be, it is a philosophy wholly unsuited to the condition and the real wants of mankind as a fallen race'.[30] Platonism, for Hartford, undermined Michelangelo's efforts to express the message of Christianity in his work. In contrast, Woolner's concern with the disciplining of the Michelangelesque body through prayer marks a recognition of its fallen nature.

However, Woolner's transformation of Michelangelo's Renaissance Platonism is also specifically marked as a move from the generic body towards the specificity of modern naturalism. Woolner himself made this connection when he loudly declared on one occasion that a life drawing by William Mulready was worth more than the whole Sistine Chapel ceiling. He seems to have thought that Michelangelo's figures were theatrical in pose, complaining of their 'vulgar display'.[31] His emphasis on the controlling function of the mother is, therefore, significant as a response to Michelangelo's aesthetic waywardness; Michelangelo's inclination to Mannerist theatricality is repressed by modernity. Woolner's mother brings the merits of a Mulready, painter of intimate poetic genre, to bear on the legacy of Michelangelo, the stylistic idiosyncrasies of which are construed in modern naturalistic terms as childlike fidgeting.

This, then, is how Woolner classicizes the Ruskinian account of the grotesque, by defining his own modernity in the figure of the mother, controlling and redirecting the dominant Renaissance sculptural inheritance epitomized by Michelangelo. Tendencies that had 'degenerated' into Mannerism and the Baroque are redeemed by domestic naturalism. Such dangerous inclinations correspond in sculpture to those in painting that had been rejected by early Pre-Raphaelitism: the de-naturing of art by the formulaic devices adopted by Raphael's followers. By constructing a complex dynamic of freedom and containment, Woolner asserts authority over the High Renaissance while integrating a conception of the stability of the ideal into a form which refers to eruptions and traces of aberrant bodies within modernity.

Grotesque nature

The achievement of civilization is visualized as drapery's capacity to conceal excess materiality, its function to smooth over the disturbing eruptions bubbling up from the pedestal. This point leads us back to the main group. The drapery hanging over the principal relief acts like a curtain that has been pulled back to reveal hitherto hidden physicality. The modern child stands on the pedestal, having been implicitly 'born' from it, freed from partially formed matter into full humanity. By extension, then, the pedestal also functions as a metaphor of the physical basis of humanity and, therefore, of motherhood. The modern mother's dress is hitched up to reveal 'obscenities' lying beneath it, obscenity from which the child has emerged. The pedestal's iconography of lust, physical gratification and uncontained flesh corresponds to this. The category of the grotesque, then, provides Woolner with a means to represent the pornographic rupturing of bodily containment, to conjoin the Rabelaisian and Classical body.

This point leads us back to *Puck*, his early exercise in the grotesque, and its concern with the struggle for existence in uncontained nature. *Puck* was discussed by Charles Darwin at the beginning of *The Descent of Man*. Darwin labelled a formation in the ear of the sculpted figure the 'Woolnerian tip', reproducing a drawing made by Woolner himself to illustrate the feature. Woolner had told Darwin that his depiction of Puck's ears arose from observations of an inverted point in the human ear. He believed that these formations were vestiges of ancestral pre-humans, a view supported by Darwin.[32] For Woolner, then, bodily deviations could be signs of a connection with a primeval past in which the grotesque was fact. Puck-like 'missing links' were constitutive of modern human identity. Modernity was characterized by a consciousness of its own biological/sexual link with a monstrous past.

The vestiges of this past were of course evident in fossil remains. That Woolner connected relief sculpture in his mind with fossils is evident in his portrait bust of the geologist Adam Sedgwick, into the base of which he had carved a 'fossil' fish.[33] The fossil is incomplete, breaking up into scarred fragments. Like the figures in Woolner's pedestal reliefs, it is trapped in materiality, the form of its body half lost, returned to undifferentiated stone. This connection between the aesthetic logic of relief as partial formation and the fossilized remains of 'undeveloped' forms of life points to the evolutionary relationship of the modern and the primitive, leading to a consideration of Woolner's depiction of the modern child.

As we have seen, the double process of articulation and effacement in *Civilization* operates as the emergence of form from undifferentiated matter ('figures from stone'); the full separation of independent identity (modern child); and the effacing of primitive obscenity (the mother's dress). This move corresponds to that between the aesthetic categories of grotesque, real and ideal. Construed in this way, maternal discipline is the suppression of the grotesque possibilities of the child's body.

The only point at which the language of the grotesque might be said to be appropriate to the central group is in the depiction of the modern child's face, lips pursed out, deviating from Classical bodily restraint as he seeks gratification from his mother. Similar statues of pouting, squirming children had been described as 'grotesque productions' by contemporaries.[34] The mother's discipline is intended to instil in the boy a mastery over his restless body. Unlike the pedestal figures, the contours of the modern child's body are coherent, his indiscipline restricted. His upward gaze clearly continues the upward-reaching arm and upturned faces of mother and child in the pedestal. But the presence of his mother blocks and stabilizes his movement. In this respect her compositional function with regard to her own child is comparable to her blocking of violence in the relief of the charioteer.

As we have seen, the barbaric family in the relief partake simultaneously of a desire for civilization and the urge for destruction. This ambiguity is constituted by the compositional relationship between the barbaric/grotesque group and the civilized/ideal group. The primitive child is connected to the modern child by the paralleling of their actions. The one looks towards the meat, while the other purses his mouth for a kiss. Both are preparing to experience oral gratification, the moment of sensuous experience eternally deferred by the point at which the action is poised. In the modern scene, however, the deferral of gratification is built into the narrative and the structure. The rigidity of the sculpted image *realizes* the civilizing function of maternal discipline, as she insists that the child say his prayers before he receives his kiss. The 'moral' of the sculpture is the necessity for this act of deferral.

Woolner, then, uses the stone of the sculpture to epitomize absolute instances of physicality (fossils) and discipline (rigidity). By doing so, Woolner also counters Ruskin's distaste for sculpture disconnected from architecture.[35] Ruskin had claimed that 'sculpture, separated from architecture, always degenerates into effeminacies and conceits'.[36] Woolner's mother epitomizes a positive 'effeminizing' process. Woman's Mission to suppress the grotesque and constitute the sublime is initiated by the barbaric, and completed by the modern mother. The upward gaze of the child rests on the modern mother's face. This act of recognition is the affirmation of fulfilled identity, the antithesis of the faceless Celtic worshippers and the blank, masked, denigrated figure of the O'Sheas' scold. It is clear that Woolner hoped his 'Lady', as he refers to the modern mother, would appear as the epitome of beauty. Writing to Pauline Trevelyan he stated that,

of all the difficulties, that of the Lady's face is the greatest. I am in despair almost to think of it. I know about five ladies whose faces I should like to model for the express purpose of studies for this one head: for my object is to make her so beautiful that all shall admit her face admits of no improvement. The labour before me is tremendous; but the Chinese proverb says 'Aim at perfection and you shall be above mediocrity': and on this ground I must not exactly grovel in despair.[37]

Woolner is, of course, referring to his own 'ideal aims', which have to be realized by real models, for the face marks the equation of the ideal with completed, individualized humanity. His Lady's beauty must, therefore, deviate from Classical convention, for, as Patmore said, this is 'a kind of beauty with which we cannot hope to compare'. Or as Walter Pater wrote of Winckelmann's conception of the Greek sculptural ideal, 'living in a world of exquisite but abstract and colourless form, he could scarcely have conceived of the subtle and penetrative, yet somewhat grotesque art of the modern world'.[38] Woolner's Lady is impassive. She looks down at her pouting infant with expressionless placidity. This is part of her civilizing function: the arresting image of the beautiful, in contrast to the physically arousing sexual body of the barbaric mother. But as Woolner implicitly recognizes in the above passage, the ideal continually escapes realization. As the figures move up from shapeless lumps, caricatures and grotesques towards a recognition of their own alienation from perfection, they also move towards a modernized Classicism in which is figured the completion of a civilization never to be attained. In this Woolner marks the irretrievable seeping of the grotesque into the aesthetics of modernity even as he seeks to label it as a sign of the barbaric, forever to be wiped away.

Notes

1. Woolner, A., *Thomas Woolner RA, Sculptor and Poet: his Life in Letters*, London: Chapman & Hall, 1917, p. 7.
2. Another exploration of the 'rich' quality of the grotesque with reference to Woolner occurs in the *National Magazine*'s discussion of *Puck*, which it engraves (*National Magazine*, January 1857, p. 8). Walter Bagehot's article 'Wordsworth, Tennyson and Browning: or Pure, Ornate and Grotesque Art in English Poetry' (*Literary Studies*, 2 vols, London: Longman, 1879) locates the modern grotesque in Browning's collection *Dramatis Personae*, the 1868 edition of which includes a poem about Woolner's sculpture *Constance and Arthur*. The poem describes the sculpture as 'a glory' arising from 'obstruction' and 'defect' (Browning, R., *Poetical Works*, Oxford: O.U.P., 1975, p. 496).
3. Schlegel, A.W., *A Course of Lectures on Dramatic Art and Literature*, trans. Rev. A.J.W. Morrison, London: H.G. Bohn, 1846, p. x.
4. The title *Civilization* is that used by the National Trust, owners of Wallington Hall. Woolner never gave the sculpture a title, referring to it in his letters as 'The Trevelyan Group'. In different publications it has been variously titled *Mother and Child, The Lord's Prayer* and *Prayer* (Read, B., *Victorian Sculpture*, New Haven and London: Yale University Press, 1982, p. 185; Smiles, S., *The Image of Antiquity: Ancient Britain and the Romantic Imagination*, New Haven and London: Yale University Press, 1994, pp. 145–46). None of these titles adequately indicates the meaning of the work. Woolner's letter to the Trevelyans describing the iconography asserts that the work depicts scenes 'symbolising Civilization itself'. See Trevelyan, R., *Wallington*, London: National Trust, 1994, p. 28.
5. The circumstances of the commission are discussed in detail by Raleigh Trevelyan; see Trevelyan, R., *A Pre-Raphaelite Circle*, London: Chatto and Windus, 1978, and Trevelyan, *op. cit.* at note 4, pp. 28–29, 63–4.
6. The subtitle of the Pre-Raphaelite magazine *The Germ* was 'thoughts towards nature in poetry and art'.
7. By 'object of representation' I mean to imply that which the representation intends, or seeks to manifest through its procedures. This would include both objects (things) in the usual sense, but also what Ruskin called 'Truth', encompassing ethical values, political functions and so on. Thus, for Brown in *Work*, the object of representation is not only the record of clothing, equipment and other depicted features, but also the dynamics and patterns constitutive of modern social relations.

8. For a subtle discussion of the structural paradoxes of *Work*, with reference to the problem of environing the act of labour through vision, see Trodd, C., 'The Laboured Vision and the Realm of Value: Articulations of Identity in Ford Madox Brown's *Work*', in Harding, E. (ed.), *Re-Framing the Pre-Raphaelites*, Aldershot: Scolar Press, 1996, pp. 61–80.
9. Cited from the Trevelyan Papers, Newcastle University Library.
10. *Art Journal*, 1856, p. 378. The sculpture was also engraved and discussed in Digby Wyatt's *The Industrial Arts of the Nineteenth Century*, London: Day and Son, 1851, vol. 2, plate LXI. De Bay's reliefs are much cruder than Woolner's. In the front relief, depicting the murder, the fleeing Cain appears to be dropping his club, which hangs above the prostrate Abel. On the right side a tied sheep on a stone represents Abel's sacrifice; Cain's is depicted on the left. At the rear is the Tree of Knowledge. See Fusco, P., and Jansen, H.W., *The Romantics to Rodin: French Nineteenth Century Sculpture from North American Collections*, Los Angeles: Alpine Press, 1980, pp. 226–27. The marble version in the Dahesh Museum, New York, seems to have lost its base with the reliefs. See Dahesh Museum, *Religion and the Rustic Image in Late Academic Art*, New York, Dahesh Museum, 1997, p. 1.
11. This figure is close to Rossetti's 'fleshly' work at this date, in particular *Venus Verticordia* (1864–1868). The composition, in which figures are too large for the spaces that contain them, is also characteristic of Rossetti. Figures with arms raised in prayer towards a vision beyond the frame occur in several of Rossetti's paintings. His illustrations to his sister's poem *Goblin Market* also contain large female figures surrounded by grotesque 'goblin' males.
12. Wright, T., *A History of Caricature and Grotesque in Literature and Art*, London: Virtue, 1865.
13. Fairholt, an engraver and antiquarian, published an article entitled 'Grotesque Design' (*Art Journal*, March 1862, pp. 89–92). He engraved all the illustrations for his own and Wright's publications on the subject. Illustrated chapters from Wright's forthcoming book were published in the *Art Journal* at intervals throughout 1863. These concentrated on medieval grotesques. Ancient Celtic culture is not discussed by Wright. Woolner states in a letter dated August 1862 that he is beginning work on the reliefs (Trevelyan Papers).
14. James O'Shea, the most talented of the carvers, had been Ruskin's protégé. Sadly, however, 'the delight in the freedom and power which would have been the elements of all health to a trained workman were destruction to him ... I hoped he would find his way in time, but hoped, as so often, in vain.' See Ruskin, J., *Works*, ed. E.T. Cook and A. Wedderburn, 39 vols, London: George Allen, 1903–1912, vol. 16, p. 525.
15. In an early letter about work on the Oxford museum Ruskin praises Woolner and the O'Sheas in successive sentences. See Ruskin, *op. cit.* at note 14, vol. 16, p. 227.
16. See Cunningham, C., and Waterhouse, P., *Alfred Waterhouse 1830–1905: The Biography of a Practice*, Oxford: Clarendon Press, 1992, pp. 34, 35. Woolner was friendly with Waterhouse, carving decorations in his home. Likewise, one of the O'Sheas cut decorative work in Woolner's London studio. See Read, *op. cit.* at note 4, p. 238. The O'Sheas have become legendary figures. The most famous story connected with them is that after arguments with the college congregation over their decorative work, they carved into the building caricatures of the congregation as parrots and owls (see Ruskin, *op. cit.* at note 14, vol. 16, pp. xlviii–l; Hunt, W.H., *Pre-Raphaelitism and the Pre-Raphaelite Brotherhood*, 2 vols, London: Macmillan, 1905, p. 159). As a result, satirical carvings have generally been attributed to the O'Sheas often despite uncertain evidence. Since they were working-class carvers, the decorative work done by the O'Sheas and others was often not considered sufficiently important for the recording of precise information about authorship; see Blau, E., *Ruskinian Gothic*, Princeton, N.J.: Princeton University Press, 1982, pp. 181–82; Brooks, M., *John Ruskin and Victorian Architecture*, London: Thames and Hudson, 1989.
17. The Assize courts were seriously damaged in World War II. They were finally destroyed in 1957, a plan to restore them having been rejected by the city council. The sculptures were removed and placed in the new court building, though some gargoyles found themselves in school playgrounds. Woolner's most important sculpture, a statue of Moses, was smashed, perhaps deliberately, by the workmen who were removing it – it had never been liked by Mancunians. See *The Manchester Guardian*, 13 September 1957; *Manchester Evening News*, 10 September 1963, 20 May 1996, 29 May 1996. I am indebted to Mr Francis Law for these references.
18. The two capitals each depict four scenes. One illustrates *Ye Pillory, Ye Punishment By Ye Wheel, Ye Punishment By Ye Weights* and the bridle, entitled *For Scolding Women*. The other shows *Ye Guillotine, Ye Stocks, Saxon Hanging* and *Torture by Pouring Down Ye Throat*. *Saxon Hanging* is copied from one of Fairholt's illustrations to an article by Wright discussing Saxon punishment (see Wright, T., 'The Domestic Manners of the English in the Middle Ages', *Art Journal*, April 1851, pp. 113–15). *Ye Stocks* may also be derived from another illustration on the same page. The inclusion of hanging, still practised at the time, is an oddity. The choice may refer to the contemporary debate over the abolition of public hanging, considered 'primitive' by many. It was eventually abolished in 1868.

19. Fairholt, F.W., 'On a Grotesque Mask of Punishment Obtained in the Castle of Nuremburg', *Memoirs of the Historical Society of Lancashire and Cheshire*, vol. vii, 1854, p. 62.

20. Fairholt's theory may explain the decision to place the capitals in the entrance of the building, a transitional point between exposed and enclosed spaces. The ambiguity of the iconography, by which either the punishments or the crimes can be read as abhorrent, places the images within an account of the grotesque as a product of fundamental contradictions within experience – a view articulated by Ruskin (*op. cit.* at note 14, vol. 11, pp. 178–82). Fairholt also illustrated a scold's bridle in an article published in the *Art Journal*. He lists known bridles in Britain, claiming that the 'grotesque appearance' is most pronounced in one in Staffordshire. See Hall, Mrs S.C., and Fairholt, F.W., 'Pilgrimages to English Shrines: Chertsey and its Neighbourhood', *Art Journal*, 1852, pp. 155–57.

21. *Art Journal*, 1856, p. 114.

22. This position is clearly comparable to Coleridge's famous distinction between the Fancy and the Imagination, a distinction that included attempts to examine the grotesque. See Coleridge, S.T., *Lectures 1809–1819: On Literature*, ed. R.A. Foakes, London: Routledge, 1987, pp. 217ff. For a detailed examination of the relation between the sublime and grotesque in Ruskin see Helsinger, E.K., *Ruskin and the Art of the Beholder*, Cambridge, Mass.: Harvard University Press, 1982, pp. 111–39.

23. Ruskin, *op. cit.* at note 14, vol. 8, p. 217; Smith, L., *Victorian Photography, Painting and Poetry*, Cambridge: Cambridge University Press, 1995, pp. 68–79.

24. The iconographical implications of the mother's groping gesture and the conception of inchoate spirituality it implies may have been influenced by Longfellow's account of primitive religion in *Hiawatha* (1855). Justifying his use of 'savage' myths, Longfellow writes in the Introduction to *Hiawatha* that,

> ... in even savage bosoms
> There are longings, yearnings, strivings
> For the good they comprehend not,
> That the feeble hands and helpless,
> Groping blindly in the darkness,
> Touch God's hand in that darkness
> And are lifted up and strengthened ...

Longfellow's humanism can be usefully contrasted with Browning's more complex and difficult exploration of primitive theology in *Caliban Upon Setebos* (1864), a poem well known to Woolner. Like Woolner, Browning generates irresolvable confusion within the text, which continually tends towards conceptual illegibility. (See also Nicola Bown's analysis in Chapter 6.) For Bagehot the poem epitomized the grotesque. Interestingly, Browning's poem about Woolner (see note 2) was placed in *Dramatis Personae* almost immediately after *Caliban Upon Setebos*.

25. Trevelyan Papers, 10 February 1857.

26. Hartford, J., *The Life of Michelangelo Buonarrotti with Translations of his Poems and Letters*, 2 vols, London: Longmans, 1857, vol. 2, p. 44.

27. The grotto, designed by Buonatalenti, is in the Boboli gardens, Pitti Palace, Florence. The imagery is of rural pursuits: hunting dogs, wild animals and folkloric figures. The thick stucco accumulations over the figures mimic layers of calcification in natural grottoes.

28. Woolner, T., *Pygmalion*, London: Macmillan, 1881, pp. 54–55. In this poem, the legend of the birth of Galatea (here called Ianthe) is rationalized as the superstitious response of ancient people to the unprecedented naturalism of Pygmalion's art. They confuse his model with the sculpture.

29. This use of Michelangelo can be traced to De Bay's sculpture, which also draws on Michelangelo as a means to depict childish restlessness. The pose of Cain is clearly Michelangelesque, while that of Abel is Raphaelesque. Cain is derived from the Medici Chapel *Day* and, perhaps, the *Madonna of the Stairs*; Abel's relaxed, expansive gestures resemble those of the Christ child in Raphael's *Madonna of the Goldfinch* and *Madonna del Passeggio*. This conforms to the conventional distinction between the harmonious sweetness of Raphael's style and the troubled 'terribilità' of Michelangelo's. For a discussion of the relationship between 'savage' angularity and 'innocent' purity in De Bay's work see Dahesh Museum, *op. cit.* at note 10, p. 1.

30. Hartford, *op. cit.* at note 26, vol. 2, p. 145.

31. Hunt, *op. cit.* at note 16, vol. 2, p. 225. Woolner was notoriously opinionated and dogmatic. The remark was made at an exhibition of photographs of the Sistine ceiling. Woolner's barbaric mother partly resembles Michelangelo's thick-set fallen Eve. Ruskin also took a dim view of Michelangelo's work. Woolner's words resemble Ruskin's opinion of *The Last Judgement*: 'all that shadowing, storm-

ing and coiling of his, when you look at it, is mere stage decoration, and that of a vulgar kind'. (Ruskin, *op. cit.* at note 14, vol. 21, p. 102). Woolner himself quoted Mulready's own criticisms of Michelangelo's draughtsmanship; see p. 8 of Woolner, T., 'Where to Draw the Line: A Word to Students', *The Magazine of Art*, November 1891, pp. 7–11.

32. Darwin, C., *The Descent of Man and Selection in Relation to Sex*, London: John Murray, 1871, p. 5.

33. Amy Woolner's biography of her father refers to a visitor who thought the fossil had actually been uncovered in the stone from which the bust was carved (see Woolner, A., *op. cit.* at note 1, p. 234). Sedgwick, one of Darwin's tutors, was an opponent of the theory of evolution. He wrote an important early critique of the *Origin of Species*. See Hull, D., *Darwin and his Critics: the Reception of Darwin's Theory of Evolution by the Scientific Community*, Cambridge, Mass.: Harvard University Press, 1973, pp. 159–66. The damaged fossil may be a humorous reference to Sedgwick's considerable age and damaged condition. He was notoriously accident prone, often breaking his bones in falls during geological expeditions. The bust does not reveal damage to his eye, but does emphasize his craggy, uneven, features. See the *Dictionary of National Biography*.

34. Tallis, J., *Tallis's History and Description of the Crystal Palace and the Exhibition of the World's Industry in 1851*, 3 vols, London: John Tallis & Co., 1852, vol. 1, p. 42; Palgrave, F.T., *Handbook to the Fine Art Collections in the International Exhibition of 1862*, London and Cambridge: Macmillan, 1862, p. 36.

35. In a letter to Lady Tennyson Woolner writes that Ruskin 'openly avows that he "hates sculpture"'. (Woolner, A., *op. cit.* at note 1, p. 138). Woolner feared that Ruskin's influence over Lady Trevelyan would cause difficulties. His attempts to incorporate aspects of Ruskinian thinking may have been intended to defuse such potential problems.

36. Ruskin, *op. cit.* at note 14, vol. 16, p. 228.

37. Letter from Woolner to Lady Trevelyan, 18 August 1859, Trevelyan Papers.

38. Pater, W., *The Renaissance*, ed. K. Clark, London: Collins, 1961, p. 212.

5.1 Thomas Woolner, *Puck*, 1847
5.2 Thomas Woolner, *Civilization*, 1857–1867

5.2

5.3

5.5

5.4

5.3   Thomas Woolner, *Civilization*, detail: 'Druids Sacrificing Victims in a Wicker Cage'

5.4   Thomas Woolner, *Civilization*, detail: 'Barbaric family group'

5.5   Thomas Woolner, *Civilization*, detail: 'Attacking charioteer'

5.6   F. W. Fairholt, 'Illustrations of Medieval Grotesques', from T. Wright, *A History of Caricature and Grotesque*, 1865

5.7   The O'Shea Brothers, *For Scolding Women*, c1863, Manchester Assize Courts

No. 79. The Wife in the Ascendant.

No. 80. Violence Resisted.

No. 95. Grotesque Monsters.

No. 98. Horror.

5.6

5.7

5.8 John Ruskin, 'Grotesques from Rouen Cathedral', from *The Seven Lamps of Architecture*, 1848

6

'Entangled banks': Robert Browning, Richard Dadd and the Darwinian grotesque

Nicola Bown

It is interesting to contemplate an entangled bank, clothed with many plants of various kinds, with birds singing on the bushes, with various insects flitting about, and with worms crawling through the damp earth, and to reflect that these elaborately constructed forms, so different from each other, and dependent on each other in so complex a manner, have all been produced by laws acting around us...

This is the opening of the final paragraph of Charles Darwin's *On the Origin of Species by Means of Natural Selection* (1859). Summarizing the thesis which the book as a whole has put forward, Darwin uses a hedge bank, something which might be seen by anyone on a country walk, to exemplify the workings of the natural world in general. In the contemplation of the entangled bank, with its seemingly random combination of life-forms and activities, Darwin invites his reader to see the underlying order of the natural world, and to recognize that order as both inevitable and wondrous. He concludes:

Thus, from the war of nature, from famine and death, the most exalted object which we are capable of conceiving, the production of the higher animals, directly follows. There is a grandeur in this view of life, with its several powers, having been originally breathed into a few forms or one; and that, while this planet has gone cycling on according to the fixed law of gravity, from so simple a beginning endless forms most beautiful and wonderful have been, and are being, evolved.[1]

Looking at the entangled bank, scientist and reader see the interdependence of life-forms, bound together in a war for scarce resources, in the chances of eat or be eaten, adapt or die, all subject to the expendability of the individual, and to the survival of the few at the cost of the many. Yet Darwin asks his reader to recognize this vision as wonderful. Though the entangled bank is not benign, the singing birds, flitting insects and crawling worms are grand; the war of nature, famine and death are exalted; evolution by natural selection, figured by the entangled bank, is beautiful.

In this final paragraph of *Origin of Species* Darwin's claims are both scientific and aesthetic: to look at, to really see the natural world, is both to know it and to wonder at it, to investigate it and to admire it. But the beauty Darwin asks his reader to see in nature is a strange, perhaps even a shocking one, founded not on harmony, proportion, agreement, symmetry or design, but on chance and change, mutation and struggle. The 'grandeur' of the vision of the entangled bank lies in the evolution, through the process of random mutation and from the struggle for life in the face of the overwhelming chances of famine and death, of new, beautiful and wonderful forms of life. The entangled bank is a dialectical image, in which death leads to life in endlessly new and different forms. And instead of being a small instance of the grand design of nature in which God's patterns could be traced in miniature, as it might have been for earlier writers,[2] for Darwin the order of the entangled bank is entirely unplanned, existing fortuitously by virtue of the operation of the independent working of the laws leading to evolution by natural selection.[3]

Darwin's scientific and aesthetic claims were, needless to say, controversial. Even though Lyell's *Principles of Geology* (1830–1833) and Robert Chambers's *Vestiges of the Natural History of Creation* (1845) had to some degree anticipated, and indeed had helped Darwin formulate, evolutionary theory, it was the completeness of Darwin's account of the processes of natural selection and the imaginative power of his work which gave *Origin of Species* its particular importance. In this chapter I ask how contemporary representations of the natural world responded to these claims, and explore some of the ways in which nature could be interpreted and represented in the light of evolutionary theory. Looking at versions of the entangled bank by Robert Browning and Richard Dadd, I shall argue that they each struggle, in very different ways, with the implications of evolutionary theory for the perception of order and meaning in the natural world. Gillian Beer has described Darwin's writing as partaking in an aesthetic sense of the 'wondrous strangeness' of the actual, characteristic of Victorian culture in general: 'The grotesque, the beautiful and the wonderful in the everyday was a major Victorian imaginative theme. The study of "fact" was for Dickens and for Carlyle and for Hopkins an exploration of the fantastic. Darwin shared this pleasure in "making strange", in 'skimming off the familiar and restoring it, enriched and stabilised'.[4] Darwin's work made the natural world newly strange for his contemporaries, and posed the problem of how it might be represented 'enriched and stabilised' if the familiar were 'skimmed off'.

Browning and Dadd respond to the implications of Darwin's work by representing the natural world as grotesque, and they each develop a grotesque aesthetic which embodies a response to the idea of evolution. Each of these responses deals in a different way with the loss of divine inspiration as the origin and centre of the natural world, and of a transcendent, spiritual significance to be found in nature, which evolution by natural selection entails. I shall suggest that whereas the grotesque in Browning both encompasses the dialectical energy of the entangled bank and offers some consolation for the loss of a transcendent view of nature, for Dadd the grotesque is brought about by the terrible costs of trying to contain the terror, the *horror vacui*, caused by the loss of a divine designer and creator.

The first person to identify Robert Browning's poetry as grotesque was Walter Bagehot, in a review of Browning's *Dramatis Personae* and Tennyson's *Enoch Arden* (both published in 1864). Bagehot's review, entitled 'Wordsworth, Tennyson and Browning: or Pure, Ornate and Grotesque Art in English Poetry' (1864) used these terms to characterize and evaluate the qualities which, he argued, typified the poetry of these three writers. It has since become commonplace to call Browning's work grotesque, especially his representations of the natural world and its workings, though usually in a rather different sense to Bagehot's. Browning's grotesque is often thought of as made out of and representing a sense of the vital energy of the natural world.

'Sibrandus Schnafnaburgensis' (1842), an early example of Browning's grotesque manner, describes the decay of a dull, pedantic book abandoned in the garden to rot:

> How did he like it when the live creatures
>   Tickled and toused and browsed him all over,
> And worm, slug, eft, with serious features,
>   Came in, each one, for his right of trover?
> – When the water beetle with great blind deaf face
>   Made of her eggs the stately deposit,
> And the newt borrowed just so much of the preface
>   As tiled the top of his black wife's closet?
>
> All that life and fun and romping,
>   All that frisking and twisting and coupling,
> While slowly our friend's leaves were swamping
>   And clasps were cracking and covers suppling![5]

The insects invade the book, burrow into it, play in it, and make their homes out of the book's decay, so that instead of an inert leaching away of the book's substance, what is described is an active process of re-use and transformation. The verbs and participles, 'tickled and toused and browsed', 'frisking and twisting and coupling', draw attention to the natural processes at work, and to their energy. The deadly sterility of the book's contents gives way, via its decay, to the energetic otherness, the 'life and fun and romping' of the natural world. Commenting on this poem, Carol Christ remarks that 'Browning changes a lifeless, static object into a location of a crawling, vital conflux of life. Propelled by its peculiar energy, each creature tries to transform the book into its own environment. In the process, they change it from a closed, completed unit, to a continually evolving stage on which the natural elements act out their individual energies.'[6] She goes on to argue that in the 'vital conflux of life' which Browning's poems repeatedly represent, each particular element is engaged in struggle with the rest for its own place, both in the poem, hence the syntactical compression typical of Browning's work, and also in the environment. It is the struggle of these particulars for space in the poem and for existence in the world which constitutes the grotesque. 'In Browning ... the grotesque is a source of exuberance and vitality ... Browning attains his grotesque by his bizarre location of this energy.'[7]

Walter Bagehot defines the grotesque in relation to what he calls 'the type', which appears either 'pure', as in Wordsworth's poetry, ornamented, as in Tennyson, or distorted, as in Browning. The poetic grotesque

> takes the type, so to say, *in difficulties*. It gives a representation of it in its minimum development, amid the circumstances least favourable to it, just while it is struggling with obstacles, just where it is encumbered with incongruities. It deals, to use the language of science, not with normal types but with abnormal specimens; to use the language of old philosophy, not with what nature is striving to be, but with what by some lapse she has become.[8]

Bagehot's 'type' is derived from the Aristotelian idea of the form, central to Aristotle's biology and influential in science at least until the seventeenth and early eighteenth centuries. The form for Aristotle is the *telos* of natural organisms, the thing which they become by maturing, and which they are becoming in every stage of development. Forms for Aristotle are ideas embodied in the material of each organism, so that they are compound of shape and substance, and are inherited directly and identically from father to son, thus constituting the eternal and intelligible nature of each species.[9] In the 'language of old philosophy', the type is the *telos*, 'what nature is striving to be', and what, under normal conditions, it will become. It is also, to use the 'language of science' (that is, of Linnaean biology), the normal specimen which runs true to the species, whose characteristics are clearly identifiable and identically inherited from generation to generation.[10] The grotesque, for Bagehot, is equally the organism in which 'by some lapse' the form has not been achieved, and an abnormal specimen which deviates from the true species, because in both cases a departure from the type constitutes a departure from the truth. As he goes on to say, the grotesque deviation 'shows you what ought to be by what ought not to be'; the grotesque is the individual which escapes definition, the imperfect 'not-species' which has departed from its true nature.[11]

Darwin's account of the evolution of species challenges the Linnaean conception which assumes that species are constant and distinct in form, fixed both in time and in relation to other species. Evolution undermines both kinds of fixity, because new forms appear and old ones vanish, and the new species appear as mutations from the old. Evolutionary theory, therefore, proposes a conception of the species in which life-forms are fluid and can be described only for a particular moment, since chance mutation and the struggle for survival encourage not the stability of life-forms but their continual change, increase and extinction. Whereas Linnaean biology envisages the species as a type which might 'get into difficulties', in Bagehot's words, *Origin of Species* replaces this with a conception of a natural world tending to diversity rather than homogeneity, in which life-forms are fluid, mutable, unstable: as Bagehot puts it, 'struggling with obstacles, encumbered with incongruities'.

It is clear that in Bagehot's terms Darwin's evocation of the entangled bank would be an example of the grotesque. The entangled bank is a dialectical image, in which death, through change and chance, leads to life in endlessly new and different forms; it is the tangling together of the various plants and creatures in relations of mutual dependence and warfare that Darwin asks his reader to recognize as grand and wonderful, full of a strange beauty. But this is precisely the vision which appals Bagehot, for it envisages a world of types in struggle and contention, a world in which the type evolves, no longer delimited by fixed boundaries, but always in a process of change and adaptation. By implication, the horror of the grotesque lies for Bagehot in its tendency to imagine evolution, and in the interconnectedness of struggle, death and life which it represents. The grotesque as formulated by Bagehot, then, is not simply a descriptive term. Because it relies on precisely those conceptions of the order and meaning of the natural world which Darwin's work exploded, it implies a response to Darwin's challenge to fundamental scientific and aesthetic conceptions of the natural world. And Bagehot's response, his desire for the purity, the immutability and stillness of the type, is a reactionary one.

Bagehot's critique of Browning's work is that not only is it grotesque, but it positively revels in a grotesque aesthetic. One of the poems from *Dramatis Personae* he singles out for greatest censure, 'Caliban Upon Setebos', is normally taken as a satire on the so-called 'primitive mind'.[12] Looked at in relation to Bagehot's criticism, however, it is clear that Browning's grotesque too implies a response to the Darwinian vision of nature; in this case, though, the representation of nature as a grotesque entangled bank is a much more positive response than Bagehot's, one which recognizes the animating energy of Darwin's image.[13] At the same time, it imagines a way for the loss of the idea of a divinely ordered natural world, an idea which Darwin's work fatally undermined, to be made bearable. 'Caliban Upon Setebos' is a dramatic monologue in which Caliban (from *The Tempest*) speculates on the nature of his god, Setebos. Subtitled 'Natural Theology on the Island', it parodies William Paley's *Natural Theology* (1802), an immensely popular work whose appeal was dramatically diminished after the publication of *Origin of Species*. Paley argued that the wondrous adaptation of life-forms to their habitats, and the marvellous workings of the natural world, were direct evidence of the designing hand of the creator. How else might the eye have come about, except through the infinite wisdom of God attending to the minutiae of retina, lens, iris, nerves and muscles to produce a perfect organ of vision?[14] For Paley, the 'evident design and fitness' of the natural world is *prima facie* evidence of the existence and works of the deity, for 'it is only by the display of contrivance, that the existence, the agency, the wisdom of the Deity, *could* be testified to his rational creatures'.[15] This is the reasoning parodied in 'Caliban Upon Setebos'. But whereas Paley sees a harmonious and ordered natural world as the expression of the just and beneficent nature of God, Caliban sees a world of random cruelty and chance which, he reasons, mirrors the equally capricious nature of Setebos.

The opening of the poem, a description of Caliban, presents a reworking of the idea of the entangled bank:

> Will sprawl, now that the heat of the day is best,
> Flat on his belly in the pit's much mire,
> With elbows wide, fists clenched to prop his chin,
> And, while he kicks both feet in the cool slush,
> And feels about his spine small eft-things course,
> Run in and out each arm, and make him laugh,
> And while above his head a pompion-plant,
> Creeps down to tickle hair and beard,
> And now a flower drops with a bee inside,
> And now a fruit to snap and crunch...[16]

From inside the entanglement, as part of it even, Caliban speculates on the creation, attempting to deduce the nature of the creator from the natural world. However, as the opening lines suggest, and as at least one critic has argued, the natural world here is not susceptible to the kind of reasoning Paley employs precisely because it is conceived in Darwinian terms. 'Caliban, like Paley, engages in speculation about the characteristics of God based on appearances in nature. However, the nature which is the basis of these speculations is not Paley's world of rational design and order, but rather Darwin's world of random chance and the struggle for existence.'[17]

The reasoning of natural theology cannot hold in the Darwinian world because this world is ruled by chance and change, and it is not underpinned by the idea of design. If applied to this world, the reasoning of natural theology produces a capricious deity whose only order is chance, and whose actions and nature are merely a projection of Caliban's own. Yet Caliban's vision of natural processes from inside the entangled bank, 'eft-things' crawling over him and the 'pompion-plant' creeping down to tickle him, nevertheless does envision another kind of order in the natural world, despite his adherence to the fallacies of natural theology. Caliban, as it were in spite of his beliefs, perceives a dialectical order in nature. This is an order that foregrounds process and connection rather than distinction and fixity; an order in which random chances generate an energy which binds together life-forms in a tangled relation. Instead of a static one-to-one correspondence between the world and God, what is represented here is a natural world which makes its own order out of the relations between life-forms. Two passages from the poem will illustrate what I mean:

> Yon otter, sleek-wet, black, lithe as a leech;
> Yon auk, one fire-eye in a ball of foam,
> That floats and feeds; a certain badger brown
> He hath watched hunt with that slant white-wedge eye
> By moonlight; and the pie with the long tongue
> That pricks deep into oakworts for a worm,
> And says a plain word when she finds her prize,
> But will not eat the ants; the ants themselves
> That build a wall of seeds and settled stalks
> About their hole – He made all these and more,
> Made all we see, and us, in spite: how else?
> . . . .
>
> Thinketh, such shows nor right nor wrong in Him.
> Nor kind nor cruel: he is strong and Lord.
> Am strong myself compared to yonder crabs
> That march now from the mountain to the sea:
> Let twenty pass, and stone the twenty-first,
> Loving not, hating not, just choosing so.
> Say, the first straggler that boasts purple spots
> Shall join the file, one pincer twisted off;
> Say, this bruised fellow shall receive a worm,
> And two worms he whose nippers end in red;
> As it likes me each time, I do; so He.[18]

The multiplicity of the natural world and its random chances are inextricably linked. The hunting, feeding and building of the first extract are inseparable from the chances of mutilation and reward in the second. To adapt Darwin's phrase, they are 'complexly dependent' upon each other. And there is no doubt that Caliban's vision from inside the bank is a grotesque one: the focus on detail in these passages, on distortion and incongruity, for example the otter 'lithe as a leech', and on the otherness of the natural world, are all typical constituents of the grotesque.

In both these passages, while each description is made up of grotesque constituents, what links these elements together is a sense of an energetic process or relation. In the first passage, each example of a life-form 'grows out' of the previous one, syntactically speaking, so that one clause, 'the pie with the long tongue' who 'will not eat the ants' forms the basis of the next clause, 'the ants themselves...'. Activity and process, too, are continually forced to the attention of the reader because the creatures described are characterized through their activities: the auk who 'floats and feeds', the badger hunting by moonlight, the pie that 'pricks deep into oakworts for a worm', the ants building their 'wall of seeds and settled stalks / about their hole'. In the second passage Caliban's sport with the crabs emphasizes the relentlessness of the struggle for life. The 'straggler that boasts purple spots' must carry on with the 'march from the mountain to the sea', even with 'one pincer twisted off'; the 'bruised fellow' and 'he whose nippers end in red' with their worms receive their advantages only by chance, that is, by Caliban's capriciousness: there is no sense that the column of crabs will not march because Caliban stones or feeds them, merely that some will reach the sea sooner or later, more or less healthy, because of his random actions.

Bagehot's criticism of this poem implies a horror at the vision of a natural world animated by struggle and contingency which it represents, but the energy with which Browning invests this world suggests that it is not meant to provoke such an alarmed withdrawal on the part of the reader. The grotesque in Browning should be seen as a way of 'fulfilling, bodying forth, and replenishing what has seemed humdrum, inexplicable, or taken for granted';[19] Gillian Beer's description of Darwin's writing in *Origin of Species* is equally applicable to 'Caliban Upon Setebos', for in it, through the grotesque aesthetic, Browning recasts in poetic form Darwin's vision of the natural world. The entangled bank in this poem is the location not of fixed types, rational design and order, but of competing energies and evolving life-forms, and, as such, Browning's grotesque might equally well be called a Darwinian grotesque: a grotesque which can embrace Darwin's claim that the entangled bank, rather than being a terrifying chaos, is instead full of wonder and meaning.

In the context of this idea of the natural world the reasoning used by Caliban to deduce the nature of Setebos cannot hold. Jeff Karr argues that in this poem Browning does not envisage the impossibility of God, but rather the impossibility of an anthropomorphic conception of the world and of God in the wake of Darwin's work. It is simply impossible to imagine God through the contemplation of the world, because nature no longer has either man or reason at its centre.[20] But I suggest that Browning also offers his readers a consolation for the loss of a beneficent deity and of a designed, harmonious natural world in which man is the dearest and most important of God's creations; these losses constituted the grievous blow which Darwin's work dealt the Victorians.[21] In the form of the dramatic monologue, in which Caliban speaks directly to the reader, while at the same time the reader 'speaks', or reads, in Caliban's voice, Browning offers a space for the loss of a divine designer and creator to be projected elsewhere. Significantly, this space is the 'prim tive' and non-European; the reader can recognize as reassuringly familiar the reasoning which assumes a one-to-one correspondence between God and the world, and he can reject it as 'primitive'. If the world Darwin gave the Victorians was a random one, ruled by waste and chance, without progress and without design, 'Caliban Upon Setebos' assures its readers that, at the very least, though they might have to recognize the truth of that world, they do not have to conceive God in its image.

Browning's poem re-imagines the natural world made wonderful by its energy and complex relations of dependency, and implicitly recognizes that the conceptions of species and their relations formulated by 'old philosophy' and by 'science' cannot adequately explain them. In a sense, he turns round Bagehot's dictum that the grotesque 'enables you to see, makes you see, the perfect type by painting the opposite deviation. It shows you what ought to be by what ought not to be.'[22] 'Caliban Upon Setebos' makes the reader see that what is, is deviation, and that the perfect type is a consolatory fiction which supports an anthropocentric conception of both God and the natural world. Nevertheless, to imagine the natural world in such terms does indeed involve a grievous loss: of transcendent significance, of the sense of the supernatural animation of nature and, for many, mystery and enchantment. For some this loss created a terrifying vacuum in a nature from which all anthropocentric significance had been emptied out; a loss which was felt to be unbearable, and could be met only by putting the mystery and enchantment back into nature, but in another form. If one might no longer believe in the hand of the deity at work in the wondrous construction of every snail shell or convolvulus, it was still possible to imagine them the habitation of another, smaller kind of supernatural being. If man could no longer be thought of as an imperfect image of God, at the centre of a divinely ordered natural world, it might be a comfort to imagine the entangled bank, image of nature's new order, inhabited by supernatural beings a little like humans, a little unlike: fairies. Or one might take refuge in a cosmology which antedated the knowledge of nature which had caused such a loss, and thus refuse to recognize it. Both these responses shape the nature Richard Dadd imagined in *The Fairy Feller's Master-Stroke*, an attempt to picture a still-enchanted natural world which has not suffered the loss of an ordering supernatural presence, and which still manifests divine order and meaning. But because he represents the natural world as an entangled bank, Darwin's central image, what it comes to signify is the deathly sterility which is the cost of the disavowal of the entangled bank's dialectical, self-ordering energetic relations. This is what constitutes the grotesque in Dadd's painting.

Dadd's interest in fairies was longstanding. He had exhibited several paintings of fairies, most notably *Titania Sleeping* and *Come Unto These Yellow Sands* (Royal Academy, 1841 and 1842 respectively), before the journey in 1843 to Egypt and the Near East from which he returned mad, and following which he murdered his father, was found criminally insane, and was confined first to Bethlem and then to Broadmoor hospitals. It was an interest shared by many of his contemporaries, but Dadd's fairy paintings, and in particular *The Fairy Feller's Master-Stroke*, his most famous work, are among the best-known of the genre. *The Fairy Feller's Master-Stroke* (Figure 6.1) is the second of only two paintings representing fairies made by Dadd after his committal to Bethlem, and it shares stylistic features and, I shall later suggest, some thematic concerns with *Contradiction: Oberon and Titania* (1854–1858, Collection of Andrew Lloyd-Webber).[23] However, though it seems as if Dadd worked on the two pictures simultaneously, the former occupied him for much longer, despite remaining behind unfinished when he was transferred in 1864 from Bethlem to Broadmoor. Subsequently Dadd made a pencil and watercolour version of the painting, *Songe de la Fantasie* (Figure 6.2), and then wrote a poem called 'Elimination of a Picture and its Subject – Called the Feller's Master Stroke' (1865). The several versions of the image suggest that he was in some way haunted by this subject, and that he returned to it until he could 'eliminate' it from his mind. Indeed, as it was his final picture of fairies, it is tempting to read the painting as Dadd's own 'master-stroke', particularly as he painted relatively little after his transfer to Broadmoor. My discussion of the painting will show how it both represents and attempts to disavow this fascination, and will argue that, in the mad logic of the painting, the fairies come to figure a divine order in a natural world which resists relations of reproduction and inheritance at all cost.

Richard Dadd's madness is not now diagnosable as a specific mental disorder, but its two most important symptoms were beliefs that he was a descendant of the Ancient Egyptian god Osiris, and that he was persecuted by evil demons. Both of these are delusions typical of psychotic illness. In an account written for Dr Wood, the apothecary of Bethlem Hospital, he described his delusions and their consequences as follows:

> On my return from travel, I was roused to a consideration of subjects which I had previously never dreamed of, or thought about, connected with self ... My religious opinions varied and do vary from the vulgar; I was inclined to fall in with the views of the ancients, and to regard the substitution of modern ideas thereon as not for the better. These and the like, coupled with the idea of a descent from the Egyptian god Osiris, induced me to put a period to the existence of him whom I had always regarded as a parent, but whom the secret admonishings I had, counselled me was the author of the ruin of my race.[24]

Dadd conceived of his delusion as a conversion to the religion of Ancient Egypt and in particular to the cult of Osiris, to which he was introduced on his visits to the major Egyptian temples and through reading, on his return, Sir John Gardner Wilkinson's *Manners and Customs of the Ancient Egyptians* (1837). His reasoning was that the cult of Osiris was the original type of Judaic law and ceremonial: he wrote to David Roberts, of his reading of Wilkinson, that 'Moses was a Priest at Heliopolis as also his brother Aaron & they were skilled in all the wisdom & learning of the Egyptians – so they applied it to the Government of the People they led out of the Land of Egypt.'[25] The religion of

Osiris predated Judaism, and therefore had a claim to be its origin or type; moreover, the sophistication of the artefacts and buildings he had seen led him to question the veracity of the conventional dating of the Deluge. How could a people

> so highly civilised & polished acquainted with Arts & Sciences to a degree that puts to shame our puerile notions of them & at so early a date in our chronology as to make us laugh at the extreme youth which our modern antiquarians give to our Race – at any rate these Egyptians must have been a very precocious & might[y] generation to have so soon after the general destruction of the race, built such things as the Pyramids of Ghiza.[26]

In other words, Dadd appears to reject Christianity as the descendant of an earlier and prior religion, a religion which was the faith of a people whose works challenged the authority of the scriptural texts which formed the founding account of the early history of the human race and the creation of the world. As he comments, this revelation was 'so terribly astounding ... that the call upon our Faith to believe in received opinions is so great that I fear a great many will be found bankrupt in that article'.[27] But this was not the only 'call upon our Faith' to which Dadd was exposed. His father, Robert Dadd, was a sometime lecturer in geology, and therefore must have been familiar with the controversy surrounding Lyell's *Principles of Geology*, which had argued that, instead of a catastrophic deluge, the rock formations of the earth's crust were the result of infinitesimally slow processes over millions of years, thus extending the age of the earth and putting into question scriptural chronologies. Richard Dadd's marked interest in the forms and shapes of rocks, which can be seen in many of his works, suggests the influence of his father's geological interests. It is wholly possible that Dadd knew something, at least secondhand, of Chambers's *Vestiges of the Natural History of Creation* which managed to incorporate a geological account of the formation of the earth's crust and a developmental account of the descent of species within a relatively orthodox theological framework not incompatible with the anthropocentrism of natural theology: 'Man, then, considered, zoologically, and without regard to the distinct character assigned to him by theology, simply takes his place as the type of all types of the animal kingdom, the true and unmistakable head of the animated nature upon this earth.'[28]

Central to Chambers's account was the idea of the continuous variation in species through reproduction; he argued, for example, that variation was frequently caused by foetal monstrosities, and recognized the parallels between the stages of development of the human embryo and the succession of categories (fish, amphibian, reptile, bird, mammal) in the fossil record.

What links the content of Dadd's delusions with such 'calls upon our faith' is the way in which all these ideas, whether originating in archaeology, geology or natural history, call into question notions of origins, priority, inheritance and reproduction. Whether literally or symbolically, each of these discourses substituted ideas of mutation, obscure or natural origin, reversed priority and inheritance from lower to higher forms for the 'received ideas' concerning these things. Dadd's madness, then, can be interpreted as at least partially culturally determined; his delusions assert a rejection of descendants and a claim for the priority of original types. He rejected the religion of the son because it was the descendant of a religion of the sun-father, and he murdered his father in order to erase the traces of his own descent and inheritance. As the descendant of Osiris, Richard Dadd inherited not the form, or soul, of the human being which had been inherited through generations, but believed himself generated by a fresh act of supernatural creation. His psychosis, then, was intimately related to contemporary ideas about development, time and history which Darwin drew upon in formulating the theory of evolution by natural selection. Dadd may not have read Darwin's work; nevertheless, *Origin of Species* and Dadd's psychotic delusions emerged from the same entangled cultural context.

This is significant for an understanding of *The Fairy Feller's Master-Stroke* because it enables the painting to be seen as engaging with contemporary anxieties about science, nature and the supernatural, rather than as merely the isolated but rather extraordinary work of a madman produced in entire seclusion.[29] Probably coincidentally, Dadd's representation of the natural world uses the image of the entangled bank which is also Darwin's metaphor; but in this entangled bank the relations of inheritance and reproduction which make up the dialectic of life and death are denied. For what is represented here, in an attempt to assert a unique supernatural creation, is an entangled bank in which order has become alienation, generation sterility, and the processes of life are turned to deathly stasis.

The Fairy Feller's Master-Stroke is an extreme example of the fragmentation of perspective which W.F. Axton has argued is characteristic of Pre-Raphaelite landscape painting.[30] The surface of the painting is so densely packed with detail that it is almost impenetrable, and this impenetrability is intensified by the extremely compressed perspective, which appears both vertical and horizontal at once. On the one hand, the figures seem to be standing on a series of 'shelves' perpendicular to the picture plane, ending in the outcrop of rock in the top left-hand corner; on the other hand, there is no actual sign of such shelves, and the figures, when examined closely, appear to be on a parallel plane that recedes both backwards and upwards. This perspectival conundrum becomes even more puzzling when one realizes that the buff-coloured ground at the bottom of the picture, which gives the impression of a 'floor' from which the composition 'rises', is in fact an unfinished area.[31] Were the painting finished, there would be no areas of differentiation in detail, tone, colour or size to signify near or far, up or down, here or there. The overall effect is of a paradoxical recession which appears to come nearer the spectator, as if the perspective has been turned round and the figures are going to topple out of the painting, except that they are 'held' by the stalks of timothy-grass and hawkbit stretched like bars across the surface plane from left to right, so heavily painted that they stand out like an enamelled relief. These bars contain the scene; in fact, they do more, they imprison it.

In *Songe de la Fantasie* the surface of the image is even more impenetrable, the figures barely distinguishable from the background, and the bar-like stalks have become even more important, swirling and spiralling across the surface and virtually obscuring the figures. These swirls are also referred to in 'An Elimination of a Picture and its Subject...'

> Turn to the Patriarch & behold
> Long pendants from his crown are rolled
> In winding figures circle round
> The grass and such upon the mound,
> They represent vagary wild
> And mental aberration styled.
> Now unto Nature clinging close
> Now wildly out again they toss,
> Like a cyclone uncontroll'd
> Sweeping round with chance-born fold
> Unto the picture bring a grace
> Which else were wanting from its face
> But tied at length unto a stem
> Shows or should do ad finitem rem.[32]

Such obscuring diagonals can be found elsewhere in the work Dadd produced during his years in Bethlem, for example in *Crazy Jane* (1855), which illustrates a ballad in which a woman is deserted by her lover, and which is organized around a diagonal branch to which the figure clings; *Sketch to Illustrate the Passions: Grief, or Sorrow* (1854), which depicts an overgrown tomb crossed by diagonal branches; *Bacchanalian Scene* (1862), which has grasses crossing the painting downwards from right to left. Each of these pictures in different ways connotes loss of reason, whether through the depiction of madness, abandonment to the senses or mourning, and this correlates with Dadd's statement that the diagonals and spirals represent vagary, 'wild/And mental aberration styled'. But in *The Fairy Feller's Master-Stroke* and *Songe de la Fantasie* they are also 'tied at length unto a stem [which] Shows or should do ad finitem rem'; that is the tying together of the diagonals which represent Dadd's own madness in an attempt to contain it 'ad finitem rem', to the end of things. As my discussion of *The Fairy Feller's Master-Stroke* will show, such containment 'ad finitem rem' has deathly consequences.

The narrative of the picture, such as it is, is organized around the 'stroke' the Fairy Feller is poised to make, a blow that will cleave the nut in two. The nut is an obvious metaphor for fertility, one of a number with which the image is littered: the dandelion heads, plane-tree fruits and flowers are others. To cleave the nut would be to release the germ of life within it, to allow growth and change; but this will never happen. Around this arrested climactic moment, the fairies are gathered, seemingly attentive to the action yet also uninvolved in it. And looking closely at the figures, we see that only the few at the bottom of the picture are actually watching the Feller and the nut. The rest seem uninvolved either with this action or with each other. For example, the row of figures on the top 'shelf', the soldier, apothecary, farmer, tailor and so on, are, though grouped together, separate. They neither act, for there is no narrative to this part of the picture, nor interact, since they do not even look at each other. Similarly, the group of figures around the 'Patriarch' (the term comes from Dadd's poem) wearing the enormous hat in the centre of the painting seem to have little relation to one another. This lack of narrative is reinforced by 'An Elimination of a Picture and its Subject...', which devotes most of its 600 lines to describing in detail each one of these figures without making any link, narrative or otherwise, between them. The image is crowded but static, and its stasis is due not only to the moment of arrest it depicts, but also to the fact that its crowd of figures, disposed around the picture seemingly at random, have no relation to each other.

Interspersed with the fairy figures are fragments of nature: the grasses, dandelion clocks, leaves, nuts and a grasshopper, almost hidden between the soldier and a fairy blowing a horn. When we look at these details, the variations of scale, already apparent in the fairies' sizes, become very marked. All these things are out of proportion to one another, so that it is impossible to tell which are enlarged or reduced. Which are the proper size: the daisies, grass and the Feller; or the nuts, grasshopper and Patriarch; or the leaves, dandelion clocks and apothecary; or all three? It is impossible to tell what should be the scale marker for the picture, since in the bewildering confusion of scales and sizes there is no perspective to give the spectator an idea of what the 'right size' should be. It appears, then, that the scene is one in which all kinds of relation, whether narrative, perspectival, of scale or dimension, have ceased to hold, so that each separate object or figure, whether natural or supernatural, is entirely discrete. In addition, the fulcrum of the picture, the Fairy Feller's axe, is unfinished. This image which seems composed of unrelated fragments distorted into an impossible perspective, has a literal blank space right at its centre.

The Fairy Feller's Master-Stroke is another version of the entangled bank of which Darwin wrote. But while Darwin's and Browning's entangled banks are full of life and of the various forms of life in relations of complex dependence upon one another, Dadd's entangled bank is marked by a lack of relation so extreme as to be alienation. It is as if, looking at the natural world evolutionary biology conceives, what is seen is not process but stasis, not the dialectical relation of struggle, contingency, death and reproduction but a deathly stillness. The about-to-be-cloven nut, the unnaturally open daisies, the absurdly pointed breasts and huge calves of the female fairies, which should be signs of fertility, signify not reproduction but sterility. And in the top row of figures, Dadd painted a portrait of his murdered father the apothecary, half-hidden and looking over his shoulder, a reminder of his own disavowal of the processes of reproduction and inheritance. The grotesqueness of this picture, most apparent in the female figures, but equally present in the distortions of scale, the clarity of detail, and above all in the 'unnatural' juxtapositioning of unrelated figures, plants and insects, is of a wholly different cast to the energetic 'Darwinian' grotesque of 'Caliban upon Setebos'. Here is a sterile grotesque the principle of which is stasis and alienation rather than a dialectic of life and death, struggle and reproduction. 'It shows or should do', in Dadd's words, 'ad finitem rem', the end rather than the beginning of things.[33]

In some ways the confusion of perspective and scale, the frustration of the narrative, and the juxtapositioning of natural and supernatural creatures recall the image with which Paley begins *Natural Theology*: a heath on which a watch is found lying. Gillian Beer comments of this image that the scene is,

uneasily, both physical and provisional: its scale is unstable, moving rapidly between generality and articulated detail. It is at once authoritative and close to the absurd. Its project is to dramatise absurdity and misappropriated evidence, to rouse resistance, and then to satisfy our sense of congruity so that we accept as much – and more than – his analogy can imply. The Process is like that of a riddle – the yoking of unlike objects, the unlocking of shared signification – and like a riddle it gratifies and disappoints ... Both the bravura and the common sense are important in the learning process created by analogy: the abrupt shifts of scale and the fickle movements between concepts and objects set it always on the edge of fantasy, though claiming for itself a more than metaphorical status, a real presence in the natural order.[34]

The analogical purpose of Paley's image, to introduce the idea of design and purposiveness in the natural world, makes the image riddling and takes it to the 'edge of fantasy'. Beer's description of the process of analogy in Paley seems uncannily close to the 'shifts of scale and the fickle movement between concepts and objects' in Dadd's painting. However, in Paley the riddling, fantastic nature of analogy is transformative. As Beer points out, the analogy of the watch on the heath for the presence in nature of God the designer requires a transformation of 'the homely into the transcendent' like that of bread and wine.[35] Analogy is merely a way of figuring the real order and meaning in the natural world. In *The Fairy Feller's Master-Stroke* the hierarchical figure of analogy is, as it were, compressed into one level. The designed order of the natural world, directly inherited from creation, is what Paley's analogy figures. His theology and his natural history and his figurative representation of them all depend upon clearly understood notion of inheritance, priority and equivalence – precisely the things which Dadd rejected as false or corrupted. Though

Dadd's image looks as if it should be an analogy for the order of the natural world, it is in fact psychotic, literal representation of it. Instead of the hidden hand of God lying behind the analogical riddle of the watch, as it does for Paley, in Dadd's painting the fairies represent the supernatural act of creation present in the scene. If Dadd rejected the distant origins of the natural human worlds in geology, natural history and archaeology, he equally rejected the stories of a divine creation which those knowledges undermined. For Dadd, the natural and human worlds were created afresh in each generation, either by Osiris, or by the fairies. The fairies in this picture, then, represent the work of creation from nothing by supernatural power. The fairy feller does not need to split the nut, since the nut can have no meaning and purpose in this natural world which is entirely without sexual reproduction and generation, a natural world where the only creation is supernatural. The fairy feller is poised to split the nut because, in the entangled bank inhabited by fairies, it is the fairies' supernatural power which supplies order and meaning. Dadd himself hints at this in an extremely obscure passage from 'An Elimination of a Picture' which describes the feller's purpose in splitting the nut:

> The meaning thus, let's find –
> For idle pastime hither led
> Fays, gnomes, and elves and suchlike fled
> To fix some dubious point to fairies only
> Known to exist, or to the lonely
> Thoughtful man recluse
> Of power a potent spell to loose
> Which binds the better slave to worse
> Swindles soul, body, goods & purse
> T'unlock the secret cells of dark abyss
> The power which never doth its victims miss
> But may e[n]gorge when truth appears
> When fail or guns or swords or spears
> For some such end we may suppose
> They've met since day hath made its close
> Night's noon time haply extra bright
> By fairie power made all so alight
> Doubtful if night or day might reign
> To certain be in mind revolve again
> And say that common nature is not true.[36]

Like the whole of the poem, these lines are difficult to interpret, but the implication here seems to be that 'fairie power' has something to do with the reversal of the natural order, that it makes 'common nature ... not true', and that this reversal has something to do with the way in which life forms are bound together, 'which binds the better slave to worse', and in which their forms or natures are transmitted through the generations 'T'unlock the secret cells of dark abyss/The power which never doth its victims miss'. It seems from this passage that the idea of the fairy world, filled with unnatural powers, in which common nature is untrue, and in which the secrets of cells are unlocked, is horrible or frightening for Dadd, and that the mystery of the fairies' purposes, which are known to only themselves and him, the lonely Thoughtful man recluse, is a burden rather than an enlightenment. There is no doubt that Dadd's psychosis, in part a response to a world from which stability, order and meaning had been torn, gave him back the vision of a world in which order and meaning were themselves terrifying.

Dadd's static grotesque is not 'Paleyite', since it refuses the hierarchies of meaning which suffuse Paley's natural world with beneficent divine purpose. It is, rather, 'Darwinian': not because it represents Darwin's entangled bank through a grotesque aesthetic, as Browning does, but because, like Darwin, Dadd rejects modes of repesenting the natural world which see its hidden order as metaphysical. For Darwin, the order of the entangled bank, though hidden, is material; it is the dialectical order of generation, struggle, death and life figured in the tangling together of life forms. For Dadd, since natural and supernatural exist in the same literal way, there can be no hidden order to the entangled bank; creation and creator, natural and supernatural are equally present within an enchanted world in which there is no distinction between them. But the cost of this vision, and the reason why it is grotesque, is because it is unable to admit the processes of life. It is stuck in a timeless and deathly moment of the arrested, continuous present in which, because there is no past, there can be no future.

Dadd's repeated return to the entangled bank in the various versions of *The Fairy Feller's Master-Stroke* bears witness to his horror at the image and his struggle to contain it. By imprisoning the bank within its swirls and bars, by pinning it down under its obsessively detailed surface, he attemped to control the force and vitality of the entangled bank. But the incongruities of form and scale, the incoherence of perspective, and the impotence of the narrative show how this attempt at control produces the distortion typical of the grotesque: the type, as it were, *in extremis*. *The Fairy Feller's Master-Stroke* is a deeply disturbing image because what it represents is the price of disavowal. It offers a deathly vision of the natural world in which the 'lifely' dialectical connection between life and death is arrested, in order to contain the terror of the randomness and contingency which are central to Darwin's account of evolution, and the tainted inheritance from father to son which is implied by evolution, by history, by archaeology and by geology. Whereas Browning's and Darwin's natural worlds teem with life and death, Dadd's is stuck in a moment of deathly stillness. In order to hold off the terror of the 'war of nature ... famine and death' which produces the 'forms most beautiful and wonderful [which] have been, and are being, evolved', *The Fairy Teller's Master-Stroke* represents a natural world in which no evolution, no birth, no death, no future can take place, because relations of dependence and reproduction, struggle and chance, that is, the processes of life, are themselves disavowed.

Darwin asked his reader to recognize the entangled bank as wondrous and beautiful, but perhaps that was not possible for his contemporaries, in view of the shockingly new vision of the natural world it embodied. Browning's response, as Bagehot's criticism implies, was to frame the entangled bank as grotesque, and in this way to give expression to the wonderful, dialectical energy of the image. For Dadd, however, the grotesque became a way of taming and holding still the energies of nature, of insisting that nothing in nature has changed, and that nothing can change. Dadd concludes his poem, 'For nought as nothing it explains/ And nothing from nothing nothing gains.' It is because the dialectic of the entangled bank cannot be tolerated in this painting that its action is arrested and forms of relation are reduced in it to an alienated sterility and stasis. But the cost of this is a nothingness, from which nothing can come, as Dadd himself admits. If one refuses the lifely dialectic of the entangled bank, if one recoils in fear and horror, if one refuses to recognize loss, then nature, as it does in Richard Dadd's vision, stops dead.

Notes

I am grateful to David Booth for his most perceptive reading of an earlier draft of this chapter, and for his patience in helping me to rethink the argument of several sections of it.

1. Darwin, C., *On the Origin of Species by Means of Natural Selection*, ed. Gillian Beer, London: O.U.P., 1996 pp. 395–36.

2. The emphasis in pre-nineteenth-century natural history on the classification of specimens and species was motivated in great part by the belief that all life-forms were related parts of the great divine plan, and linked by a natural classification that it was the task of naturalists to discover. This belief was underpinned by natural theology; William Derham, for instance, argued in *Physico-Theology, or, Demonstration of the Being and Attributes of God from His Works of Creation* (1713) that observation of the created world would lead to knowledge of the deity. Prior to the early nineteenth century, and later in Britain, natural history was principally concerned, not with the relationships of life-forms to each other and to the environment, but with their place in the natural classification of the divine order. 'By gathering together and comparing representatives of as many species as they could, some naturalists hoped to discover the natural classification system that related all living things to each other' (Larsen, Anne, 'Equipment for the Field', in Jardine, N., Secord, J., and Spary, E. (eds,) *The Cultures of Natural History*, Cambridge: Cambridge University Press, 1996, p. 358).

3. Even before Darwin's formulation of the laws of evolution by natural selection, the entangled bank was, arguably, a key metaphor through which the workings of the natural world were conceptualized. Compare, for example, these instances from the *Journal of Researches*:

> On every side were lying irregular masses of rock and torn-up trees; other trees, though still erect, were decayed to the heart and ready to fall. The entangled mass of the thriving and the fallen reminded me of the forests within the tropics... The number of living creatures of all Orders, whose existence intimately depends on the kelp, is wonderful. A great volume might be written, describing the inhabitants of one of these beds of sea-weed. Almost all the leaves, excepting those that float on the surface, are so thickly incrusted with corallines as to be of a white colour. We find exquisitely delicate structures, some inhabited by simple hydra-like polypi, others by more organized kinds, and beautiful compound Ascidiae. On the leaves, also, various patelliform shells, Trochi, uncovered molluscs, and some bivalves with their place are attached. On shaking the great entangled roots, a pile of small fish, shells, cuttle-fish, crabs of all orders, sea-eggs, starfish, beautiful Holuthruiae, Planariae, and crawling nereidous animals of a multitude of forms, all fall out together... I can only compare these great aquatic forests of the southern hemisphere, with the terrestrial ones in the inter-tropical regions.

(Darwin, C., *Journal of Researches into the Geology and Natural History of the Various Countries Visited During the Voyage of the Beagle*, London: Dent, 1906 (originally published 1839), pp. 199–200, 228–29.) The recurrence of the word 'entangled' here in the context of the multitudinousness and interdependence of life-forms suggests that, even at this stage, Darwin saw entanglement as the underlying order of the natural world.

4. Beer, G., *Darwin's Plots: Evolutionary Narrative in Darwin, George Eliot and Nineteenth-Century Fiction*, London: Ark Paperbacks, 1985, p. 81.

5. Browning, R., *The Poems*, ed. John Pettigrew, Harmondsworth: Penguin, 1981, vol. 1, p. 419.

6. Christ, C., *The Finer Optic: The Aesthetics of Particularity in Victorian Poetry*, New Haven and London: Yale University Press, 1975, p. 68.

7. *Ibid.*, p. 71.

8. Bagehot, W., 'Wordsworth, Tennyson and Browning, or Pure, Ornate and Grotesque Art in English Poetry', *Literary Studies*, 2 vols, London: Longmans, 1879, p. 375.

9. See Lear, J., *Aristotle: The Desire to Understand*, Cambridge: Cambridge University Press, 1988, pp. 15–54, for an account of Aristotle's theory of form, which Lear summarizes as follows (pp. 19–20):

    we should conceive the end as being the (*fully actualized*) form. For the form is and has been its nature throughout its development. The form is *both* that toward which the process is directed – 'that for the sake of which' the process occurs – *and* that which is directing the process. It is an immature organism's nature simply to be a member of that species in the fullest, most active sense. This, for Aristotle, is one and the same nature: the active, dynamic form which, at varying levels of potentiality and actuality, is at work in the appropriate matter.

    For Aristotle, understanding the forms of organisms is the key to understanding the rationality of the natural world, and the constancy of forms from generation to generation embodies these rational structures (p. 54):

    Animals, therefore, strive for immortality in the only way open to them: by reproducing their kind. In this way the species exists eternally. Now, while the parents may pass on family resemblance between one generation and the next, what primarily remains through the continuing change of generations is the formal, intelligible structure of each species. It is the intelligibility of each species that is truly eternal.

10. Lisbet Koerner notes that Carl Linnaeus's system of classification was derived ultimately from Aristotelian principles, whilst he also subscribed to the doctrines of natural theology, themselves a Christian interpretation of Aristotelian biology. See Koerner, L., 'Carl Linnaeus in his Time and Place', in *The Cultures of Natural History*, *op. cit.* at note 2, pp. 145–62.

11. For a rather different discussion of Bagehot's conception of the grotesque, see Armstrong, I., *Victorian Poetry: Poetry, Poetics and Politics*, London: Routledge, 1993, pp. 284–86. Armstrong relates Bagehot's grotesque to religious typography: 'in attempting to establish the pure, fixed, universal theological Type against the Grotesque, Bagehot, even though using the Type metaphorically, exploits its conservative propensities' (p. 285). She also suggests, without developing the idea, that the Type is also 'evolutionary'.

12. Bagehot wrote of 'Caliban Upon Setebos' that:

    Mr Browning has undertaken to describe what may be called *mind in difficulties* – mind set to make out the universe under the worst and hardest circumstances. He takes 'Caliban', not perhaps exactly Shakespeare's Caliban, but an analogous and worse creature; a strong thinking power, but a nasty creature – a gross animal, uncontrolled and unelevated by any feeling of religion or duty. The delineation of him will show that Mr Browning does not wish to take undue advantage of his readers by choice of nice subjects.

    (*Op. cit.* at note 8, pp. 377–78.)

13. Browning read *Origin of Species* on its publication, and followed the debate which ensued. In December 1859 Browning met an American Unitarian, Theodore Parker, who was also an amateur biologist. His *Discourse of Matters Pertaining to Religion* is another text Browning may well have had in mind when writing the poem. Compare, for example: 'A man rude in spirit must have a rude conception of God. He thinks the deity like himself. If a buffalo had a religion, his conception of the deity would probably be a buffalo' (Browning, *op. cit.* at note 5, p. 1158). Phillip Drew implies that Browning's reading of *Origin of Species* must have been a superficial one, and that he failed 'to notice that Darwin had added quite a lot to the idea of evolution which had been current in the 1830s' (Drew, P., 'Browning and Politics', in Armstrong, I. (ed.), *Writers and their Background: Robert Browning*, London: G. Bell, 1974, p. 147). Whether or not Browning immediately and consciously

grasped all the implications of Darwin's work, it is hard to believe that he would not have responded to an image of such power and vibrancy as the entangled bank.

14. This is the argument made in the opening chapter of Paley, W., *Natural Theology: or Evidences of the Existence and Attributes of the Deity, Collected from the Appearance of Nature*, London: R. Faulder, 1802. Paley takes the example first of a watch and then the eye as instances of perfect design and fitness for purpose. Design and fitness presuppose a divine creator, for such perfection cannot have arisen by accident.

15. Paley, *op. cit.* at note 14, p. 42.

16. Browning, *op. cit.* at note 5, p. 805, ll. 1–11.

17. Karr, J., 'Caliban and Paley: Two Natural Theologians', *Studies in Browning and his Circle*, **13**, 1985, pp. 37–46; p. 39.

18. Browning, *op. cit.* at note 5, pp. 806–807, ll. 46–56, 99–109.

19. Beer, *op. cit.* at note 4, p. 81.

20. Karr, *op. cit.* at note 17, p.45. See also Beer, *op. cit.* at note 4, pp. 49–76, for an account of Darwin's own struggles against anthropomorphism in *Origin of Species*.

21. Beer, quoting Freud, describes Darwin's work as the 'second blow' to man's narcissism: the first being the Copernican revolution and the third being, of course, the discovery of the Unconscious. See Beer, *op. cit.* at note 4, pp. 12–18, for a discussion of the effects of this 'blow' on Victorian culture and mentality.

22. Bagehot, *op. cit.* at note 8, p. 375.

23. For a full account of Dadd's life, see Allderidge, P., *The Late Richard Dadd: 1817-1886*, London: Tate Gallery, 1974. The two pictures clearly share some thematic concerns. The central figures in *Contradiction: Oberon and Titania* are framed by a tangle of plants and insects which push against the surface of the picture-plane. Dadd's rejection of reproduction, inheritance and generation which underlies his psychotic delusions, and which, I will argue, are central to understanding Dadd's representation of the natural world, is figured metonymically by the huge malachite egg supported by an extremely fragile pillar to the top right of the painting. Like the splitting of the nut in *The Fairy Feller's Master-Stroke*, the precarious poise of the egg, which could so easily fall and break, signifies the imminent destruction of the possibility of reproduction. And of course a malachite egg could not, in any case, ever be fertile.

24. Cited in *ibid.*, pp. 22–24.

25. Cited in *ibid.*, p. 39.

26. *Ibid.*

27. *Ibid.* A much more detailed discussion of the origins of Dadd's belief in Osiris can be found on pp. 79–81 of Lippincott, L., 'Murder and the Fine Arts or, a Reassessment of Richard Dadd', *The John Paul Getty Museum Journal*, **16**, 1988, pp. 75–94. Lippincott argues that Dadd's conviction of the priority of Osiris leads him to reverse conventional typological relationships, which see non-Christian religions as versions of the Christian type. Thus she reads *Mercy: David Spareth Saul's Life* (1854), a subject which has the conventional typological meaning of a prefiguration by David of Christ, as a representation of Osiris staying the sacrifice of human captives, a subject Dadd had seen repeatedly pictured on the walls of the temples he had visited.

28. Chambers, R., *Vestiges of the Natural History of Creation*, London: John Churchill, 1845, pp. 272–73.

29. Patricia Allderidge contends that after his confinement Dadd 'produced only variations, increasingly idiosyncratic, on the themes which he was already handling; and his own development, marked by a progressive drive back to his inner resources to replace the ever receding stimuli of the world from which he had been cut off, proceeded, as it were, within a vacuum' (Allderidge, *op. cit.* at note 23, p. 41). This implies that the later pictures should be interpreted in purely formal terms, or that they should be regarded as 'pure fantasy', unmediated by any discursive or pictorial context. She also remarks that 'it would be misleading to single out insanity as having more effect on his painting than as part of his whole formative experience ... Delusional material – Osiris, devils and the like – does not intrude into his painting' (*ibid.*, p. 43). My argument is that Dadd's insanity is derived at least in part from his 'whole formative experience', and that, on the contrary, *The Fairy Feller's Master Stroke* can only be properly understood if it is seen as containing 'delusional material', itself derived from the world from which he was isolated.

30. Gillian Beer chose *The Fairy Feller's Master-Stroke* as the front cover illustration to *Darwin's Plots* precisely because it so much resembles an entangled bank.

The spectator's visual apprehension of such paintings is disturbed, if not confused, by their ambiguities and contradictions, and his comprehension is baffled by the plethora of glaring details, each and every one of which is crying out for narrow inspection. The spectator is thus forced out of his comfortably static, distant relationship to the picture-surface and into a succession of radically different, constantly altering perspectives, as he tries to read detail, comprehend masses, and gradually build up some sense of how everything works together.

(Axton, W.F., 'Victorian Landscape Painting: A Change in Outlook', in Knoepflmacher, U.C., and Tennyson, G.B., *Nature and the Victorian Imagination*, Berkeley and London: University of California Press, 1977, pp. 304–305.)

31. Dadd's method was to work out the composition in great detail in monochrome and then painstakingly to fill in the picture little by little in colour. There are several unfinished areas, the main ones being the 'floor' at the bottom of the picture and the Fairy Feller's axe at its centre.

32. Cited by Allderidge, *op. cit.* at note 23, p. 129.

33. Interestingly, this echoes Aristotle's dictum: 'For what is, cannot come to be (because it is already) and from what is not, nothing could have come to be' (Physics, 1.8), which Jonathan Lear glosses thus: 'from nothing, nothing could come to be. But nor can something come to be from something, for something already exists and thus cannot come to be' (Lear, *op. cit.* at note 4, p. 55). Dadd's poem, which is to 'eliminate' his picture, returns to echo the Aristotelian conceptions of form and generation underpinning the religious ideas which both he and Darwin, in very different ways, rejected.

34. Beer, *op. cit.* at note 4, pp. 83–84.

35. *Ibid.*

36. Dadd, *op. cit.* at note 32, ll.117–36.

6.1 Richard Dadd, *The Fairy Feller's Master-Stroke*, 54 × 39 cm, c1855–1864

6.2 Richard Dadd, *Songe de la Fantasie*, 38 × 31.5 cm, 1864

7

Monsters and monstrosities: grotesque taste and Victorian design

Shelagh Wilson

In 1906 Robert Wallace Martin, potter of Southall, finally succeeded in firing a large fountain on which he had been working for over six years (Figures 7.1, 7.2). It is remarkable for its use of the grotesque. Grotesque heads and bodies and distorted, twisted forms are supported on a plinth in the form of a huge curving shell. The undulations of the shell reveal small caves inhabited by anthropomorphized birds. The shell recalls the Renaissance grotto-esque, the remarkable caves, fountains and grottoes designed to stir conflicting fascination and anxiety, summed up by Leonardo as the 'fear of the threatening dark grotto, [and] desire to see whether there were any marvellous thing within it'. This combination of lure and threat is evident in Martin's fountain. As a total composition it combines rippling organic beauty when seen from afar with detailing both repellent and compelling upon closer inspection. The grotesque creatures vary between the semi-recognizable dolphin-like forms and the large animalistic 'monstrous heads' which grow dramatically from the upper section, threatening to lean out and topple the fountain. They cause disruption both to the sensibilities and to the composition. But a total effect of horrific, violent, uncontrolled bodily energy is mitigated by humour and by expert modelling of the forms.

The fountain is partly a product of Wallace Martin's desire to contribute to a tradition of ambitious ceramic creations such as the grottoes of the great French potter and Protestant martyr Bernard Palissy (1510–1590). As we shall see, Palissy's influence is central to Victorian debates about the function and scope of the grotesque in design, and to the wider problem of organic realism. For Wallace Martin, a devout member of the Plymouth Brethren, Palissy also represented the creative aspirations of the pious and humble craftsman, aspirations given cultural weight by Ruskin's conception of the independent workman-designer in the medieval sense, whom Ruskin had claimed was the only person capable of producing the truly Noble Grotesque.

For Wallace Martin this fountain was to be the pinnacle of his career, an object of 'wonder' which he hoped to enter in the Royal Academy Exhibition. To his brothers, attempting to keep the family pottery business afloat, it was an expensive folly and anachronism that took him away from the profitable lines of humorously grotesque bird- and face-jugs which appealed to the fin-de-siècle taste for the bizarre. For us, however, this late attempt to give form to many of the most powerful Victorian ideas about the value of the grotesque in design can serve as a useful summation of the complex and often contradictory functions of grotesque imagery. Wallace's hopes for his fountain's success at the R.A. indicate more than a simple desire for recognition. They identify the continuing mythic power of Ruskin's invocation of the grotesque as the natural aesthetic of the labourer. For Ruskin, cultural recognition of the grotesque was a sign of the ability of a society to value and respect rather than to repress the seemingly incoherent thoughts and fantasies of the powerless. This was of great importance to Wallace, whose own marginalized, eccentric ideas were clearly considered an embarrassment by patrons of the Martin brothers, for whom his devotion to his fountain represented a wilful refusal to respond to their demands.[1] Wallace dreamed that the fountain's success would bring a commission to create what he called a 'grotesque corner' in a garden, recreating Palissy's lost great grottoes.[2]

If the influence of Ruskin and Palissy indicate Wallace's most serious aims as an artist of the grotesque, his more commercial work indicates the importance of alternative connotations of the term within design. The Martin brothers successfully sold humorous grotesque pots, adapting to the tradition of the Toby jug and the tobacco jar the caricatures popularized in books of 'Grotesqueries' and in the work of Lewis Carroll and Edward Lear.[3] Cosmo Monkhouse made exactly that connection in his 1882 review of Wallace's work: 'We have a hundred young sculptors who will model you a Venus or an Adonis as soon as look at you; but who save Mr. Martin could give you a Boojum or a Snark in the round?'.[4] The high art connotations of the term 'sculptor' here indicate the importance of the distinction between a ceramicist such as Wallace and a 'real' artist, whose work might actually be displayed at the R.A., as Wallace's fountain never was.[5] Monkhouse's contrast of classical beauty with the humorous grotesque draws attention to this distinction and to the complex questions of cultural status, social class and aesthetic value that are implicated in the separation of 'craft' from 'art'. Ruskin's own attempts to grapple with this problem were fraught with difficulty, both theoretical and practical, as is testified by his frustrated efforts to work with the 'wild' Irish stone-carvers, the O'Shea brothers.[6] Probably influenced by the O'Sheas' work, Wallace's fountain caused difficulties because it sought to enter this difficult terrain;[7] as long as his grotesque fantasies could be restrained by humour and presented as tobacco boxes and spoon warmers they could be praised 'as a quaint fancy' which has never 'been so successfully indulged in work of a sculpturesque character since the days of gargoyles'.[8]

Wallace Martin had trained in the 1860s in the studio of the sculptor Munro and had worked as a potter since the 1870s. His work was always marked by spirited individuality and love of natural and grotesque forms. Wallace's most characteristic pots are grotesque birds, caricaturing actual and stereotypical figures of the day, described by Monkhouse as 'Sam Slick and Solomon rolled into one' (a reference that combines Biblical authority with a fictional craftsman-satirist).[9] He also produced distorted grotesque 'pre-adamite' and 'antediluvian' animals, 'gaping boobies' as well as 'face'-jugs, in which the clay of the jug twists and teases into a leering head (Figure 7.3). Such images derive from a long tradition of fantastical design, dating back to the Gothic, though, like other Victorian images of animals, they are informed by the contemporary preoccupation with natural history. As we shall see, such Victorian fascination with bodily realism clashed with the values of design reformers, preoccupied with an aesthetic of decorum: with policing the boundaries of forms. In such conditions the grotesque becomes a problem of both taste and meaning. Wallace's fountain epitomizes this. Locked in an ambiguous space between the threatening and the absurd, the ambitious and the decorative, it was considered by the Martins' critics to be both portentously pointless and repulsively fascinating.[10] Eventually, Wallace was forced to finish work on it before he had completed his full design. It was never sold.

Wallace's failure to achieve the impact for which he had hoped with his fountain is indicative of the declining fortunes of Victorian thinking about the grotesque in design. The term 'Victorian' was already beginning to signify a unique kind of tastelessness, a tastelessness which partakes of the freakish and grotesque. The philosopher David Stove locates the high point of such feeling in 1934 when 'Victorian Architecture was all at once the object of universal detestation, or rather horror.' Stove coins the phrase *horror victorianorum*, by which he means 'that horror which even nowadays is felt, at least to a slight degree, by almost everyone who visits a display of Victorian stuffed birds under glass, for example, or of Victorian dolls and dolls' clothes'.[11] Stove was writing in the late 1980s, towards the end of his life, but he remembered the 'quality of the horror', the 'intensity' with which this was felt in the 1930s.[12] Certainly there is ample evidence to corroborate this view. In *The Conquest of Ugliness*, a book typical of many promoting Modernist design, John Milne located the Ugliness of the title in 'the Victorian era', which produced 'hideous monstrosities'.[13]

Horror, monstrosity, the un-dead quality of stuffed birds and dressed dolls: these writers clearly evoke the disturbances characteristic of the grotesque. Here, though, the response is wholly negative. The dark fears described by Leonardo are unmixed with excitement at the prospect of 'marvellous things'. The Victorian grotesque slides towards complete abjection. It is clear, though, that in design the concept 'Victorian' is locked into the grotesque in complex ways. The irony is that the origins of the anxieties that led 'Victorian' to become shorthand for hideous design are to be seen in the way the terminology of the monstrous and grotesque is increasingly used from the 1850s by design reformers attacking so-called 'high' Victorian design. It was the Victorians themselves who first condemned 'Victorian' design. This debate centred on the problematic relationship between taste, function and realism. As I intend to show, this relationship produced a tension between competing values that resulted in objects characterized by just those features which theorists such as Thomson and Hollington have identified as necessary to the power of the grotesque.

Grotesque bodies of design

Philip Thomson in defining the grotesque distinguishes several 'notions', such as extravagance and exaggeration, which are relevant to a discussion of Victorian design. But undoubtedly abnormality is the most crucial and goes some way to explaining the simultaneous revulsion and fascination which characterizes so many responses to 'High' Victorian design. Thomson suggests that:

amusement at a divergence from the normal turns to fear of the unfamiliar and the unknown once a certain degree of abnormality is reached ... [This] is responsible perhaps more than anything else for the not infrequent condemnation of the grotesque as offensive and uncivilised, as an affront to decency and an outrage to 'reality' and 'normality' – or, expressed in the less obviously moralistic language of aesthetic criticism, as tasteless and gratuitous distortion or forced, meaningless exaggeration.[14]

For many Victorian writers this tension between humour and horror is central to the problem of the grotesque. Ruskin insists that the grotesque is a combination of the ludicrous and the fearful, but places his emphasis on the latter, stressing the seriousness of grotesque imagery. The *Art Journal*, reviewing Ruskin's book, thought that 'no effort upon the part of this writer will ever raise the meaning to a heroic sense', and that the 'qualities of grotesqueness will always be associated with the ludicrous'.[15] One of the journal's writers, F.W. Fairholt, concluded his article 'Grotesque Design', which discusses eccentric antiquities, with an apology for writing about something so trivial and meaningless.[16]

This debate rehearses the conflicts we saw at work in responses to Wallace Martin's fountain. The grotesque is acceptable while it knows its place as a form of amusement, but once it gets ideas above its station it becomes threatening. Indeed, even Ruskin's most ardent followers in the Arts and Crafts

Movement chose to ignore this aspect of his thinking. This attitude seems to have been widely shared for, with few exceptions, such as Dresser, writers and designers merely adopted the example of two carved griffins used by Ruskin to illustrate the 'noble' and 'ignoble' grotesque. The griffins, together with the terms 'noble' (true) and 'ignoble' (false) grotesque, appear in design articles such as pieces by Mrs Haweis in the *Art Journal*, but they are used as mere 'buzz' words, completely severed from the complexity of Ruskin's argument.

The eccentric door-knockers and pokers discussed by Fairholt are consistent with the typical comic grotesques made by the Martin brothers. Their eccentricity defines them as objects of humour. When humour seems absent, then the language of horror and monstrosity begins to emerge. This is of particular importance to the debate about the limits of realism in design which ran though the Victorian period and was so closely connected to popular fascination with natural history. Stove's reference to stuffed birds indicates the importance of this aspect of Victorian culture to the *horror victorianorum* he describes. When a ceramic depicting a boa constrictor killing a hare was exhibited in 1878, the absence of humour in this physically realistic image of conjoined bodies was clearly too much for one reviewer:

There is also one disagreeable object: it is a group in majolica of a poor hare, life size, being crushed in the coils of a boa constrictor, the swallowing operation being just commenced at the nose of the victim, which has already disappeared in the gaping mouth of the serpent. This group has no use but to give the sensation on leaving the stall, of having woke up from a hideous dream.[17]

Monstrosity, the fearful, the repulsive, objects being 'not where one would expect to find them' and the nightmare allusion occur repeatedly in these Victorian commentaries on design. However, there is a much more careful distinction being made here than the wholesale condemnation of an entire culture to which Stove refers. The feelings described by this reviewer form part of a journalistic and critical debate on taste. The placing of objects, their forms, their connection to one another: these concerns become increasingly important to commentators on design as Victorian manufactures proliferated. There is a fear of uncontrolled and uncontainable productive energy, of commodities compounded of irreconcilable or garbled principles of design, thrown up against one another in jumbled 'battles' of styles, or placed incongruously in bizarrely inappropriate spaces. It is a fear that modern manufacturing will create a culture of the grotesque.

This anxiety about excess and confusion informs much Victorian rhetoric about design reform. When these concerns were repeated and amplified by Modernists, the real circumstances from which they originated tended to become obscured. In particular, an often self-conscious love of the grotesque, anathema to reformers, has been repressed. Even the recovery of and subsequent celebratory attitude to 'Victoriana' which began in the 1960s is, in some respects, scarcely more helpful than the earlier prejudice against Victorian design.[18] These attitudes have led to a paucity of actual objects being held in museum collections which might assist in understanding the Victorians' own idea of or response to the grotesque. Peter Floud warns of the danger of only using the seemingly enormous contemporary literature in assessing Victorian design.[19] I would argue that these problems are even more evident with 'grotesque' design, as the design reformers who were mostly responsible for establishing the main national collections were also engaged in a campaign of suppression of the grotesque, and consciously or unconsciously excluded it.[20] For instance, although Minton majolica was bought for the V&A it tended to be copies of antiques, such as the Briot jug and ewer. The thousands of items of realistic, humorous and occasionally horrible majolica ceramics – which are what actually sold in huge numbers – are almost totally absent. The *Boa and Hare*, mentioned above, can only be known from the reviews of the various exhibitions, none of which were illustrated.

The objects discussed in this chapter were intended to be seen at close quarters, handled and frequently used; the grotesque effect such as the surprise of a frog discovered at the bottom of a mug on finishing a drink can be lost in reproduction. It is this sense of physical contact, of connection with the body, which is so important when considering the grotesque in design. The reviewer who was so horrified by the *Boa and Hare* was responding to the almost palpable sense of bodily experience, of one creature being forced into another. This is just the kind of encounter encouraged by the modelled frog in a mug, which would appear to 'swim' up the surface as you swallowed your drink, threatening to jump into your own mouth.

Many theorists have seen this spectacle of bodily transgression and invasion as an important feature of the grotesque. Its relevance to Victorian design lies in the way in which Victorians were often keen to emphasize the relationship between the transformative powers of manufacturing and the given forms and materials of the natural world. This often produced objects caught in an ambivalent condition between 'design' and 'nature'. These items are often invisible in the many guides and catalogues to the numerous nineteenth-century exhibitions, but there are good examples such as the Brazilian beetle necklace and parure exhibited in 1867 and the 'humming-bird' earrings (Figure 7.4) of *c*1875. In these, the preserved carcasses of actual creatures were hung from highly fashioned gold and silver. Such insect and animal jewellery was popular throughout most of the Victorian period. Contemporary commentators were often at a loss to explain this 'perversity': the wearing of flies, bees, even earwigs in places on the exposed body where they should not be. There is a disquieting disruption in the idea that such adornments, designed to emphasize the feminine and beautiful, result in a body being covered in flies. What should be swatted or got rid of in aversion stands out, glinting upon the shoulder. The obverse of this incorporation of corpses is the use of the most expensive materials to model highly realistic insects. Flies or bees were often beautifully executed in minute detail. An 1867 exhibit had an 'opal body, and wings and head set with rubies, brilliants, emeralds, and sapphires'.[21]

Queen Victoria cherished a bracelet given, and possibly designed, by Prince Albert. On it, around the delicately engraved gold band, a frighteningly lifelike spider pursues a fleeing fly. She publicly wore this unlikely royal adornment throughout her life. Not surprisingly, manufacturers were keen to translate this royal grotesque into items for a wider public. One example was advertised by Wainwright's, a Birmingham jewellery manufacturer, in 1881: 'Ye Spider and Ye Flie, a most charming novelty'. A novelty was all these mass-manufactured items could be. In the process of reducing the detailing and intricate modelling of the best examples, and with the exclusion of the gemstones which imparted the malicious sparkle to the originals, the whole spirit of the grotesque is lost. This example is still a reasonably expensive item; by the time the motif is stamped out in a base metal for 1d as a cheap fairing, it can only act as a pale aide-mémoire to the original grotesque impression of these jewels.

As the vogue for insects grew it was to reach extremes so bizarre as to be incomprehensible to those conditioned to late twentieth-century attitudes. By the late 1860s 'Bonnets and veils were covered in every kind of beetle ... from rose-beetles with their bronze and green carapaces to stag beetles ... Parasols were liberally sprinkled with ticks, with grasshoppers, with hornets. Tulle scarves and veilings sometimes had on them artificial bed-bugs.'[22] The mounted humming-birds mentioned above unite the Victorian love of taxidermy, novelty, exotic plumage, with a grotesque fascination with the actual body, desecrated, disembowelled and then reconstructed as ornament. There is a need to represent the whole bird, albeit denuded of wings. The use of the glowing breast feathers as a mere abstract ornament is rejected. The fully rounded body, with head and protruding beak, is needed to produce the effect that only realism can achieve. Today we may still feel Stove's horror at a cultural climate that would delight in such an object.[23] The richly plumed hats and popular 'butterfly-wing' pictures are sufficiently abstract in design to keep thoughts of the source of the raw material in abeyance. But the humming-bird earrings, worn to sway as the head turns, force a direct confrontation with the fact that this beautiful decorative object is a dead animal.

Dead nature, undead art

These earrings are just one example from the now little-known Animal Products Museum, which was a core part of the South Kensington Museum. It was intended to illustrate the decorative and practical uses for the many exotic animals brought back by Victorian explorers and natural scientists, in order that the public might be 'gratified by a passing glance at such a general collection of useful and ornamental products as has never before been available for inspection'.[24] It is not surprising that the Animal Products Museum has languished in obscurity. It seems to have been something of an embarrassment to the early curators at South Kensington, whose programme of design reform was not easily adapted to the function of this part of their empire. I will consider in detail the reasons for this later. But the crucial point is this: for reformers 'grotesque' was a particular style of design, a playful use of fantastical floral and animal forms. It took its place among other styles within what came to be labelled the 'grammar of ornament'. What this grammar sought to exclude was an *illicit realism* within design, a form of bodily presence that transgressed the proper formal boundaries of an object.

We tend to think that fear of the body was a characteristically Victorian experience. It is, however, arguable that the opposite is the case, at least in design. Victorian fascination with natural history is well known. Lynn Barber has argued persuasively that the massive popular interest stemmed mainly from its image as a useful, healthy and above all godly pursuit to which diligent amateurs could contribute.[25] The heady Victorian cocktail of belief in progress, trade, divine mission and science lies behind much of this unbridled enthusiasm for discovering, eating, shooting and stuffing the animal kingdom. Popular scientific ideas combined interest in the practical use and transformation of nature with equal stress on the preservation or re-creation of its original form. Palaeontological discoveries led to the reconstruction of dinosaurs; strange, hitherto almost mythical beasts were brought back, alive and dead, to London Zoo or the taxidermists' waiting hands. As Barber points out, Victorian natural history books, while claiming to offer 'improving instruction', retailed 'fascinating facts, bizarre, curious and extraordinary anecdotes', invariably stressing 'the most strange and exotic aspects of their subject'.[26] In other words, popular natural history hovered at the borders of the grotesque. As in the notorious case of the 'Elephant Man', scientific marvel and circus freak merged together.[27]

This sense of the freakish or exotic specimen is implicit in the humming-bird earrings. Similar characteristics are evident in examples of animal tableaux shown at the Great Exhibition of 1851. These anthropomorphic scenes included *The Schoolmaster at Home* (Figure 7.5) exhibited by the expert German taxidermist Ploucquet, which was widely admired. *Schoolmaster Severity*, as this scene from the 'Collection of Comic Creatures' became popularly known, and others, inspired a whole school of British taxidermists including Walter Potter (1835–1918).[28] Potter produced such touching tableaux as *The Rabbits' Village School* and *The Kittens' Wedding*.[29] In these the contradiction between the presence of death (animal corpses) and the simulation of living experience and sentiment produces the sensation of the grotesque for modern viewers. The difficulty is in knowing whether this same sense was experienced by the Victorians themselves. *The Strand* magazine illustrates an armchair (Figure 7.6) covered with the skin of a 'man-eating' tiger which had ripped to death a 'a little white girl, ten years of age'.[30] The skin is arranged so that it appears to be leaping over the back of the chair, teeth bared, eyes glinting. Nearby is a footstool made from the face of a leopard, its mouth bent into a benign smile by the shape of the upholstery. Again, the object exists in an ambivalent space, caught between a series of contradictions: savagery within domesticity; bodily laceration turned to bodily comfort; horror within amusement. There is, however, little hint in *The Strand*'s comments on this 'ingenious' use of animal skin that these doublings are characteristic of the grotesque.

Certainly, enthusiasm for bizarre uses for animals existed at all levels of society. The royal family displayed their 'big game' in a variety of novel furniture items: a bear dumb-waiter, a giraffe chair (Figure 7.7), a baby elephant hall porter's stand as well as a complete set of 'Antler' furniture ordered by Prince Albert for Osborne House. The artist Landseer designed a macabre throne-like chair made to incorporate a series of animals he had shot. His 'Antler' coat-rack was copied and was popular in gentlemen's clubs, as was the use of stuffed monkeys as swinging lights. In fact demand for these was still so great in the 1890s that monkey supplies were becoming hard to find.[31] For the middle classes there were prepared taxidermic scenes which formed part of the range of items to put under 'shades', as the Victorians called the glass domes which sat on a turned wooden base. But undoubtedly it is the stuffed birds under glass which characterize Victorian taste. The new middle classes who could not yet indulge in hunting, shooting or fishing could house a stuffed trophy of the harvest.

All of these designs display 'double bodies'. This is most apparent in the tiger chair, in which the tiger's natural shape is imposed over the alien structure of the chair. This double body is characteristic of Victorian faith in both realism and manufacture. As in the case of insect jewellery, it was not necessary to use actual animal remains to achieve this effect. The popularity of shooting is also reflected in a variety of heavily carved sideboards which won prizes at the Great Exhibitions. The undoubted carving talents of Robinson of Newcastle and the Warwickshire school were displayed in the realistic carving of the chase and of dead game. Again, decoration involves adding forms which threaten to overwhelm the functional shape of the object, producing effects similar to the bursting, erupting bodies on Wallace Martin's grotesque fountain. These are just the kinds of designs ritually labelled monstrous by design reformers and Modernists.

Such sideboards, albeit in a slightly more restrained form, provided an essential site for the many dishes required for displaying, serving and eating the game, fish and other increasing variety of food, and all its sauces and condiments, which proved to be another arena for the grotesque to flourish. The majolica ceramics of Minton (and others) united the Victorian love of technology, novelty, humour, and often unlikely subject matter. Vibrant and colourful cheeky monkeys rode teapots; a vulture wrestling with a snake (Figure 7.8) somehow performed the function both of handle and spout. Manufacturers vied with each other for the most unlikely subject matter for umbrella stands. The glazes perfected by the French potter Arnoux at Minton produced a large range of lifelike, even dazzling colours on earthenware bodies. The perfection of the technique eventually enabled Minton's to exhibit such wonders as the 30ft-high St George's fountain at the 1862 Exhibition. This was publicity, a loss-leader to establish their supremacy in the highly competitive world of majolica tableware, ornaments and garden seats and planters. In majolica a rabbit pie would be served in a sea-green dish with a realistic rabbit-head handle. Oysters would be served on tiered dishes with a 'cover formed of oyster shells, coloured after nature. It makes little pretensions to art, but is of a grotesque character, and is likely to be popular in districts where it is the custom to open the oyster at table.'[32] Much majolica was more fantastic in colour and subject matter, but still often humorous, like the punch bowls cradled on an outstretched, grinning Mr Punch. Surviving majolica indicates that there was a great use of realism in items such as lettuce-leaf salad dishes.[33]

This popular realist British majolica was often referred to as 'Palissy ware' after the 'rustic ware' of Wallace Martin's hero, the Renaissance potter Bernard Palissy. Palissy's colourful dishes were often rather crudely glazed, but had life and vitality. The decoration was very realistic, supposedly cast from the dead bodies of the various lizards, frogs and snakes which are accurately modelled and coloured against backgrounds of green foliage. These fully formed creatures would appear inside bowls, or on pitchers encrusted with shells. This super-realism produced a very grotesque effect, which, when combined with the heroic tale of the potter's life, proved irresistible. Henry Morley's influential *Life of Bernard Palissy the Potter* (1852) recounted a tale of success in the face of adversity, of a noble, self-taught, Protestant artist struggling for years to perfect his glazes, refusing compromise, bringing his family to the brink of ruin, but at last achieving fame, recognition and royal patronage.[34] Palissy ware was also revived in France by potters such as Aviseau, but the French makers tended to copy the grotto and rustic themes in dishes of a similar size and function, whereas the English were inspired by the spirit, colours, and use of lifelike relief forms.[35] The public love of realistic relief or 'real' objects was not shared by the growing number of 'design reformers' who were seizing control of the institutions in the 1850s. Even Ruskin, often thought to be the champion of realism, who was developing his theory of the grotesque as Morley's book on Palissy was published, seems not to recognize Palissy as a producer of the 'noble' grotesque.[36]

Killing the grotesque: Palissyite versus Puginite design

All the items discussed above may be said to form part of this Palissyite tradition, tied into preoccupation with natural history, a science of which Palissy himself was a pioneer. Like Palissy's work, they set the modelling of natural forms against the functional structures of objects. In doing so, they create a space for the fantastic within design, allowing, as in the case of the tiger-chair, complex and conflicting emotions to enter into the actual *encounter* with objects. This is the grotto-esque as Palissy and Leonardo understood it. It is just this tradition, however, that was to be subjected to assault by reformers, so much so that the very existence of the style I have called 'Palissyite' has been obscured.

Once Henry Cole (1802–1882), an ambitious civil servant, began his work on design reform, his view on what constituted 'good' design powerfully influenced the political establishment. His opinion was strongly informed by his Utilitarian beliefs and increasingly by the writings of A.W.N. Pugin. Pugin had condemned the monstrous distortion of 'objects of ordinary use simply because the artist ... has embodied some extravagance to conceal the real purpose for which the article has been made'.[37] Cole's conversion to Pugin's 'true principles' was not immediate, as can be seen in his writings and his own design work. In 1846 a company Cole had founded under the name of Summerly's Art Manufactures won several prizes, including one for a tea service designed by Cole himself (Figure 7.9). This tea-set, probably the only known design by Cole, is a strange hybrid and incorporates the Palissyite grotesque features of animal heads as spouts and handles. A contemporary commented 'the teapot is poor in form and bad in character. The mouth is formed of a lion's head, whilst the knob of the cover consists of a sheep's head – a combination very *outré*, to say the least.'[38] This attack, combined with the growing criticism of naturalism in design by writers such as Ralph Wornum, may have encouraged Cole to abandon this form of decoration. It is possible to detect in the text of Cole's next venture, *The Journal of Design and Manufactures*, a changing attitude towards the grotesque. There is a shift in language.

There is a move to use the word 'grotesque' to conflate 'ugly' with 'deeply cut' decoration which disrupted the surface of the design. The oyster dish previously mentioned had, as we saw, few 'pretensions to art, but is of a *grotesque* character'. This presumably refers to the Palissy-like high-relief depiction of oyster shells, as the phrase occurs again in describing a hop-pattern jug by Minton:

In the *hop* pattern the ornament is placed upon the jug rather in the spirit of its form, which is of a bold, picturesque, we should rather say *grotesque* character – not, however, in depreciation of it. The character of the original design, which was still more *grotesque*, with much bolder outlines and depth of shadows, has been tamed down, we presume, to suit the exigencies of manufacture.[39]

Here the author has to be careful to stress that the word 'grotesque' is *not* a deprecatory term; presumably elsewhere it is. The favourite grotesque subject of mythical beasts devouring each other, in what seems from the illustration to be a crisp and lively interpretation, albeit as a gas bracket (Figure 7.10), is singled out as bad design:

It is [a] ... 'vulgar piece of absurdity, ... rubbish ... in which the highest merit aimed at appears to be the elaboration of *monstrosity*, without even the limited excuse which artists may sometimes claim for its occasional introduction, and, which helps to sanction the presence of the hideous faun of the ancient master, or the grinning monkeys of mediaeval art – the faculty of enhancing pure tranquil grace and beauty by the exhibition of deformity on a pitiful scale. Abstract monstrosity is, per se, neither more nor less than absolutely disgusting, and this therefore, is to a considerable extent the character of this piece of design.'[40]

This language of disgust and revulsion, often associated with the grotesque, was already being used by the *Art Union* journal by 1846. Curtain-pole ends were described as 'odious ... all, without exception, being deformities such as every cultivated eye would turn from with disgust'.[41] This strong language, given the often seemingly innocuous objects singled out for opprobrium, indicates the strength of opinion underlying the design debate in the 1840s and 50s which would surface so publicly in criticism of the 1851 Great Exhibition. The language of the grotesque was being applied in design to certain objects which, often for entirely other reasons, became increasingly unacceptable. The principle of abstraction and stylization of nature in two-dimensional flat pattern, as advocated by Pugin, was adopted even for three-dimensional objects. With the publication of Owen Jones's *The Grammar of Ornament* (1856) clean, stylized patterns adapted to machine manufacture were elevated to design orthodoxy. What Jones calls the 'grotesque' is just another kind of pattern.[42]

Cole's brand of keen Utilitarianism inclined him to reject the fantastical and counter-functional Palissyite tradition.[43] Instead, he sought to educate a wider public in the True and False principles of design, creating for the new Museum of Manufactures a collection of objects 'Intended to illustrate FALSE PRINCIPLES of Decoration' where he displayed a special, catalogued collection of 'types of what should be avoided' (Report of 1852). This 'House Full of Horrors' quickly became a laughing-stock. Dickens's journal *Household Words* published an article by Palissy's biographer Henry Morley, satirizing Cole's conception of false principles. The hapless Mr Crumpet who visits the Department of Practical Art at Marlborough House 'to look over the museum of ornamental art' sees the 'pattern of my own trousers ... my pocket-handkerchief', and on his return home realizes that he 'had been living among horror up to that hour'. Having 'acquired some Correct Principles of Taste' his life becomes a nightmare as he is constantly confronted by false taste, until he is terrified out of his wits by exposure to a 'Butter-fly-inside my cup! Horr-horr-horr-horr-ri-ble!'[44] Morley here ridicules poor Crumpet's incipient *horror victorianorum* by championing the humorous, grotesque device of an insect, albeit tamed to a flat representation, in the bottom of a pot.

This leading story in *Household Words* was followed by Dickens's own satire in *Hard Times*, which ridicules Cole in the figure of the Government Officer who lectures school children (known only by numbers) on True and False principles of design.[45] Dickens objects to these 'Commissioners of Fact' who wish to regulate the people's taste and forbid 'in any object of use or ornament, what would be a contradiction in fact'. The grotesque in design would be, of course, impossible if design were to be limited to the 'combinations and modifications (in primary colours) of mathematical figures which are susceptible of proof and demonstration': the ultimate goal of Utilitarian taste, as Dickens sees it. Dickens's own vivid descriptions of objects and interiors counter this dehumanizing geometry, becoming metaphors for character as the warm-hearted Sissy ('girl number twenty') announces her simple love of realistic horses on wallpaper, or flowers on carpets. He attacks those Utilitarian killjoys who would deprive the poor of the myriad of fancies and novelties newly available 'to adorn their lives so much in need of ornament'.[46] It is appropriate that Dickens, who contributed so much to the grotesque in literature, should defend design, which by now included all decorative arts, from being placed in so rigid a strait-jacket. In this, his views are in tune with Ruskin's.[47]

Like Morley, Dickens satirizes the distaste felt by reformers when confronted by Palissyite realism. The Government Officer implicitly identifies Sissy's taste as grotesque, while she considers it natural. For the Officer, 'quadrupeds going up and down walls' is a revolting aberrance, a contradiction that must be repressed. Like Mr Crumpet's sudden, gagging sense of physical invasion by the 'insect' in his cup, the Officer's response is one of incipient horror at a grotesque culture that cannot recognize itself as such. Because he sees realist design as intrusively physical, he is disturbed by 'a carpet having a representation of flowers upon it', as this will mean crushing the flowers as you walk on them.[48] The Officer creates a fearful sense of the natural world breaking into the cleansed space of manufactured objects in the home, just as if the tiger skin might suddenly revive and leap from its chair.

Christopher Dresser: redesigning the grotesque

The proto-Modernist thinking of Cole and the reformers, then, presupposes an engagement with the grotesque. Though it seeks to suppress it, it actually calls it into being as a sense of horror at misplaced, monstrous forms and the derangement of nature. For reformers, abstraction was a protection against the horror of the grotesque. Nevertheless, as we have seen, the term 'grotesque' is sometimes used in a positive way by reformers. Generally, they are thinking of the kinds of decorative design associated with Raphael: the very 'grotesques' condemned by Ruskin as degraded and trivial. The vogue for Japanese and primitive art encouraged the trend towards abstraction in design, while also offering new sources for this decorative grotesque in a form more acceptable to those trained in South Kensington's principles than the rather wild and uncontrolled vision presented by Ruskin. This can be seen most clearly in the writing and design work of Christopher Dresser (1834–1904).[49] His views on the idea of the grotesque altered between the publication of *The Art of Decorative Design* (1862) and *Principles of Decorative Design* (1873). In 1862 his manual warns against use of forms that may create a bizarre human effect, 'ornamental composition such as tends to suggest the human countenance or any monster, should be scrupulously avoided'. But he encourages the use of imaginary ornamental animals such as a particular Chinese dragon which 'is all that could be desired, being vigorous, energetic, grotesque, and ornamental', but only because it is not 'a representation of any existing creature, but a mere ornamental animal'.[50]

This denial of the grotesque realistic form is understandable in Dresser, who trained throughout the reign of Pugin's True and False principles, assisting Jones by illustrating 'the geometrical arrangement of natural flowers' for *The Grammar of Ornament*.[51] Earlier, reference was made to a definition of a gas-bracket as a monstrosity because it was imagined not to resemble a known beast. Dresser inverts this, allowing only the abstract monster to be admitted as grotesque. Dresser, like his contemporary William Morris, later to coin his famous dictum against having any object that 'was neither useful nor beautiful', grew to manhood aware of the tidal wave of 'monstrous and ridiculous' objects where novel and winsome treatments of animals either obscured the ostensible use or became the subject of a decorative object.

As a product of the Schools of Design, Dresser studiously avoided such pitfalls, but his introduction to Japanese art probably inspired his realization that the spirit and power of the grotesque could give a work an energy which propelled it far beyond the ordinary. The grotesque, 'addresses our sense of humour; it presents the comic element in art, and when it appears in a very droll form, affects the spirits as powerfully as the keenest wit'.[52] Although sharing Ruskin's view of the power of the grotesque, Dresser differs entirely in seeing the grotesque as a product of the intellect. Not surprisingly for one whose two-dimensional designs for manufacture were increasingly his main source of income, he rejected the idea of the imagination of the rude craftsman.

In the late 1860s Dresser produced several designs which illustrate the development of his use of the grotesque. In 1867 he designed several different grotesques for Minton's cylindrical vases. These range from large, colourful flattened beetles for cloisonné vases, through chameleons rendered as decorative pairs, to a rather sinister half-skeletal, half-insect-like figure, which Dresser referred to as 'an old bogey' (Figure 7.11). The latter, which seems not to have been used widely for production, epitomizes Dresser's principle of the grotesque, 'that the further the grotesque is removed from an imitation of a natural object the better it is, provided that it be energetic and vigorous-life-like'.[53] One unusual departure from Dresser's usual flat design is a vase for Minton's with a large, high-relief modelled scarab beetle on the side. The alarming effect is dispersed by the pattern on the back, which forms a face, reminding the user that it is a motif and not a monstrous beetle.

'Old Bogey' is certainly bizarre, but is it really grotesque? It is certainly not a 'true' or a noble grotesque in the Ruskinian sense. In terms of Dresser's work it is a vital form which enables him to step into the marvellous abstract patterns that represent some of his best work. From the skeleton motifs and the flattening out of forms he is able to develop designs which

> embody chiefly the idea of power, energy, force, or vigour and in order to do this, I have employed such lines as we see in the bursting buds of spring, when the energy of growth is at its maximum ... I have also availed myself of those forms to be seen in certain bones of birds which are associated with the organs of flight, and which give us an impression of great strength, as well as those observable in the propelling fins of certain species of fish.[54]

The idea of the grotesque as a well-spring, a freeing form which enables the designer to make significant shifts in direction, is exciting. However, Dresser's move into abstraction was too avant-garde, and the designs and the few pieces of ceramics that resulted can be read only as an indication of his theoretical position and what might have developed.[55]

By 1873 the *Principles* already indicates Dresser's reversion to a much more mundane use of the grotesque. It becomes a 'principle' of

> a less noble character than ... those which we have already noticed as entering into ornament yet remain to be mentioned. Man will be amused as well as instructed; he must be pleased as well as ennobled by what he sees. I hold it as a first principle that ornamentation, as a true fine art, can administer to man in all his varying moods, and under all phases of feeling. Decoration, if properly understood, would at once be seen to be a high art in the truest sense of the word, as it can teach, elevate, refine, induce lofty aspirations, and allay sorrows; but we have now to notice it as a fine art, administering to man in his various moods, rather than as the handmaiden to religion or morals.[56]

Dresser tries to justify his dislike of 'the truly horrible or repellent ... simply repulsive [grotesque]' which can be placed in other cultures and periods such as the 'hideous "evil spirits" of Gothic and the Celtic "anastomosis", or network, of grotesque creatures'. The role of the grotesque is to act as a foil to beauty and to provide humour. Dresser has a curiously modern concern not to 'awaken a sense of pain' in any life-like creature, whereas that which suggested 'no thought or feeling induced no sense of pain'.[57] This idea may have been influenced by John Bell, whose rather eccentric article on 'The Senses in Art' had warned against any appeal to the sense of pain.[58] Dresser's successful commercial designs of the early 1870s incorporate a series of humorous incidents, such as cats meeting and parting and a 'frog frieze' of dancing frogs (Figure 7.12). His designs increasingly reflected the new interest in 'Japanese' motifs. Many incorporate huge beetles and the range of insects which would appeal to the wider public market referred to earlier. 'Nothing is worse than a feeble joke, unless it be a feeble grotesque', wrote Dresser in 1873, something which was entirely forgotten in a series of static, rather dull and definitely humourless 'grotesques' (his word) intended as borders and suggested for the 'nursery' or 'smoking room', in *Studies in Design* (1876).

Dresser's insistence that 'a grotesque must reveal, by its nature or formation, knowledge on the part of its producer' led to his intellectualization of the grotesque as a concept, but only produced a rather controlled grotesque in his design work. In the 1880s his designs for the Linthorpe Pottery Co. in Middlesbrough, a philanthropic concern to provide local employment, are much freer and more 'primitive'. But these grotesque forms are not from the designer's imagination, but the result of yet more exploitation of obscure cultures, in this case the pre-Columbian pottery of South America.

By the 1870s the 'closed world' of high Victorian design was breaking down. The immense confidence and love of novelty that characterize the period were increasingly declared tasteless, almost barbaric. The Aesthetic Movement, which abhorred dark, rich colours and monstrous objects, was influential, and its adherents would join the followers of Cole to prepare the way for increasing abstraction and simplicity at the expense of the grotesque.

In addition, the effects of Darwin's theories led ultimately to a dampening down of enthusiasm for natural history, which was ceasing to be an amateur hobby. The idea of a complex ecosystem of which man was only a component part rather than master began to undermine confidence in the world as a never-ending source of food, raw materials and adventure. As a Creationist, Wallace Martin, locked in a pre-Darwinian conception of nature, could ignore modern science, continuing to see the grotesque in terms of a world made by God's creative fancy.[59] His evangelical fervour, like Ruskin's, gave an intensity to his grotesques, an intensity impossible for an urbane rationalist such as Dresser. But this conception of nature was increasingly obsolete. By the 1880s books stressed watching rather than capturing nature; binoculars and cameras would increasingly replace nets and guns. Animals, once fierce, could become friends. Beatrix Potter replaced Walter Potter as the expert in humanizing rabbits. This is reflected in the growing popularity of illustrated children's books and in wallpaper such as Dresser's dancing-frog friezes. The grotesque had returned to a form of the comic; the disturbing power it possessed in the mid-century had been lost. Ruskin's 'Art arising from irregular and accidental contemplation of terrible things; or evil in general' rarely appeared in design. As he had predicted, it was now mainly to be experienced in literature. The genres of horror and science-fiction were well established by the 1890s. Grotesque design joined other signs of the freakish and bizarre, surfacing in mystery stories such as the Sherlock Holmes canon, where horror increasingly came from within, the realm of psychology projected onto the social world, visible as inexplicable objects which set the scene for a crime.

Notes

1. A patron of the Martins, the architect Sydney Greenslade, wrote an account of his visit to their pottery works. The manuscript is not easy to decipher, but his attitude seems to have been one of embarrassment when shown the incomplete fountain. Wallace's antics 'preaching the word' are also treated unsympathetically, and are connected to his work, revealing his disjointed, 'grotesque' mentality: 'Poor Wallace when he got on to the religious mania of his he proved a terrible "bore". Curiously unevenly balanced mind had he, making the most hideous grotesque – and believing the narrowest of beliefs – a strict Plymouth brother' (Greenslade papers, Southall Reference Library).
   The poet and sculptor Thomas Woolner probably had Wallace Martin in mind when, in his poem *Pygmalion*, he wrote of a 'baseborn' would-be sculptor whose innate vulgarity cheapened the high arts. His sculptures were 'grotesque, ridiculous', so

   > To our chief potter I commended him
   > Who cheerfully gave work of comic heads
   > Fashioned to pots, and any odd device
   > His fancy might invent, which products would
   > Be taken in large numbers by the crowd.

   See Woolner, T. *Pygmalion*, London: Macmillan, 1881, p. 87.

2. See Haslam, M., *The Martin Brothers Potters*, London: Richard Dennis, 1978, p. 138; Amico, L.N., *Bernard Palissy: In Search of Earthly Paradise*, Paris, New York: Flammarion, 1996, pp. 49–81. Wallace had been encouraged by the patronage of Sir Frank Crisp, who shared his taste for the fantastic and grotesque. Sir Frank commissioned hobgoblins and reptilian figures for a grotto in the grounds of his Henley-on-Thames home. According to Ernest March these figures would have given his nightmares, 'if viewed unexpectedly'. See Haslam *op. cit.* above, p. 84.

3. The most famous of these artists was Ernest Griset, whose drawings of animals were very popular. His French counterpart, Grandville, was also well known. See Haslam, *op. cit.* at note 2, p. 84; Hood, T., *Griset's Grotesques: or Jokes Drawn on Wood*, London: Routledge, 1867.

4. See Monkhouse, C., 'Some Original Ceramicists', *Magazine of Art*, vol. 5, p. 444. There are some connections between Martin ware and the drawings of Lear. Henry Holliday's illustrations to Carroll's *The Hunting of the Snark* may also have been influential. Some scenes contain Martin-like creatures.

5. Before founding the pottery, Wallace had attempted to establish himself as a sculptor, but had failed to make a living. Several plasters for relief and portrait sculptures were exhibited at the R.A. One relief, *The Woodland Spring*, was engraved and praised by the *Art Journal*. It is similar in style to Munro's work. See Haslam, *op. cit.* at note 2, pp. 21–22; Read, B., and Barnes, J., *Pre-Raphaelite Sculpture: Nature and the Imagination in British Sculpture, 1848–1914*, London: Lund Humphries, 1991, pp. 111–30.

6. Employed on Woodward's new Oxford Museum as 'independent' decorative carvers, the O'Sheas fell foul of the authorities because of their wilful 'destruction of university property' by carving animals into the stone as they chose. Like Wallace Martin in his youth, James O'Shea produced some conventional narrative and portrait relief sculpture. His satirical carving of the university Convocation as parrots and owls was described by Cook and Wedderburn as 'like a piece of the

160   VICTORIAN CULTURE AND THE IDEA OF THE GROTESQUE

Middle Ages; just such a story may one read into many a grotesque and grinning gargoyle of some old cathedral'. See Ruskin, J., *Works*, 39 vols, ed. E.T. Cook and A. Wedderburn, London: George Allen, 1903–1912, vol. 16, pp. xlviii–l.

7. Haslam, *op. cit.* at note 2, p. 87.
8. Monkhouse, *op. cit.* at note 4, p. 444.
9. Sam Slick, Yankee clock-maker, was a cracker-barrel social commentator invented by the humorist Thomas Chandler Haliburton (1796–1865). An anti-establishment figure, he contrasts with the definitive, Biblical wisdom and social authority of Solomon.
10. Haslam, *op. cit.* at note 2, pp. 134–39.
11. Stove, D., *The Plato Cult and other Philosophical Follies*, Oxford: Basil Blackwell, 1991, p. 19.
12. Stove's book is a complex, quirky and bullish Positivist critique of Modernist philosophy, centring on Popper. He also makes swipes at more fashionable Post-Modern writers such as Foucault, but generally treats them as beneath his contempt. At the book's heart is an affirmation of dull-but-honest Victorian philosophers of science. The date 1934 is important, as it marked the publication of Evelyn Waugh's *A Handful of Dust*, construed by Stove as the archetypal Modernist satire of Victoriana, epitomized by the conclusion of the narrative in which Toby, the central character, is forced to live out his days in a ludicrous Heart of Darkness, deep in the Amazonian jungle, trapped by a tribal leader who insists that he read to him excerpts from the works of Dickens. Thus Victorian seriousness – the civilizing missions of Exploration and Empire – is turned into a grotesque parody of itself, under the aegis of Dickens, master of the Victorian grotesque. Earlier in the novel, Toby's tasteless neo-Gothic family seat is said to have been designed by Pecksniff, the hypocritical architect in *Martin Chuzzlewit*, one of Dickens's most grotesque characters. The mansion is seen as both 'amusing' and heavily oppressive.
13. Milne, J.A., 'Beauty in Merchandise', in De La Valette, J. (ed.), *The Conquest of Ugliness*, London: Methuen & Co., 1935, p. 21.
14. Thomson, P., *The Grotesque*, London: Methuen, 1972, pp. 24–26.
15. *Art Journal*, 1856, p. 114.
16. Fairholt, F.W., 'Grotesque Design', *Art Journal*, March 1862, p. 92. This article discusses decorative and functional objects which use fantastical animal figures or bizarre combinations of mechanism and realism. He treats them as objects of curiosity and amusement.
17. Bergesen, V., *Majolica: British, Continental and American Wares, 1851–1915*, London: Barrie & Jenkins, 1989, p. 64. The reviewer was writing for the *Pottery and Glass Trades' Review*. The boa constrictor and hare, probably modelled by A. Carrier de Belleuse, is described by Bergesen as 'one of the most repulsive pieces of majolica ever produced'. Similar models of animals consuming one another survive. See Jones, J., *Minton: The First Two Hundred Years of Design and Production*, Shrewsbury: Swan Hill, 1993, p. 132.
18. The rehabilitation of 'Victorian' as a style for home decoration, pub design and themed 'heritage' museums cannot assist an understanding of countless objects which no longer exist. It rather creates an oversimplified view based on a handful of stereotypical images, many of which were imaginary in the first place.
19. Floud, P., 'Victorian Furniture', in *Concise Encyclopaedia of Antiques*, vol. 5, London: Connoisseur, 1953.
20. A practice which seems, unfortunately, to be continuing; *The Times* reports the destruction of many Victorian items in museum collections, curators having been told that lottery bids are liable to be turned down if museums show too great a fondness for aged taxidermic specimens and other such 'curiosities'.
21. Flower, M., *Victorian Jewellery* (rev. ed.), London: Cassell & Co., 1967, p. 134.
22. *Ibid.*, pp. 33–34.
23. The response to this slide when shown in lectures is an almost universal gasp of horror. Even our University's slide librarian, inured to much gruesome modern art, felt impelled to add '(yuck)' after the title on the label. Interestingly, there has been very recently a revival of such aggressive emphasis on animal bodies in fashion and jewellery. Alexander McQueen's 'Eclect Dissect' show included models wearing dead ravens and bird skulls. See the *Guardian*, 8 July 1997, p. 5; *Independent on Sunday*, 14 September 1997, pp. 1, 8. There are connections here with contemporary avant-garde fascination with grotesque somatics, evident in the work of Hirst, the Chapmans and others. In 1989 an artist was prosecuted for exhibiting a bust wearing earrings made from freeze-dried human foetuses.

24. *Guide to the South Kensington Museum*, London: South Kensington Museum, 1857.
25. Barber, L., *The Heyday of Natural History*, London: Jonathan Cape, 1980, pp. 14–26.
26. *Ibid.*, p. 19.
27. Howard, M., *Victorian Grotesque: An Illustrated Excursion into Medical Curiosities, Freaks and Abnormalities, Principally of the Victorian Age*, London: Jupiter, 1977.
28. Potter's museum of taxidermic scenes still exists and has been moved from Sussex to Devon where it is now part of the 'Jamaica Inn' Daphne Du Maurier Museum.
29. See Lambourne, L., *Ernest Griset: Fantasies of a Victorian Illustrator*, London: Thames & Hudson, 1979, p. 35; Tallis, J., *Tallis's History and Description of the Crystal Palace and the Exhibition of the World's Industry in 1851*, London: John Tallis, 1852.
30. *The Strand* magazine, 1896, p. 277.
31. *Ibid.*, p. 275.
32. *Journal of Design and Manufactures*, vol. 1, 1849, p. 15.
33. The work of George Jones, Joseph Holdcroft, Simon Fielding and others is discussed in detail by Dawes. Some objects humorously play on the idea of animals eating one another, such as a Royal Worcester teapot in the shape of two fish, in which the spout is being 'swallowed' by the pot. See Dawes, N.M., *Majolica*, New York: Crown, 1990, pp. 132, 112–22.
34. Morley's book was republished in many editions. Moreover, there was a spate of more popular versions of Palissy's life, including several novels. Evangelical publications aimed at the working classes presented him as a model hard-working and pious craftsman (e.g. 'A Noble Working Man of Olden Times', *The British Workman*, August, 1864, p. 462). He was discussed by Smiles and other authors who specialized in inspirational stories of great men. At least two paintings illustrating episodes from his life were exhibited at the RA. See Arts Council of Great Britain, *Great Victorian Pictures: Their Paths to Fame*, London: Arts Council, 1978, pp. 85–86.
35. This could also be because in France Palissy was taken up by the small art-potter who produced mainly decorative wares, whereas in England majolica was made by several large manufacturers who needed to make functional wares in addition to the decorative pieces. For a detailed discussion of Palissy's influence see Amico, *op. cit.* at note 2, pp. 189–217.
36. Ruskin's comments on Palissy suggest that he admired his work, but was unable to adapt his theory of the Noble Grotesque to accommodate it. His comments are generally very positive. See Ruskin, *op. cit.* at note 6, vol. 16, p. 428; vol. 20, p. 290. Ruskin seems to have been developing his theory up to April 1853, when it was published in volume three of *The Stones of Venice*.
37. Pugin, A.N.W., *True Principles of Pointed or Christian Architecture*, London: J. Weale, 1841, p. 24.
38. *Art Union*, 1846, p. 204. This competition, not unreasonably considered by many to have been a 'fix', seems to have been the extent of Cole's personal venture into actual design although Summerly's Art Manufactures continued with other designers until 1852. See Cole, H., *Fifty Years of Public Work*, London: Bell and Sons, 1884, p. 178.
39. *Journal of Design and Manufactures*, vol. 1, 1849, p. 16.
40. *Ibid.*, p. 110.
41. *Art Union*, 1846, p. 4.
42. Jones, O., *The Grammar of Ornament*, London: Day & Son, 1856, p. 123.
43. Cole's *Journal* directly attacked Palissy's influence in 1849, claiming that 'we have never been able to admire, with the enthusiasm of the true antiquary, the taste which guided Bernard in the peculiar form he gave to his manufacture. The idea of dishes with lizards, caterpillars, cupids and all kinds of nasty creatures' inside was repulsive (*Journal of Design and Manufactures*, vol. 1, 1849, p. 160).
44. Morley, H., 'A House full of Horrors', *Household Words*, December 1852, pp. 266–70.
45. K.J. Fielding puts forward a convincing argument that Dickens intended this piece as a direct satire with Henry Cole as the Government Officer (see Fielding, K.J., 'Charles Dickens and the Department of Practical Art', *Modern Language Review*, **XLVII**, 1953, pp. 270–77). However, Cole's close associate Richard Redgrave emerges as the critic most opposed to the use of super-realism, the novel and strange in design: all essential elements of the grotesque. In his criticism of the Great Exhibition we recognize that condemnatory language of Victorian design as 'bad taste' and 'vulgar': 'the hunger after novelty is quite insatiable... and happy is the man who lights upon something, however outré, that shall strike the vulgar mind'. (See Redgrave, R., *Supplemental Report on the Exhibition of 1851*, London: HMSO, 1852, p. 710).

46. Dickens, C., *Hard Times*, ed. G. Ford and S. Monod, New York: W.W. Norton, 1969, p. 192. Cole seems to have learnt from this upbraiding; the Museum of Manufactures was disbanded and its objects spread through the collections and largely lost. Several of these objects were brought together as part of the RCA's centenary exhibition by Clive Wainwright, who has indicated a long-term ambition to recreate the display (Wainwright, C., 'Principles True and False: Pugin and the Foundation of the Museum of Manufactures', *Burlington Magazine*, **CXXXVI**, no. 1095, June 1994, p. 362).

47. Ruskin acknowledged Dickens's role as a champion of the grotesque in the character of the working man. In the *Stones* he identifies the crucial shift that has taken the grotesque from the realms of design and into that of literature. Ruskin perceives that:

    The classical and Renaissance manufactures of modern times having silenced the independent language of the operative, his humour and satire pass away in the word-wit which has of late become the special study of the group of authors headed by Charles Dickens; all this power was formerly thrown into noble art, and became permanently expressed in the sculptures of the cathedral.

    (Ruskin, *op. cit.* at note 6, vol. 11, p. 173.)

48. Dickens, *op. cit.*, at note 46, pp. 51–52. Dickens here refers to a pet hatred of reformers. In a debate between Ruskin and the Puginite reformer George Wallis, Wallis referred to carpets with realistic flowers on them as the epitome of debased design: 'ladies, epecially, in spite of the best geometric designs, insist upon roses done in wool'. Ruskin attacked this argument by specifically invoking Palissy. He did not see why 'as the first thing we usually did to make the ground fit to be walked upon by any festive procession was always to strew flowers upon it ... we should refuse to have flowers on our carpets, lest we should stumble over them'. Seizing on a reference by Wallis to the revival of Palissy ware, Ruskin pointed out that Palissy's 'noble' achievement proved the falsity of Puginite principles; 'if we were not allowed to have flowers on our carpets, why were we to have vipers on our plates?'. See Ruskin, *op. cit.* at note 6, vol. 16, p. 248. For an account of *Wallis* see Bøe, A., *From Gothic Revival to Functional Form: A Study in Victorian Theories of Design*, Oxford: Basil Blackwell, 1957, pp. 44, 50, 72.

49. Dresser was a star pupil from the Schools of Design, who in the 1860s was becoming recognized as a considerable designer (see Halén, W., *Christopher Dresser, a Pioneer of Modern Design*, London: Phaidon, 1990, pp. 12–17). Interested in nature – his honorary doctorate was awarded for his work in botany – he was ideally placed to be affected by the changes wrought by new discoveries in the 40s and 50s. Dresser was a massively prolific designer who worked for many of the country's major manufacturers of glass, ceramics, metalware and furniture. He also published articles and books which made a major contribution to nineteenth-century design. His full significance has only been recognized in the last 20 years.

50. Dresser, C., *The Art of Decorative Design*, London: Day & Son, 1862, p. 165.

51. Jones, *op. cit.* at note 42, p. 3.

52. Jones, *op. cit.* at note 17, p. 90.

53. Dresser, C., *Principles of Decorative Design*, London: Cassell, 1873, p. 26.

54. *Ibid.*, p. 17.

55. I am referring here to designs for vases for Josiah Wedgwood & Sons in 1867 and some of the Minton pieces of a similar date.

56. Dresser, *op. cit.* at note 53, p. 25.

57. *Ibid.*, p. 26.

58. *Journal of Design and Manufactures*, 1851. John Bell was an artist and designer who may have taught Dresser at South Kensington. He produced grotesque designs for Wedgwood and Minton. See Dawes, *op. cit.* at note 33, pp. 23–25; Cole *op. cit.* at note 38, p. 182.

59. Wallace may have known the theories of fellow Plymouth Brother, Philip Gosse, for whom geological evidence of the world before 4000 BC was nothing more than a chimera. Evidence of the 'past' was created along with the earth. Various explanations for fossil remains circulated among Fundamentalist groups, including deliberately deposited diabolic temptations to unbelief and divine testing of faith. Both views imply that prehistoric animals are deceptive fantasies. Such ideas may lie behind Wallace's fascination with invented 'pre-Adamite' creatures. Haslam discusses Wallace's response to Darwin (Haslam, *op. cit.* at note 2, p. 84). Ruskin also had an antipathy to Darwinism; see Beer, G., *Darwin's Plots*, London: Routledge and Kegan Paul, 1983, pp. 275–76.

7.1/7.2 Robert Wallace Martin, *Grotesque Fountain*, 1906, details

7.3

7.3 The Martin Brothers, *Examples of Martin Ware*, 1882

7.4 Earrings made from mounted hummingbirds, c1875

7.5 H. Ploucquet, *The Schoolmaster at Home*, tableau exhibited at the Great Exhibition, 1851

7.6 'Man-eating tiger mounted as an Arm Chair', from *The Strand Magazine*, 1896

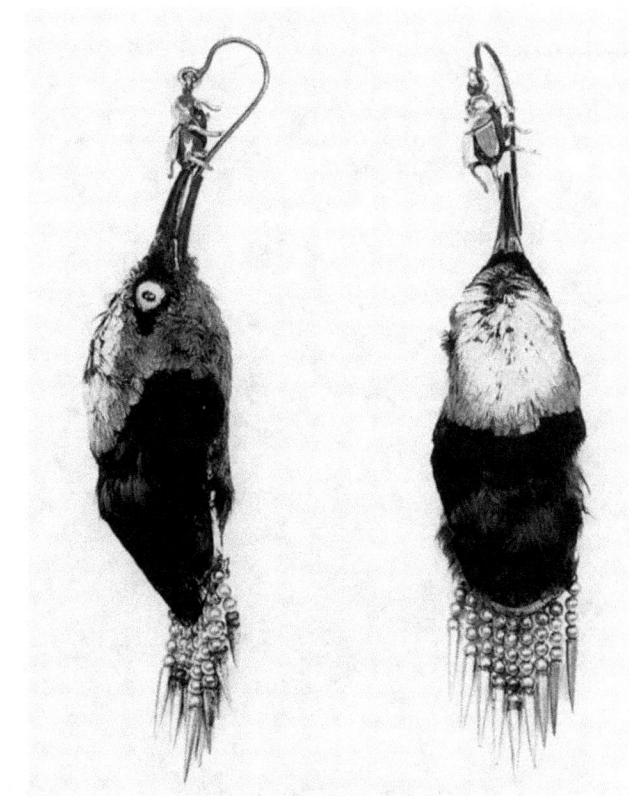

7.4

7.5

7.6

CHAIR MADE FROM A BABY GIRAFFE.

PET MONKEYS MOUNTED ON A FLOOR LAMP.

PET MONKEY HOLDING CANDELABRA.

died, and, although her grief was great, she resolved to have her dead darling turned into something useful as well as ornamental. In life that monkey had been phenomenally active — tweaking the noses of dignified people who least expected it; and the sorrowing mistress couldn't bear to think of the poor little thing as a mere stuffed specimen grinning idiotically beneath a glass case. Therefore was that pet monkey — which is seen in the next illustration — set up as a candle-holder, grasping in its little fists the polished brass sconces, and with quite an eager, officious air.

This set another fashion, and before long a West-end firm (Messrs. Williams and Bach, of New Bond Street) was doing a roaring trade in animal and bird lamps. The designs of many of these are remarkably ingenious. Here is another monkey lamp, in the design of which two active little fellows are supposed to be frolicking together, the topmost monkey bearing the oil-well after the manner of Atlas, with his tail coiled around the cross-bar, while his playfellow is scrambling

which belongs to that mighty Nimrod, Mr. J. Gardiner Muir, of "Hillcrest," Market Harborough. This chair, as may be seen in the accompanying reproduction, is made from a baby giraffe, which, with its mother, was shot by Mr. Gardiner Muir, near the Kiboko River, in British East Africa. The design is by Rowland Ward, of Piccadilly. In the photograph will be noticed a little dog on the seat of the chair; this is the hunter's little Scotch terrier, "Punch."

It is quite astonishing to learn how many defunct animals are called upon to throw light upon things. I refer, of course, to animals converted into lamps. Some years ago a certain lady's pet monkey

7.7 'Types of animal furniture', from *The Strand Magazine*, 1896
7.8 Majolica glazed 'Vulcan and Python' teapot, 1879

7.9   Henry Cole, design for a tea service, c1845

7.10   Design for a grotesque gas bracket, 1849

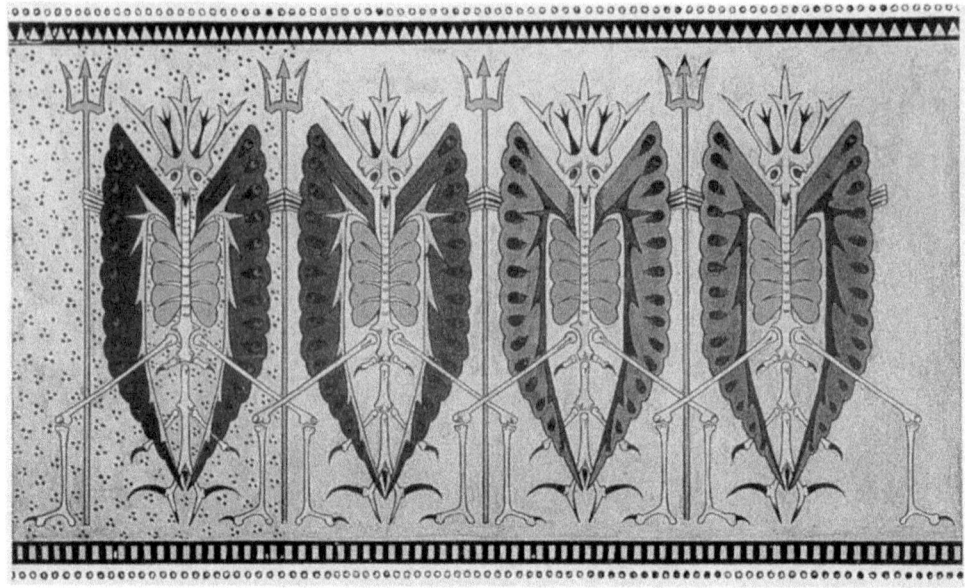

7.11 Christopher Dresser, *Old Bogey*, 1867

7.12 Contrasting grotesque frogs: (left) Christopher Dresser's *Frog Frieze*, 1871, and (above) Wallace Martin's *Frog*, c1900

7.13 E. J. Sullivan, 'Omar with the Ungainly Vessels', illustration to Fitzgerald's *The Rubáiyát of Omar Khayyám*, 1913

8

Turning back the grotesque: G.F. Watts, the matter of painting and the oblivion of art

Colin Trodd

Where is the grotesque in late Victorian painting? How can it be located and with what values is it associated? This chapter argues that, by attending to the conceptual and critical frameworks provided by cultural discourse, it is possible to track the spaces in which the grotesque was figured in visual and textual forms. The central argument of the chapter is simply this: articulations of the grotesque are entwined with readings of the body; that the desire to register the spiritual body generates the oblivion of ideal form; that the representation of physical power or force becomes a process of entangling and effacing the 'primitive' in the human frame. The grotesque bodies forth as both truncation and profusion of form: at once reduction of the body and extension of its physical powers, it is both rupture of the body as ideal sign and projection of the body as vital energy. This doubling process, in which the grotesque is at once kenotic power and kinetic process, generates some particularly intriguing work in late Victorian culture, where certain readings of evolutionary theory could project the fusion of the empirical and the metaphysical.[1] For instance, in the case of the painter G.F. Watts, the grotesque is the inescapable materiality of a process that, wanting to announce the presence of the spiritual body, becomes entangled with the articulation of primal traces in the human frame.

Absorbed by the idea of the transcendental, fascinated by theosophy, concerned with the condition of national health and intelligence, promulgator of the 'law of combat', student of evolutionary theory, advocate of Greek art and author of *Our Race as Pioneers*, Watts is an amalgam of the differential traces that mark the territory of late Victorian culture.[2] Identified as sage, magus, saint and mystic, his voluminous writings are a bizarre conflation of the bardic and the quotidian; this is a language that wants to be gnomic and luminous, opaque and penetrating.[3] Victorian and Edwardian commentators are drawn to what they see as the spiritual qualities of an art that searches for the Universal or the Absolute. In his own writings the painter rejects the anthropomorphic God of Christian orthodoxy and projects a 'visionary' art that oscillates and hesitates between abstract Theism, in which the world is designed for man, and immanent vitalism, in which a 'life-force' generates all forms of material existence in a ceaseless tide of violent flows.[4]

Hovering between romantic materialism and evolutionary biology, Watts's later paintings generate networks of conflicting and contradictory forces in and around their articulation of the body and its role within narrative structures. If this chapter sets out to examine the representation of the body in such late paintings as *She Shall be Called Woman, Evolution, Experientia Docet, Love and Death, The Genius of Greek Poetry* and *Eve Repentant*, it does so in order to explore the ways in which such works, by seeking to register ideal form, are drawn to a force that disfigures or dissolves it.

What is interesting about Watts's work is that the registration of the primal in the body occurs within an aesthetic that is grounded in a classical vision of the human form as a composite of ideal parts.[5] However, instead of the noble completion and solidity of form associated with the 'Phidian' tradition to which he aspires, many of Watts's later works are marked by their formal disintegration and 'deliquescence'. In such cases the body becomes the place of endless blockage: hovering between the ideal and the material, and often turning away from the picture-plane, it seems to get in the way of more measured or primal representations of itself. What do such processes reveal? Were they part of a deliberate pictorial or conceptual strategy involving the grotesque?

I would argue that in the presentation of the body as a form of material blockage – a place where energy and violence intermingle or collide – the grotesque is locked into the process of biological development. Unlike Brown, for whom Cromwell is an unhomely presence because energy can never incarnate the nature of the being to which he aspires, Watts attempts to efface all signs of the grotesque from the material form of the body.[6] However, this process of elimination is always about to lead to the oblivion of art itself. In such paintings as *She Shall be Called Woman* (Figure 8.1), materiality is at once ubiquitous and elusive, at once the invisible vitality that suffuses form and the registration of a space where life seems to be the outcome of the spiritualization of matter.

In surveying the critical interpretations of Watts there is one historical source that places the artist within the landscape of the grotesque. G.K. Chesterton's brilliant essay presents Watts's painting as the quintessential record of the 'atmosphere' of the late nineteenth century because of its ability to connote doubt and faith: here is a mode of painting which contains within itself the signs of 'sceptical idealism' and the values of 'cosmic utilitarianism'.[7] At the same time, the efficacy of such work is discovered in its opposition to what Chesterton calls the 'metaphysical pathos of unity': the belief that unity is valuable in itself, or that the process of absorption is spiritually elevating.[8]

Chesterton is attacking what he identifies as the 'formless' nature of late Victorian thought, which he associates with orientalism, spiritualism and evolutionary theory. The first of these – orientalism – is taken to contain the other two in that it combines violence and fate; and he identifies Cecil Rhodes as its chief representative. Rhodes, he asserts, 'had no principles whatever to give to the world. He had only a hasty and elaborate machinery for spreading the principles he hadn't got. What he called his ideas were the dregs of Darwinism which had already grown not only stagnant, but poisonous.'[9] It should not come as any great surprise that Watts was greatly interested in orientalism, spiritualism and evolutionary theory, that in Rhodes he saw the conflation of force and will: physical evidence to support his claim that all life was informed by the same vital law.[10]

Chesterton discovers his negative trinity of forces in many aspects of late Victorian cultural life. Hostile to Impressionism, which he associates with a general indifference to definition, order and structure, he sees in Watts the last heroic attempt to resist this relativizing impulse. Identified as a key cultural practice, Impressionism refers to all forms of art and thought in which fluidity becomes a series of frozen moments. Such quasi-epiphanies are to be rejected. With regard to painting, Impressionism is, he claims in his book on Blake, ' the substitution of atmosphere for shape, the sacrifice of form to tint'; and he discovers in this attitude an ecstatic secularism which truncates the powers of the imagination and cancels the contact between things.[11] He attacks Impressionism, then, because it is a false materialism.[12] Indeed, Chesterton wants to demonstrate that the importance of Watts lies in his understanding of 'the God-like materialism of art'.[13] Not only are Watts's paintings rooted in the mystery of matter, they are, even when they seem to be at their most 'abstract', attempts to grasp and picture the strangeness of being, the inexplicable presence of things. His vision is taken to be moral, a record of an engagement with the world as it is.[14] Watts is presented as the author of a synthetic philosophy in which painting and ethics are unified, and where art recedes to a place prior to its own foundation. At this point Chesterton echoes Mrs Barrington, Watts's friend and biographer, for whom the painter tries 'to embody in art an echo of the essential interests of life; something more complete in its suggestiveness to the whole of human nature than mere artistic completeness could ever be'.[15]

Defining Watts's style as more primitive than pagan, Chesterton sees in it evidence of a desire to return to an expressiveness that precedes the birth of allegory: this style of painting 'might have been upon the tower of Babel'.[16] Associating the idea of origin with visions of the unknowable, Watts 'paints like one upon a tower looking down the appalling perspective of the centuries towards fantastic temples and inconceivable republics'.[17] If painting is a pilgrimage in which the artist pictures, not the drama of history, but the mysterious physicality of life, then Watts is a painter for whom painting is a vision of the primal *in* vision.[18] The painter as wanderer wonders at the wanderings of matter:

> In the whole range of Watts's ... art there is scarcely a single example of the ordinary and arbitrary current symbol, the ecclesiastical symbol, the heraldic symbol, the national symbol. A primeval vagueness and archaism hang over all the canvases ... like frescoes from some prehistoric temple. There is nothing there but the eternal things, clay and fire and the sea, and motherhood and the dead.[19]

Watts, who imagined his work forming a vast cycle called *The House of Life*, is identified with a mode of picturing from which all residual traces of iconography have been effaced; he is identified, that is, with a vision that claims that life is not reducible to language, to allegory.[20] His mastery of what Chesterton calls 'perspective' is a realization of the mystery of human experience and its expressive value; and because Watts assimilates the strangeness of matter into the nature of his art, Chesterton wants to penetrate this art of penetrative seeing. The registration of the importance of Watts's art is associated with his capacity to grasp the material identity of things. Identifying light as the sign of a force that generates and envelops nature, Chesterton outlines two approaches to it in Victorian painting. The 'pagan' position of Watts, which 'deals always with a light shining on things', is explained as a stoical acceptance of the natural realm; the 'Christian' position of the Pre-Raphaelites, which shows light shining through things, is defined as a self-torturing pursuit of the numinous.[21] Establishing a dichotomy between opaque and transparent colouring, Chesterton sees in transparency a denial of the organic nature of things; it is a violent rupturing of the body and a laceration of its form by an impulse that acknowledges organic life through its fragmentation. In contradistinction to the haptic vision of the Pre-Raphaelites, he discovers in Watts a recognition of the ludic physicality of matter. His 'iridescent' colours enact

> the dawn of things; it is the glow of the primal sense of wonder; it is the sun shining on the childhood of the world ... it is a light shining on things, not shining through them. It is a light which exhibits and does honour to the world, not a light which breaks in upon this world to bring it terror.[22]

The body, in resisting the violence of light, is an integral part of the matter of the landscape in which it materializes. Furthermore, Watts is taken to see in matter the bardic nature of art as the endless wandering between language and representation. Watts's achievement is marked by his ability to make of painting something that restores art to a 'mythic' state without the deployment of myths. Generating expressive and communicative compositions without the framing powers of narrative, Watts, it seems, locates the power of the image in a moment before art, thus 'remembering' the unknowable place where art would dwell. This 'indescribable primalism', Chesterton informs us, produces 'autochthonous colours' from 'the palette of creation', locking the artist into an endless disruption of classical vision.[23]

In his own writings Watts articulates the nature of painting as the search for universal norms, eternal forms and foundational values. Such principles are realized when art is seen as an engagement with the 'generic and general'; and if such art makes use of 'the simplest forms' from 'the mass of infinite detail', it presents 'a grand whole to the mind'.[24] Art, generating 'cosmopolitan' subjects that unite all mankind, is 'a medium for giving vitality to such interchange of ideas as are common to all nations'.[25] However, this desire for unity and completion is made through processes in which civilizing energy is always about to become pure violence: culture is both untranscendable truth and a supplement to more 'basic' impulses and forces of life; and so 'the struggle for existence'

> cannot be suspended without loss. The law of combat is the law of life. When a man is comfortable and has all that he wants, his fibres are relaxed. He is no longer pressed by the daily and hourly contest which is the condition of a strenuous life. Hence all races tend to decay when they achieve comfort. And that law of combat is what you ignore in your opposition to War. War is the ultimate form – gross, rude, horribly painful ... but the culminating point of the rock of combat which is the condition of progress ... The principle, movement, may in humanity be explained by impulse to activity; it is as certain as in the solar systems, and must, being a natural law, have its safety-valve, its outlet. This has always been war. The competition of commerce [is] the accumulating irritation of interests always threatening and preparing for war, inevitable war.[26]

Culture may aspire to incarnate the idea of the beautiful, but the social life in which it is made is a product of pure conflict: 'Civilization admits of no standing still', because 'the law of expansion is the law of vitality ... Civilization is like a flood, a mighty overwhelming flood.'[27] How, we might ask, do such pronouncements connect with Watts's paintings? What bearing does the idea of violence have on his art? We can begin to address these issues by examining how Watts deals with the body.

If Watts associates the function of art with the desire to make manifest the Ideal or Complete Body, the process of making art is bound up with a need to control the effusions that characterize the body as a material form. The body is both a lost unity and a process of physical development that will culminate in Absolute Purity. The search for expressive beauty is thus a movement between an original purity that is about to be restored, and a pure essence that must be imagined because it is yet to be realized. However, in its attempt to articulate the purity of origins, painting becomes entangled with a primal physicality that seems to preclude the idea of beauty that we find in his essays.[28] This doubling process takes the form of, on the one hand, a mode of 'spiritual' evolution in the case of *She Shall be Called Woman*, where the body embodies the autotelic power of Pure Consciousness; and, on the other hand, with *Experientia Docet: Tasting the First Oyster* (Figure 8.2), a type of evolutionary materialism in which the body is placed within the developmental processes of the natural world. In the first image the body 'speaks' nature and gives it form; in the second it is formed by and emerges from a more primal moment of evolutionary development. We have in these images two readings of the relationship between human identity and the natural realm. Firstly, the body is the source of a power which, enveloping nature, presents the natural world as a discharge of energy that spiritualizes matter; and secondly, the human animal, framed by the emptiness of a primordial landscape, repeats the postures of other primates in a space marked by its 'bovine grotesqueness'.[29]

To confirm that Watts locks the body into the idea of the grotesque we must return to Chesterton, for whom the term is associated with 'size, vitality, variety, energy and ugliness'.[30] In the case of Watts, however, he draws attention to his representation of the back: 'The back is the most awful and mysterious thing in the universe: it is impossible to speak about it. It is the part of a man that he knows nothing of.'[31] That is to say, the back is the grotesque: it is an unknowable place within the body; it is the body turned away from itself. Eschewing the classical tradition, where the back registers the symmetry of movement and power, Chesterton presents the back as the *strangeness* of the idea of place. As we will see, it is certainly possible to read the back as grotesque by treating it as the location of primal signs of 'animal' physicality. This, of course, is not Chesterton's position. Instead of seeing the back as a turning away back into evolutionary history, he sees the back in terms of the pure mystery of the quotidian. Like Browning, for whom he had nothing but respect, Chesterton associates Watts's vision with the grotesque, meaning the capacity to see the strange presence of objects in the world.[32] Watts's achievement, then, is to find in the back the primal entanglements of nature:

This is the deepest, the oldest, the most wholesome and religious sense of the value of nature – the value which comes from her immense babyishness. She is top-heavy, a grotesque, as solemn, and as happy as a child. The mood does come when we see all her shapes like shapes that a baby scrawls on a slate – simple, rudimentary, a million years older and stronger than the whole disease that is called art.[33]

Chesterton stresses the capacity of the back to announce its own essential mystery by resisting allegory. In *Love and Death* (Figure 8.3) he finds in the back, that is, in the idea of the grotesque, a presence that blocks the presentation of painting as a code whose final meaning lies behind the symbols it uses.[34] We can also cite *The Sower of the Systems* (Figure 8.4), where the Creator is seen turning away from the picture-plane into indeterminate space and matter. The paradoxical nature of such imagery will become apparent when I produce a supplementary reading of Chesterton's engagement with Watts and the grotesque. However, I want first to return to one of his larger 'cosmological' paintings.

She Shall be Called Woman is, so Watts informs us, not the Eve of Genesis, but a vision of the 'incarnation of the spirit of our time, and a hope for the future. It is intended to express the very essence of life – strong, fresh, vital, electric – an embodiment of the ideal inheritance of humanity from its mother, of the spiritual, the loving, the beautiful'.[35] Thus, the purification of the body – the process of detaching it from instincts, and affirming in the materiality of life an expenditure of the spiritual – becomes a way of absorbing the figure into the textures of nature. In such a moment of creation it is impossible to determine the agency of form and generation: distinctions between nature and the body are avoided by a process of painting that insists on the integration of things. In order to preserve the true character of the human form the body becomes a network of landscape motifs: clouds, grass, ground, flowers, birds are energized by a light that seems to emanate from this subject. The body, simultaneously formed and dissolved by a transfiguring luminosity, is at once the oblivion of matter and its purest articulation.[36]

She Shall be Called Woman may be an attempt to picture the powers of the mind as the generative force of matter – as the process by which the subject-object division is obliterated – but the painting also works to undermine what Watts defines as the formal dignity of the body. That is, the fragmentation of presentation – which isolates and draws attention to zones of the body in such a way as to suggest difference rather than unity, as well as the depiction of the body as that which emanates light – contradicts Watts's recommendation that 'the flesh is most lovely in colour' when it is free from 'violent shadows or strong colour'.[37] This contradiction takes the following form. On the one hand, the violation of the materiality of the body as flesh is the necessary pre-condition for the articulation of the union of the body and nature; on the other hand, Watts writes that in purifying painting of violent effects the body *becomes* nature and begets matter. It would seem that the violence of painting as matter – as process of inscription and structure of transcription – both affirms the power of the body *and* violates its material form. Violence, in fragmenting the body, unifies it with spirit; violence, in overcoming unity, is entangled with, but cannot express, the universal order of things.

For Watts, war is the condition from which art seeks to escape in order to establish and register its identity; but war, or perhaps we should speak of violence, is also the ground of its articulation. Moreover, violence seeps from the representation of matter into the matter of his art. A visitor to his studio, comparing his technique with that of Leighton, observed: 'He covers his brush with paint and makes nice, long, deep, firm strokes ... you paint with everything except the brush ... with nasty old bits of paper, and with your thumb.'[38] Here the act of painting is pictured as a return to a primal encounter with matter as the body generates imagery by ignoring the instruments of painting. As we have seen, Watts projects the evolution of life in terms of the spiritualization of matter: in returning to the origin of human existence his cosmic histories are to embody the teleological structure of life; there is no intention of associating evolution with the primitive as something valuable in itself. However, despite his desire to liberate painting from the thraldom of physicality, the process of painting becomes the endless affirmation of matter embodied by the 'gestural' nature of his working methods. If it is not possible to escape such violence, there seems to be little sense of a movement *away* from matter into spirit; painting becomes the convulsive equivocation between two conceptual registers.

As we have seen, commentators were intrigued by his rugged or virile methods of painting; but how did this expenditure of energy find expression in Watts's confrontations with nature? The blankness of *Experientia Docet* enables Watts to avoid any direct confrontation with the contents of contemporary scientific belief.[39] This self-declared admirer of Darwin does not articulate nature as a matrix of erasures, nor does he see the earth as a series of traces whose inscriptions are forever in the process of cancellation or affirmation.[40] Indeed, organic life is marginalized by a landscape where the writings of geology, zoology and biology are absent. This painting not only effaces allegory, it also erases those signs by which contemporary scientific discourse, reading nature as a collection of multiple temporal planes, discovered warring processes of organic growth in the volatile surface of the earth. Such picturing labours to resist the logic of Watts's ur-law of life: the law of combat. Nature, he writes, 'delights in conflict! Life is conflict ... The law of creation is movement and conflict ... Conflict means conquest or defeat.'[41] Elsewhere he affirms that 'the poet ... ignores the condition of conflict and its necessity, especially that state of effervescence amongst men which leads to war'.[42]

Although he states that 'art has struggled for life', the surface of the earth, unlike the surface of many of his paintings, remains neutral.[43] For Darwin, the earth is a volatile surface, or rather a series of inscriptions, imprints or traces. In the earth Darwin sees networks that trace the history of natural forces. This treatment of matter is, of course, extended to the human body, which Darwin presents as a record of its own evolutionary history. Seeing it as an amalgam of differential traces that register the profusion of matter, Darwin detaches the body from the aestheticist narratives of Romantic Theism and Natural Theology. And it is through Darwinian theory that we can examine the way in which the biological 'facticity' of the back is locked into expressions of the grotesque.

By drawing attention to the back in such paintings as *Love and Death* and *Eve Repentant* (Figure 8.5), Watts brings into focus that part of the human form that, as Darwin writes, 'retains ... rudimentary and useless structures [and] repetitions'.[44] If man still 'bears in his bodily frame the indelible stamp of his lowly origin', the back is pictured as a cluster of signs and erasures, in this case the *os coccyx* at the base of the spine.[45] To be sure, Watts frames a 'vestigial' element of the body that declares that human evolution involves irregularity, rupture and loss; the apparent blankness of the base of the back contains traces of the missing tail possessed by our ancestors.[46] It is in this 'mingling' of the human and the animal – a mingling that Watts would have regarded as a form of illicit or deviant symbiosis – that we find the registration of the grotesque. As both surface and sign, the back is bodied forth as a form of corporeal palimpsest: it is the place where 'pure' representation cannot purge itself of material life, because it is where biology is buried in the home of art.[47] With the back the 'divine law' of evolution is written out by the facts of evolutionary biology.[48]

I am not suggesting that Watts was attracted to the back because it allowed him to 'transgress' classical art theory by affirming the distortion, deformation and defacement of its visual norms; and there is no evidence to suggest that he intended to assimilate the grotesque into his account of the development of the human life. Indeed, a cursory glance at his writings confirms that he sees in the back the essential syntax of art. However, this 'architectonic' approach is always locked into a process that stresses the ineluctable coupling of the beautiful and the grotesque. It could be said, then, that if the grotesque is buried within his classical aesthetic, the back is the place of both its suppression and its articulation.

Simultaneously the site of profusion and truncation, the back becomes a multiple register of the aberrant nature of a self-dismembering modern experience: 'what is called the backbone', he writes, 'is formed of bones placed one upon another, making it a very beautiful and flexible column'. However, both the structural integrity of the spinal column and the physical beauty of the back are destroyed by the shapes of modern fashion that, compressing the body, weaken the muscles formed by nature. Therefore,

the separate bones will sink one upon another in consequence of the weight of the head and upper part of the body; loss of height and power of movement being the consequence ... No artificial support can supply the place of Nature's beautiful design and perfect arrangement. Nor is this all the mischief. The general form produced by the arrangement of the ribs is actually reversed. The cavity containing the heart and lungs is contracted, these being grievously impeded in their vital functions; the ribs crumpled together are occasionally driven into the lungs, causing death – and all for what? For pleasure? Certainly not. For beauty? No less certainly not. For nothing but the gratification of a most depraved taste. In this indifference to, this defiance of natural laws, does not the highly refined lady ... place herself on a level with the squaw who sticks a bone through her lip to make it hang down below her chin?[49]

Imprisoning the body in violating matter, fashion cannot represent the authentic aesthetic quality of the human form. If it cannot embody the ideal type to which the body aspires, it must contort and collapse the body into a grotesque sign of atavism. In truncating the back, fashion turns it back to face itself. The sense of expelling from the back its purity or power is registered when he refers to his desire to turn 'criminals, tramps and loafers' – the signs of social degeneration – into a collective or 'national backbone'.[50] This resurfacing of the grotesque in the space of beauty, this eradication of the aesthetic by primal violence, is a dominant theme that informs Watts's ideas about art, culture and society from the 1870s.

Such points are useful in our attempt to face the full complexity of Watts's style, technique and subject-matter. By examining the 'invisible' materialism of a range of paintings we can propose a reading of his art that questions the view, so dominant in the late Victorian and Edwardian periods, that his allegorical or metaphysical tendencies are self-grounding.[51] Those paintings where the back acts as a central compositional and formal element block or efface the values to which the idea of transcendence aspires. Instead of revealing the spiritualization of matter, such paintings declare that the apparent movement away from matter asserts the ineluctable, incoherent and incongruous materiality of the body as physical form. Thus we are obliged to confront the two questions Watts wants his art to overcome: is nature framed by force or by an author; is nature self-generating or is it structured by some 'external' power? By drawing attention to and framing the back, Watts produces a number of images that work against their declared attention to return both art and the body to the unity of ideal form.

Even where the representation of the back is not at issue – in, for instance, *Evolution* (Figure 8.6) or *The Genius of Greek Poetry* (Figure 8.7) – it is not only a case of the return of the primal body, but of drawing attention to the primal *in* the body. In *Evolution*, evolution seems to be a process of dissolving bodies; this is a realm in which fecundity is a form of degeneration or oblivion. Instead of repeating the standard pictorial logic of narrative art, the central figure, in being drawn to the left, is drawn to 'the past'. With *The Genius of Greek Poetry*, the logic of disintegration and fragmentation works against any possible articulation of universal coherence or unity; this is an image where form has become force: here the main figure observes in nature violence and mutation rather than plenitude and continuity. Cultural formation appears to be trumped by evolutionary process. The dominating view of this painting, established by Mrs Barrington in her catalogue of the New York exhibition of 1884, claims that Watts replicates the anthropomorphic vision of Greek culture, where 'all the effects and moods of nature weave themselves in his imagination into semi-human existences'.[52] Maybe. But is it not also the case that we witness a scene in which stasis, symmetry and serenity are overcome by agitated movement as the main figure views his own origin or demise? Here looking involves the figure in an act that acknowledges the primitive source of human nature; or, vision declares his future destruction by figures, all of whom seem to embody the law of combat as 'universal conflict'.[53]

Watts writes that 'the human form is the highest expression of beauty'; but in *The Genius of Greek Poetry* the ideal form of the body is effaced as the pose of the central figure works against formal coherence.[54] Such fragmentation erases narrative clarity, as the arc above the head of the central figure hesitates between human form, abstract shape and moment of evolutionary development. Vision eliminates the classical ideal: instead of an image that returns us to a moment of cultural authority, we are confronted with a primal scene of indeterminate form and dismembered representation. If Watts desires to personify nature as the conflation of Mind and Design, this intention is frustrated by a mode of picturing that presents nature as a set of traces, networks and forces.[55] The clouding of composition, the coming into being of primitive humanoid forms in the background, and the attitude of the central figure, suggest tension rather than stasis, profusion rather than order. Here energy becomes pure discharge, as violence mingles with representation in a space where things seem to hover between articulation and oblivion.

As it is possible to register a connection between Watts's work and a certain reading of the grotesque, how, we might ask, did he conceptualize the grotesque? There are two ways of addressing the question. Firstly, we know from his writings that Watts was concerned with the articulation and deployment of power. It is in what we might call the violence of violence – that is, illegitimate force not sanctioned by law – that Watts sees the grotesque. Violence is grotesque when it constitutes an elaboration to the 'natural' level of the rules that govern nature. The grotesque is life as pure profusion: the crowding out of law by needless growth; the oblivion of generation. The grotesque is the crowd, which in *The Genius of Greek Poetry* emerges from the vaporous space beneath the arc. The only way to picture the crowd is as a rupturing of the aesthetic: here the Michelangelesque figure becomes a witness to a process over which he has no narrative authority. In this vague, luminous, troubling painting the decomposition of form produces a disorientating space that sees the mingling of things in a process of endless veiling.[56]

The second way in which Watts deals with the grotesque – and again this draws attention to forces and powers that negate the pure body of art – is through his cultural criticism. It is not surprising that Watts identifies the grotesque with popular culture and the interests of the masses, for whom caricature is identified as the archetypal form of art.[57] He thus names Hogarth as the embodiment of the 'grotesque in style'.[58] 'Grotesqueness', however appropriate in certain contexts, is always the pollution of high art because it is the imperfection of expression; and of Hogarth he writes:

because the material conditions did not permit of an appeal to a sense of nobility, no appreciation, no loudly expressed opinion of his just claims by the best writers will ever be able to place him by the side of the greatest painters. Though he was in reality greater than most, he was forced to speak in a dialect, and cannot therefore compete with those poets who had command of all the treasures of language.[59]

In certain contexts, fusing both these readings of the grotesque, Watts conflates anarchic force with the idea of the extension of the body into the amorphous mass of the crowd. At such moments the energy of the crowd seems to parody his own sense of physical decrepitude:

I hear around me the tramp of armed men and the hurry of others hastening to claim the right to live, and feel, I can't tell you what a desire to be among them somehow. If I had the singer's gift I would lend them some aid, but as it is, I almost feel too small to live, and very often life is a positive pain to me for want of mental lungs powerful enough to breathe the strong air. What a nuisance it is to be less than oneself.[60]

Entangled with the idea of oblivion, the grotesque is at once the agitation of matter and the deformation of the aesthetic. When Watts addresses the nature of grotesque painting, it is, he claims, the attempt to make art ugly; and such ugliness results from the localization of expression, or any form of practice that, denying the 'essential truths of nature', produces 'exaggeration'.[61] In contradistinction, Watts asserts that his art searches for a way of articulating the desire to 'lift the veil that shrouds the enigma of being'.[62] However, this desire to picture art as the escape from the residual grotesqueness of matter into the transcendent purity of form-as-being is undermined by the very nature of his pictorial style. We have seen that Watts's work can be characterized as a drawing attention to *and* an avoidance of the signs that comprise the human body. This movement is away from matter: pigments are used to express a desire to reach a level of pictorial clarity in which colour and light both embody and transcend their physical bases. For Watts, however, the processes of labour, because they are repetitive rather than developmental, are signs of failure: they do not record the progressive unfolding of art as the transvaluation of form, technique and subject. 'I haunt', he writes, 'the footsteps of the great dead.'[63] Like Brown, he experiences late-coming, and it plays upon his sense of the worth of his labour. Unlike Brown, he presents his failure in Darwinian, or, more accurately, Spencerian terms, when he refers to himself as an example of 'the survival of the unfittest'.[64]

The desire to see in creativity the transmutation of physical into mental power is a marked feature of the way in which Mrs Barrington defines the value of Watts's achievements. Whereas his 'magnetic' sculptures reveal an 'instinctive sensibility for form' and exert 'a kind of mesmeric influence', some of his paintings are 'regulated' or 'laboured'.[65] She herself, in comparing 'Celtic' and 'Phidian' approaches to art, sees in Watts an eternal battle between the Grotesque and the Classical. Watts embodies the desire for the impossible reconciliation between the endless agitation of matter and the pure serenity of form.[66] She writes: 'How happy, simple and unagitating is the art of the noble Phidian procession, so serene and composed in its dignified beauty compared to the mystery of the half-hidden Slav passion surging out in intricacies of musical sound, and to the straining, appealing gesture in the sculpture of the

Celt'.[67] The irony is that if she, like Watts, presents Classical art as the zenith of creative value, such beauty of form is deemed inaccessible to his 'melancholy' modern consciousness, whose 'yearning , passionate' nature is the endless entanglement of the physical and the spiritual. Watts may love colour, but because his colours are autumnal rather than spring-like, they are 'murky ... too suggestive, I think, of decay'.[68]

This confusion in matter, this concealing of beginnings and endings, is the very nature of Watts's art. To be sure, the sense of the density of matter, where the grotesque is the ineluctable condition of material life, is caught at the most prosaic of levels. Even at the level of technique, Watts – who spends so much of his time searching for the perfect transparency of form – cannot escape the agitation of matter.[69] Thus painting becomes the surfacing of violence in the place of inscriptions and erasures built up, in many cases, over a period of 30 years or more. Instead of revealing the elegance and purity of form, painting registers the endless movement and 'evolution' of matter; and instead of affirming self-registration, each work becomes a palimpsest: the outcome of 'perpetual re-touching, a scumbling of half dry paint dragged over the surface in such a fashion as always to leave the possibility of further work tomorrow'.[70]

Notes

1. Symons, J.A., 'Caricature, the Fantastic, the Grotesque', in *Essays Speculative and Suggestive*, London: Chapman Hall, 1890, pp. 15–43.

2. The three volumes of his collected thoughts, compiled by his wife, read like a parody of Ruskin's capacity to deny the application of the law of the division of labour to intellectual life. Covering everything from agriculture to zoology, Watts's essays and maxims were 'managed' and edited into shape by his second wife. That he lacked Ruskin's creative and literary skills can be seen from a cursory glance at any of these documents. See Watts, M.S., *G.F. Watts, Annals of an Artist's Life*, 3 vols, London: Macmillan, 1912 (hereafter referred to as M. Watts).

3. It may well be the case that Watts re-fashions himself through his contemporaries' image of him as a painter in search of the True Source of Art and Life. Indeed, for many of his colleagues, some of a decidedly practical and prosaic nature, he was the embodiment of the idea of art. Here is the landscape painter, etcher and art critic P.G. Hamerton: 'It seems to me that you are living in a region of thought which is not only far above art as a trade, but even above art as a profession' (see M. Watts, vol. 2, p. 173). Other examples of this attitude can be found in the correspondence collected by his wife. See the letters by Sir Clifford Allbut and F.W.H. Myers, *ibid.*, vol. 2, pp. 180, 185, 187; p. 324.

4. Watts, for whom evolutionary theory confirms the teleological nature of life, writes that 'the evolution of the idea of goodness in the mind of man [is] leading up to the knowledge that love is all' (M. Watts, vol. 2, p. 139). In such moods this cosmic altruism could be applied to the nature of orthodox Christianity which, by dint of its exaggerated ornamentation and customs, is assimilated into the language of the grotesque. His wife writes: 'He believed in the next century the Christian creed would have to be purified from encrustations' (vol. 2, p. 243). Elsewhere he asserts that the very idea of religion must be detached from the ugly (vol. 2, pp. 244–45), and that Christianity would evolve into the church of the 'universal Self' (vol. 3, pp. 324–25). Other useful sources concerning his ideas about theological, cosmological and spiritual matters can be found in vol. 2, pp. 2, 166; vol. 3, pp. 31, 36. Valuable material concerning his religious ideas can be found in Stewart, D., 'Theosophy and Abstraction in the Victorian Era', *Apollo*, November 1993, pp. 298–303.

5. M. Watts, vol. 2, p. 80.

6. Although I have not pursued the idea here, it would be possible to examine paintings such as *Mammon* as a 'Wattsian' variant of the 'political' grotesque associated with Carlyle and Brown; and it is interesting to note that the careers of these two very different artists overlapped because of their connections with cultural life in Manchester. Watts seems to have been rather touched that the notoriously pugnacious Brown saw something significant in his art. See M. Watts, vol. 1, pp. 244, 261, 276, 318–19. Watts and Brown are identified as heroic figures beyond the commercial logic of the modern art academy in Spielmann, M.H., 'The Work of G.F. Watts', *Pall Mall Extra*, 1886, pp. 1–20. See Trodd, C., 'The Authority of Art: Cultural Criticism and the Idea of the Royal Academy in mid-Victorian Britain', in Pointon, M., and Binski, P. (eds), *National Art Academies in Europe 1860–1906: Educating, Training, Exhibiting*, Oxford: Basil Blackwell, 1997.

7. Chesterton, G.K., *G.F. Watts*, London: Duckworth, 1904, p. 18.

8. *Ibid.*, pp. 9–16.

9. Chesterton, G.K., *A Miscellany of Men*, London: Methuen, 1912, p. 202.

10. Watts's political philosophy moves between Tory Paternalism, embodied in his 'rural' vision of Compton, and quasi-'cosmic' Social Darwinism, which acknowledges the evolutionary nature of the Imperial Imperative. Although more work must be undertaken in the area of his scientific and cultural readings, it does seem that there are points of contact between his later ideas and the literature of Vitalism. Like Watts, Driesch seeks to 'spiritualize' evolutionary theory and presents teleology as 'an irreducible peculiarity of the phenomenon of life' (Driesch, H., *The History of Vitalism*, London: Macmillan, 1914, p. 176). By the 1880s and 1890s Watts would have agreed that the processes of life were to be understood as autonomous, 'obeying their own laws' (*ibid.*, p. 178). For Watts's opinions on oriental culture, evolutionary theory and Rhodes, see M. Watts, vol. 2, pp. 243–45, 267–69, 272, 277; vol. 3, p. 282. 'Our Race as Pioneers', his definitive engagement with Social Darwinian Imperialism, is found in vol. 3, pp. 277–94. Watts was sufficiently impressed by Rhodes to include his portrait in *The Hall of Fame* series of eminent Victorians that he donated to the National Portrait Gallery. See Ormond, R., *G.F. Watts: The Hall of Fame*, London: HMSO, 1976, pp. 5–11, for further details.

11. Chesterton, G.K., *William Blake*, London: Duckworth, 1910, pp. 17–18.

12. It should be pointed out that the identification of Impressionism with violence is not restricted to Chesterton. Walter Bayes, the painter and critic, applauds Watts's capacity to oppose Impressionism and its 'violent attempt to capture the crude appearance of fleeting facts'. Never 'vulgar or commonplace', Watts creates images from which 'the coarse and the material have been eliminated' (Bayes, W., *The Landscapes of G.F. Watts*, London: Duckworth, 1907, pp. ix–xi). Watts claims that evolution reveals the inadequacy of the idea of 'Impressionism' (M. Watts, vol. 2, p. 293). A detailed account of Chesterton's attitude to 'Impressionism' is provided by Coates, J., *Chesterton and the Edwardian Cultural Crisis*, Hull: Hull University Press, 1984, pp. 191–209.

13. Chesterton, *op. cit.* at note 7, p. 20.

14. Mrs Watts stresses the moral nature of Watts's project and states that he referred to a class of his paintings as 'ethical reflections' (M. Watts, vol. 2, p. 139).

15. Barrington, E.R., *Reminiscences of G.F. Watts*, London: George Allen, 1905, p. 119.

16. Chesterton, G.K., *Robert Browning*, London: Macmillan, 1903, p. 24.

17. Chesterton, *op. cit.* at note 7, p. 34.

18. He presents the evolution of art as a movement from the purity of perceptual engagement to a form of decorative delicacy. See M. Watts, vol. 3, p. 27.

19. Chesterton, *op. cit.* at note 7, p. 33.

20. His comments on the non-allegorical nature of his work can be found in M. Watts, vol. 1, p. 183; vol. 2, pp. 180, 188. Chesterton seems to have been drawn to Watts's relaxed attitude to early mythic forms, structures and beliefs. Unlike the works of Muller, which Watts had read, the three volumes edited by Mrs Watts do not assert that mythic expression is a corruption of religious culture; that myth is grotesque in its desire to demonstrate the physical is not an attitude we can associate with Watts. See Muller, F.M., *Comparative Mythology*, London: A. Smyth Palmer, 1856, pp. v–20; M. Watts, vol. 2, p. 190; Coates, *op. cit.* at note 12, pp. 143–52.

21. Chesterton, *op. cit.* at note 7, p. 33.

22. *Ibid.*.

23. *Ibid.*, pp. 65, 59.

24. M. Watts, vol. 3, p. 41.

25. *Ibid.*, vol. 2, p. 213.
26. *Ibid.*, vol. 3, p. 291; Stead, W.T., 'Interview with G.F. Watts', *Review of Reviews*, **150**, June 1902, pp. 567–77.
27. M. Watts, vol. 3, pp. 280–81.
28. See Fry, R., 'Watts and Whistler', *The Quarterly Review*, 1905, n. 202, pp. 607–23, reprinted in Reed, C. (ed.), *A Roger Fry Reader*, Chicago and London: The University of Chicago Press, 1996, pp. 25–38, for a contrasting view of the relationship between classical aesthetics and the body in Watts's paintings. Claiming for Watts a superiority over Whistler, Fry is impressed by the forceful articulation of the human form in an art where idealism is rooted in the observation and understanding of the vital processes of the body as a physical structure.
29. Mullen, C., *G.F. Watts*, London: John Roberts, 1974 (unpaginated).
30. Chesterton, G.K., *The Defendant*, London: Hodder and Stoughton, 1901, p. 115.
31. Chesterton, *op. cit.* at note 7, p. 62.
32. Chesterton, *op. cit.* at note 16, pp. 148–66.
33. Chesterton, *op. cit.* at note 30, p. 49.
34. Chesterton, *op. cit.* at note 7, pp. 63–65.
35. M. Watts, vol. 2, pp. 202–3.
36. *Ibid.*, vol. 2, pp. 138–41; Stewart, *op. cit.* at note 4, pp. 298–301.
37. M. Watts, vol. 3, p. 236.
38. Mullen, *op. cit.*, at note 29.
39. It was not uncommon for commentators to allege that Watts's authority was the result of a poetical conflation of 'art' and 'science'. Mrs Barrington, for instance, (*op. cit.* at note 15, p. 120) claims that in balancing these two processes they are carried

    into the most technical qualities of his art ... He aims at combining great precision and exactness in rendering the essential truths of form and the delicate gradation and harmony which are found in nature's colouring, with a free, loose touch which gives a palpitating, tremulous quality to the surfaces of painting, and approximates, he thinks, the atmosphere in nature.

40. M. Watts, vol. 1, p. 203; vol. 2, p. 142.
41. *Ibid.*, vol. 3, p. 325; Darwin, C., *The Origin of Species*, London: John Murray, 1859, pp. 291–343.
42. M. Watts, vol. 2, p. 295.
43. *Ibid.*, vol. 3, p. 263.
44. Darwin, C., *The Descent of Man and Selection in Relation to Sex*, London: John Murray, 1871, vol. 1, pp. 186, 29.
45. *Ibid.*, vol. 2, p. 405.
46. *Ibid.*, vol. 1, pp. 29–30.
47. It should be noted that although he uses the term 'grotesque' to describe at least one of Watts's paintings, Henry James's reading of *Love and Death* is through the standard allegorical frame. See 'The Picture Season in London', *Galaxy*, August 1877, and 'London Pictures', *Atlantic Monthly*, 1882 reprinted in Sweeney, J.L. (ed.), *The Painter's Eye: Notes and Essays on the Pictorial Arts by Henry James*, London: Rupert Hart-Davis, 1956, pp. 130–52, 202–15.
48. M. Watts, vol. 3, p. 297; Norris, M., *Beasts of the Modern Imagination*, London and Baltimore: Johns Hopkins University Press, 1985, pp. 37–41.
49. M. Watts, vol. 3, p. 224.
50. *Ibid.*, vol. 3, p. 307.
51. See Spielmann, *op. cit.*, at note 6, pp. 9–18; Monkhouse, C., *British Contemporary Artists*, London: William Heinemann, 1895, pp. 6–31; Bayliss, W., *Five Great Painters of the Victorian Era*, London: Sampson Low, 1902, pp. 99–101; Barrington, *op. cit.* at note 15, pp. 131–32; Shrewsbury, H.W., *The Visions of an Artist*, London: C. Kelly, 1918, pp. 82–83.
52. Barrington, *op. cit.* at note 15, pp. 93, 131, 132.
53. M. Watts, vol. 3, p. 325.

54. *Ibid.*, vol. 3, p. 8.
55. This desire to articulate mind through matter, a marked feature of his portraits, is explored in Barlow, P., 'Facing the Past and Present: The National Portrait Gallery and the Search for "Authentic" Portraiture', in Woodall, J. (ed.), *Portraiture*, Manchester and New York: Manchester University Press, 1997, pp. 233–36. The scumbled surfaces of the paintings, the viscous nature of the medium and the density of technique, are, for Barlow, signs of a desire to register the difficulty in assimilating the ineluctable but elusive presence of the body into the formal language of the portrait.
56. The curious combination of the ethereal and the physical – the sense in which the clouding of form is also a crowding of the image by things coming into being – is caught in *Chaos*. Here the fusion of irregular or disparate forms and spaces suggests primal force rather than 'organic' fertility. For a discussion of this work and its relation to *The House of Life*, see M. Watts, vol. 1, pp. 101–4.
57. This is how Chesterton sees the value of the grotesque: it is Life entering Art as the Voice of the People; it is popular, democratic and demotic. Where Chesterton sees vitality in the grotesque, Watts sees excess. If Chesterton associates the grotesque with the energy of the People, Watts sees in it the the force of struggling, fighting crowds and the agitation of matter. The idea that the crowd is grotesque because its physicality is a sign of atavism is articulated in Le Bon's *The Crowd*, a text that displays certain 'Wattsian' beliefs. In this work, bodies become grotesque because social combination is presented as an endless expansion of the primitive, the irrational and the violent: the power of the crowd is a discharge of primal instincts and unconscious powers directed at culture and civilization. See Le Bon, G., *The Crowd*, London: Ernst Benn, 1896, pp. 6–67.
58. M. Watts, vol. 3, p. 188.
59. *Ibid.*, pp. 188–89.
60. Barrington, *op. cit.* at note 15, p. 14.
61. M. Watts, vol. 2, p. 213.
62. *Ibid.*, vol. 3, p. 190.
63. *Ibid.*, vol. 2, p. 13.
64. Barrington, *op. cit.* at note 15, p. 14.
65. *Ibid.*, pp. 41–42.
66. Mrs Watts seeks to distance Watts from Celtic culture. Drawing upon the division established by Arnold (Arnold, M. *The Works*, 15 vols, London: Macmillan, 1903, vol. 5, pp. 1–150), she asserts that because of the absence of ornamentation, elaboration and emotional intensity in work marked by its commitment to balance, harmony, dignity of form and 'the true proportion of things', Watts's vision is pure and Greek, rather than 'confused' and Celtic. See M. Watts, vol. 2, pp. 278–79, and Watts's echo of this view in vol. 3, pp. 50–51.
67. Barrington, *op. cit.* at note 15, p. 40.
68. *Ibid.*, pp. 40, 69.
69. The subject of technique as an expression of artistic vision is an important topic in Watts's writings. His statements can be found in M. Watts, vol. 2, pp. 87–91; vol. 3, pp. 56–58, 76, 184. Not surprisingly, Roger Fry identifies technique as the key to Watts's achievements in his shrewd obituary (Fry, R., 'G.F. Watts', *Burlington Magazine*, vol. 5, 1904, p. 452). MacColl provides the classic early Modernist critique: Watts creates 'flaccid and inflated forms ... stringy and corrugated textures [and] harsh and dirty tints' (MacColl, D.S., *Nineteenth Century Art*, Glasgow: James Maclehose and Sons, 1902, p. 119). James adopts a similar attitude when he dismisses Watts's fantasies as the worst form of Victorian art. See *Harper's Weekly*, January 1897, reprinted in Sweeney, *op. cit.* at note 47, pp. 244–46.
70. Bayes, *op. cit.* at note 12, p. xiv.

8.1 G. F. Watts, *She Shall be Called Woman*, oil on canvas, 257.8 × 116.8 cm, c1875–1892

8.2 G. F. Watts, *Experientia Docet: Tasting the first Oyster*, 72 × 93 cm, 1885
8.3 G. F. Watts, *Love and Death*, 151 × 75 cm, 1875

8.4 G. F. Watts, *The Sower of the Systems*, 66 × 53 cm, 1902

8.5 G. F. Watts, *Eve Repentant*, 257.8 × 116.8 cm, 1892

8.6 G. F. Watts, *Evolution*, 70 × 64.5 cm, c1890–1895

8.7　G. F. Watts, *The Genius of Greek Poetry*, 66 × 53.3 cm, c1857–1878

Bibliography

Abbott, W.C., *Conflicts with Oblivion*, New York: Kennikat Press, 1924
Alexander, P.P., *Mill and Carlyle: An Examination of J.S. Mill's Doctrine of Causation in Relation to Moral Freedom, with an Occasional Discourse on Sauerteig by Smelfungus*, Edinburgh: Nimmo, 1866
Alexander, P.P., *Carlyle Redivivus, being an Occasional Discourse on Sauerteig by Smelfungus*, Glasgow: Maclehose, 1881
Allderidge, P., *The Late Richard Dadd: 1817–1886*, London: Tate Gallery, 1974
Althusser, L., *For Marx*, trans. B. Brewster, London: Verso, 1990
Amico, L.N., *Bernard Palissy: In Search of Earthly Paradise*, Paris, New York: Flammarion, 1996
Amigoni, D., *Victorian Biography and the Ordering of Discourse*, Hemel Hempstead: Harvester Wheatsheaf, 1993
Amigoni, D., and Wallace, J., *Charles Darwin's The Origin of Species: New Interdisciplinary Essays*, Manchester: Manchester University Press, 1995
Armstrong, I., *Victorian Poetry: Poetry, Poetics and Politics*, London: Routledge, 1993
Arnold, M., *The Works*, 15 vols, London: Macmillan, 1903
Arts Council of Great Britain, *Great Victorian Pictures: Their Paths to Fame*, London: Arts Council, 1978
Atterbury, P., *Parian Phenomenon: A Survey of Victorian Porcelain, Statuary and Busts*, London: Dennis, 1989
Axton, W.F., 'Victorian Landscape Painting: A Change in Outlook', in Knoepflmacher, U.C., and Tennyson, G.B., *Nature and the Victorian Imagination*, Berkeley and London: University of California Press, 1977
Bagehot, W., *The Collected Works*, 12 vols, N. St.-John Stevas (ed.), London: The Economist, 1974
Bagehot, W., 'Wordsworth, Tennyson and Browning: or Pure, Ornate and Grotesque Art in English Poetry', *Literary Studies*, 2 vols, London: Longmans, 1879 (first published 1864)
Bakhtin, M., *Rabelais and His World*, Indiana: Indiana University Press, 1984
Ball, P., *The Science of Aspects: The Changing Role of Fact in the Work of Coleridge, Ruskin and Hopkins*, London: The Athlone Press, 1971
Barasch, F.K., *The Grotesque: A Study in Meanings*, The Hague: Mouton, 1971
Barber, L., *The Heyday of Natural History*, London: Jonathan Cape, 1980

Barlow, P., 'The Imagined Hero as Incarnate Sign: Thomas Carlyle and the Mythology of the National Portrait in Victorian Britain, *Art History*, **17** (4), December 1994

Barlow, P., 'Facing the Past and Present: The National Portrait Gallery and the Search for "Authentic" Portraiture', in *Portraiture*, ed. J. Woodall, Manchester and New York: Manchester University Press, 1997

Barrell, J., *The Birth of Pandora and the Division of Knowledge*, Basingstoke: Macmillan, 1992

Barrington, E.R., *Reminiscences of G.F. Watts*, London: George Allen, 1905

Bate Richards, A., *Oliver Cromwell: An Historical Tragedy*, London: Effingham Wilson, 1873

Bayes, W., *The Landscapes of G.F. Watts*, London: Duckworth, 1907

Bayliss, W., *Five Great Painters of the Victorian Era*, London: Sampson Low, 1902

Beer, G., *Darwin's Plots*, London: Routledge and Kegan Paul, 1983

Beer, G., *Darwin's Plots: Evolutionary Narrative in Darwin, George Eliot and Nineteenth-Century Fiction*, London: Ark Paperbacks, 1985

Beer, G., *Arguing with the Past: Essays in Narrative*, London: Routledge, 1989

Beidler, P.G., 'The Postmodern Sublime: Kant and Tony Smith's Anecdote of the Cube', *Journal of Aesthetics and Art Criticism*, **53**, Spring 1995, pp. 177–86

Bennett, M., *Artists of the Pre-Raphaelite Circle*, London: Lund Humphries, 1988

Bergesen, V., *Majolica: British, Continental and American Wares, 1851–1915*, London: Barrie & Jenkins, 1989

Bernstein, J.M., *The Fate of Art: Aesthetic Alienation from Kant to Derrida and Adorno*, Cambridge: Polity, 1992

Blau, E., *Ruskinian Gothic*, Princeton, New Jersey: Princeton University Press, 1982

Bøe, A., *From Gothic Revival to Functional Form: A Study in Victorian Theories of Design*, Oxford: Basil Blackwell, 1957

Booth, W.C., 'Freedom of Interpretation: Bakhtin and the Challenge of Feminist Criticism', *Critical Inquiry*, **9.1**, 1982, pp. 45–76

Bosanquet, B. (ed.), *The Introduction to Hegel's Philosophy of Fine Art*, London: Kegan Paul and Tench, 1886

Boswell, J., *The Hypochondriack*, 2 vols, ed. M. Bailey, Stanford, California: Stanford University Press, 1928

Boswell, J., *The Tour to the Hebrides*, in Birkbeck Hill, G. and Powell, L.F. (eds), *Boswell's Life of Johnson*, 6 vols, Oxford: Clarendon Press, 1950

Boswell, J., *The Life of Johnson*, first published in 1791, Oxford: Oxford University Press, 1980

Boulton, J.T. (ed.), *Johnson: The Critical Heritage*, London: Routledge and Kegan Paul, 1971

Brook. C., *Signs for the Times: Symbolic Realism in the Mid-Victorian Art World*, London: Allen and Unwin, 1984

Brooks, M., *John Ruskin and Victorian Architecture*, London: Thames and Hudson, 1989

Brown, F.M., *The Exhibition of Work and Other Paintings*, London: McCorquodale and Co., 1865

Browning, R., *Poetical Works*, Oxford: Oxford University Press, 1975

Browning, R., *The Poems*, ed. John Pettigrew, Harmondsworth, Penguin, 1981

Bruce Nadel, I., *Biography: Fiction, Fact and Form*, London: Macmillan, 1984

Burke, E., *Reflections on the Revolution in France*, London: Dent, 1967

Burke, P., and Porter, R. (eds), *Language, Self and Society: A Social History of Language*, Cambridge: Polity, 1991

Bynum, W.F., and Porter, R. (eds), *Medicine and the Five Senses*, Cambridge: Cambridge University Press, 1993
Cameron, C., *Thomas Carlyle: The Father of Existentialism?*, MA Dissertation, University of Northumbria, 1994
Carlyle, T., *Critical and Miscellaneous Essays*, in 3 vols, London: Chapman and Hall, 1869 (reprint of 1839 edition)
Carlyle, T., *Last Words of Thomas Carlyle*, London: Longman Green, 1892
Carlyle, T., *Sartor Resartus*, E.J. Sullivan (illus.), London: George Bell, 1898
Carlyle, T., *The French Revolution*, E.J. Sullivan (illus.), London: Chapman and Hall, 1910
Carlyle, T., *The French Revolution*, Oxford: Oxford University Press, 1989
Carlyle, T., *Works*, ed. H.D. Trail, 30 vols, London: Chapman and Hall, 1896–1901
Cattermole, R., *The Great Civil War of Charles I and the Parliament*, 2 vols, London: Longman, Orme, Brown, Green and Longmans, 1841
Chambers, R., *Vestiges of the Natural History of Creation*, London: John Churchill, 1845
Chesterton, G.K., *The Defendant*, London: Hodder and Stoughton, 1901
Chesterton, G.K., *Thomas Carlyle*, London: Hodder and Stoughton, 1902
Chesterton, G.K., *Robert Browning*, London: Macmillan, 1903
Chesterton, G.K., *G.F. Watts*, London: Duckworth, 1904
Chesterton, G.K., *William Blake*, London: Duckworth, 1910
Chesterton, G.K., *A Miscellany of Men*, London: Methuen, 1912
Chesterton, G.K., *A Miscellany of Men*, London: Methuen, 1913
Chesterton, G.K., *The Victorian Age in Literature*, London: Oxford University Press, 1913
Chesterton, G.K., *Selected Essays*, London and Glasgow: Collins, 1936
Chesterton, G.K., *A Handful of Authors*, London and New York: Sheed and Ward, 1953
Christ, C., *The Finer Optic: The Aesthetic of Particularity in Victorian Poetry*, New Haven and London: Yale University Press, 1975
Clark, J.C.D., *Samuel Johnson: Literature, Religion and English Cultural Politics from the Restoration to Romanticism*, Oxford: Oxford University Press, 1994
Coates, J., *Chesterton and the Edwardian Cultural Crisis*, Hull: Hull University Press,. 1984
Cole, H., *Fifty Years of Public Work*, London: Bell and Sons, 1884
Coleridge, S.T., *Lectures 1808–1819 On Literature*, ed. R.A. Foakes, London: Routledge, 1987
Comte, A., *A General View of Positivism*, trans. J.H. Bridges, London: Trubner, 1865
Conrad, P., *The Victorian Treasure House*, London: Collins, 1973
Coulling, S., *Matthew Arnold and his Critics*, Athens: Ohio University Press, 1974
Crowther, P., *Critical Aesthetics and Postmodernism*, Oxford: Clarendon Press, 1993
Cunningham, C., and Waterhouse, P., *Alfred Waterhouse 1830–1905: The Biography of a Practice*, Oxford: Clarendon Press, 1992
Dahesh Museum, *Religion and the Rustic Image in Late Academic Art*, New York: Dahesh Museum, 1997
Daniel, H., *Devils, Monsters and Nightmares; an Introduction to the Grotesque and Fantastic in Art*, London: Abel-Schuman, 1964
Darwin, C., *The Origin of Species*, London: John Murray, 1859
Darwin, C., *The Descent of Man and Selection in Relation to Sex*, London: John Murray, 1871
Darwin, C., *The Descent of Man and Selection in Relation to Sex*, London: John Murray, 1890
Darwin, C., *Journal of Reasearches into the Geology and Natural History of the Various Countries Visited During the Voyage of the Beagle*, London: Dent, 1906

Darwin, C., *On the Origin of Species by Means of Natural Selection*, ed. Gillian Beer, London: O.U.P., 1996
Davey, S., *Darwin, Carlyle and Dickens*, New York: Haskell House, 1971 (reprint of 1875 edition)
Dawes, N.M., *Majolica*, New York: Crown, 1990
Delamotte, P.H., *Choice Examples of Art Workmanship, Selected from the Exhibition of Ancient and Medieval Art*, London: Royal Society for the Encouragement of Arts, Manufactures and Commerce, 1851
Dibdin, T.F., *A Bibliographical, Antiquarian and Picturesque Tour in the Northern Counties of England and in Scotland*, 2 vols, London: James Bohn, 1838
Dickens, C., *Pictures from Italy*, London: Bradbury and Evans, 1846
Dickens, C., *Hard Times*, ed. G. Ford and S. Monod, New York: W.W. Norton, 1969
Doyle, A.C., *His Last Bow: Some Reminiscences of Sherlock Holmes*, London: John Murray, 1917
Dresser, C., *The Art of Decorative Design*, London: Day and Son, 1862
Dresser, C., *Principles of Decorative Design*, London: Cassell, 1873
Drew, P., 'Browning and Politics', in Armstrong, I. (ed.), *Writers and their Background: Robert Browning*, London: G. Bell, 1974
Driesch, H., *The History of Vitalism*, London: Macmillan, 1914
Eagleton, T., *The Ideology of the Aesthetic*, Oxford: Blackwell, 1990
Eastlake, C.L., *A History of the Gothic Revival*, London: Longman, Green, 1872
Fairholt, F.W., *Eccentric and Remarkable Characters*, London: Bentley, 1849
Fairholt, F.W., *Holbein's 'Dance of Death'*, London: John Russell Smith, 1849
Fairholt, F.W., 'On a Grotesque Mask of Punishment Obtained in the Castle of Nuremberg', *Memoirs of the Historical Society of Lancashire and Cheshire*, **vii**, 1854
Fairholt, F.W., *Gog and Magog, the Giants of Whitehall; their Real and Legendary History*, London: J.C. Hotten, 1859
Fairholt, F.W., 'Grotesque Design', *Art Journal*, March 1862, pp. 89–92
Fairholt, F.W., *A Dictionary of Terms in Art*, London: Virtue, 1870
Fellows, J., *The Failing Distance: The Autobiographical Impulse in John Ruskin*, Baltimore: The Johns Hopkins Press, 1975
Fenwick, G., 'Nourishing the Curiosity: Leslie Stephen and the English Men of Letters Series', *Nineteenth Century Prose*, **22.2**, Fall 1995, pp. 95–114
Ferrey, B., *Recollections of A.N. Welby Pugin, and his father Augustus Pugin: with notices of their works*, London: E. Stanford, 1861
Ferrey, B., *Recollections of A.W.N. Pugin and his father Augustus Pugin*, with an appendix by E. Sheridan Purcell and an introduction and index by Clive and Jane Wainwright, London: Scolar Press, 1978
Fielding, K.J., 'Charles Dickens and the Department of Practical Art', *Modern Language Review*, **XLVII**, 1953, pp. 270–77
Fingesten, P., 'Delimiting the Concept of the Grotesque', *Journal of Aesthetics and Art Criticism*, **42**, Summer 1984, pp. 419–26
Fitzgerald, E., *The Rubáiyát of Omar Khayyám*, illus., E.J. Sullivan, London: Methuen, 1913
Floud, P., 'Victorian Furniture', in *Concise Encyclopaedia of Antiques*, vol. 5, London: Connoisseur, 1953
Flower, M., *Victorian Jewellery* (rev. ed.), London: Cassell & Co., 1967
Forster, J., *The Life of Charles Dickens*, 2 vols, London: J.M. Dent and Co., 1872
Foucault, M., *Power / Knowledge*, trans. Colin Gordon, Brighton: Harvester, 1980

Fraser, H., *Beauty and Belief: Aesthetics and Religion in Victorian Literature*, Cambridge: Cambridge University Press, 1986
Fredman, W.E. (ed.), *The P.R.B. Journal*, Oxford: Clarendon Press, 1975
Freud, S., 'The Uncanny', 1919, in *The Standard Edition of the Complete Psychological Works*, 24 vols, London: Hogarth Press, **17**, 1955
Froude, J.A., *Thomas Carlyle, a History of his Life in London*, 2 vols, London: Longmans, Green and Co., 1884
Fry, R., 'G.F. Watts', *Burlington Magazine*, vol. 5, 1904, p. 452
Fusco, P., and Jansen, H.W., *The Romantics to Rodin: French Nineteenth Century Sculpture from North American Collections*, Los Angeles: Alpine Press, 1980
Gardiner, S.R., *History of the Commonwealth and Protectorate*, 4 vols, London: Longmans, Green and Co., 1916
Gilchrist, A., *Life of Blake*, 2 vols, London: Macmillan and Co., 1863
Gloag, J., *The English Tradition in Design*, London: Penguin, 1947
Goldberg, M., *Carlyle and Dickens*, Athens: University of Georgia Press, 1972
Gorlin, A., 'The Grotesque', *Interior Design*, **64**, September 1993, pp. 196-97
Halén, W., *Christopher Dresser: a Pioneer of Modern Design*, London: Phaidon, 1990
Hall, S.C., *The Book of British Ballads*, London: J. How, 1843
Hall, S.C., *The Baronial Halls, Picturesque Edifices and Ancient Churches of England*, 3 vols, London: Chapman and Hall, 1845
Hall, Mrs S.C., and Fairholt, F.W., 'Pilgrimages to English Shrines: Chertsey and its Neighbourhood', *The Art Journal*, 1852, pp. 155-57
Hardie, M., *Water-colour Painting in Britain*, 3 vols, London: B.T. Batsford, 1968
Harpham, G.G., *On the Grotesque: Strategies of Contradiction in Art and Literature*, Princeton, New Jersey: Princeton University Press, 1982
Hartford, J., *The Life of Michelangelo Buonarroti with Translations of his Poems and Letters*, 2 vols, London: Longmans, 1857
Harvey, J.R., *Victorian Novelists and their Illustrators*, London: Sidgwick and Jackson, 1970
Haslam, M., *The Martin Brothers Potters*, London: Richard Dennis, 1978
Haweis, H.R., *The Art of Beauty*, New York: Harper, 1878
Haweis, H.R., *The Art of Ornament*, London: Chatto and Windus, 1889
Hawkins, J., *The Life of Samuel Johnson LL.D*, London: published by subscription, 1787
Heffer, S., *Moral Desperado: A Life of Thomas Carlyle*, London: Weidenfeld and Nicolson, 1995
Helsinger, E.K., *Ruskin and the Art of the Beholder*, Cambridge, Mass.: Harvard University Press, 1982
Hewison, R., *John Ruskin: The Argument of the Eye*, Princeton, New Jersey: Princeton University Press, 1976
Hill, N., *A Reformer's Art: Dickens' Picturesque and Grotesque Imagery*, Athens and London: Ohio University Press, 1981
Hindson, P., and Gray, T., *Burke's Dramatic Theory of Politics*, Aldershot: Avebury, 1988
Hollington, M., *Dickens and the Grotesque*, London and Sydney: Croom Helm, 1984
Hood, T., *Hood's Own: or, Laughter from Year to Year*, London: Ward, Lock and Co., 1831
Hood, T., *Griset's Grotesques: or Jokes Drawn on Wood*, London: Routledge, 1867
Hood, T.L. (ed.), *Letters of Robert Browning*, London: John Murray, 1933
House, M,. and Storey, G. (eds), *The Letters of Charles Dickens*, 4 vols, Oxford: Oxford University Press, 1965

Howard, M., *Victorian Grotesque: An Illustrated Excursion into Medical Curiosities, Freaks and Abnormalities, Principally of the Victorian Age*, London: Jupiter, 1977
Hueffer, F.M., *Ford Madox Brown, a Record of his Life and Work*, London: Longman, 1896
Hugo, V., 'Preface to *Cromwell*', in *The Dramas of Victor Hugo*, trans. B. Lelior *et al*, 8 vols, London: H.S. Nicols, 1898
Hull, D., *Darwin and his Critics: The Reception of Darwin's Theory of Evolution by the Scientific Community*, Cambridge, Mass.: Harvard University Press, 1973
Hunt, W.H., *Pre-Raphaelitism and the Pre-Raphaelite Brotherhood*, 2 vols, London: Macmillan, 1905
Ingram, A., *Boswell's Creative Gloom: A Study of Imagery and Melancholy in the Writings of James Boswell*, London: Macmillan, 1982
Jenks, E., *Thomas Carlyle and John Stuart Mill*, Orpington: George Allen, 1888
Jennings, L.B., *The Ludicrous Demon: Aspects of the Grotesque in German Post-Romantic Prose*, Berkeley: University of California Press, 1963
Jervis, S. (ed.), *Art and Design in Europe and America 1800–1900*, London: Victoria and Albert Museum, 1987, p. 78
Johnson, S., *Prose and Poetry*, selected by Mona Wilson, London: Rupert Hart-Davis, 1963 (first published in 1950)
Jones, J., *Minton: The First Two Hundred Years of Design & Production*, Shrewsbury: Swan Hill, 1993
Jones, O., *The Grammar of Ornament*, London: Day & Son, 1856
Jordanova, L., 'The Art and Science of Seeing in Medicine: Physiognomy 1780–1920', in Bynum, W.F., and Porter, R. (eds), *Medicine and the Five Senses*, Cambridge: Cambridge University Press, 1993
Kant, I., *The Critique of Judgement*, trans. W.S. Pluhar, Indianapolis: Hackett Publishing Company, 1987
Kaplan, F., *Thomas Carlyle: A Biography*, Ithaca: Cornell University Press, 1983
Karr, J., 'Caliban and Paley: Two Natural Theologians', *Studies in Browning and his Circle*, **13**, 1985, pp. 37–46
Katz, M.P., and Lehr, R., *Palissy Ware: Nineteeth-century French Ceramists from Avisseau to Renoleau*, London: Athlone Press, 1996
Kayser, W., *The Grotesque in Art and Literature*, trans. U. Weisstein, Bloomington: Indiana University Press, 1963
Koerner, L., 'Carl Linnaeus in his Time and Place', in Jardine, N., Secord, J. and Spary, E. (eds), *The Cultures of Natural History*, Cambridge: Cambridge University Press, 1996
Kroker, A., Kroker, M., and Cook, D. (eds), *Panic Encyclopedia: The Definitive Guide to the Postmodern Scene*, Basingstoke: Macmillan, 1989
Lambourne, L., *Ernest Griset: Fantasies of a Victorian Illustrator*, London: Thames & Hudson, 1979
Landow, G., *The Aesthetic and Critical Theories of John Ruskin*, Princeton, New Jersey: Princeton University Press, 1971
Larsen, Anne, 'Equipment for the Field', in Jardine, N., Secord, J. and Spary, E. (eds), *The Cultures of Natural History*, Cambridge: Cambridge Univesity Press, 1996
Le Bon, G., *The Crowd*, London: Ernst Benn, 1896
Lear, J., *Aristotle: The Desire to Understand*, Cambridge: Cambridge University Press, 1988
Lewes, G.H., 'Dickens in Relation to Criticism', *Fortnightly Review*, 1872, pp. 141–54
Lippincott, L., 'Murder and the Fine Arts or, a Reassessment of Richard Dadd', *The John Paul Getty Museum Journal*, **16**, 1988, pp. 75–94

MacColl, D.S., *Nineteenth Century Art*, Glasgow: James Maclehose and Sons, 1902
Madox Rossetti, H., *Ford Madox Brown*, London: De La More Press, 1901
Maitland, F.W., *Life and Letters of Leslie Stephen*, London: Duckworth, 1906
Marx, K., *Selected Writings*, ed. D. McLellan, Oxford: Oxford University Press, 1977
Mason, T.W., 'Nineteenth-Century Cromwell', *Past and Present* 40, 1968, pp. 187–91.
Miller, N., *Heavenly Caves: Reflections on the Garden Grotto*, New York: Braziller, 1982
Milne, J. A., 'Beauty in Merchandise', in De La Valette, J. (ed.), *The Conquest of Ugliness*, London: Methuen & Co., 1935
Milton. J., *Poems*, ed. S. Orgel and J. Goldberg, Oxford: Oxford University Press, 1991
Monkhouse, C., 'Some Original Ceramicists', *Magazine of Art*, 5, 1882, pp. 443–46
Monkhouse, C., *British Contemporary Artists*, London: William Heinemann, 1899
Morley, H., 'A House Full of Horrors', *Household Words*, December 1852, pp. 266–70
Morley, H., *Palissy the Potter: The Life of Bernard Palissy*, London: Chapman and Hall, 1852
Mullen, C., *G.F. Watts*, London: John Roberts, 1974
Muller, F.M., *Comparative Mythology*, London: A, Smyth Palmer, 1856
Musée de Saintes, *Bernard Palissy: Myth et Réalité*, Saint-Jean-D'Angély: Bordessoules, 1990
Nadel, B.I., *Biography, Fiction, Fact and Form*, London: Macmillan, 1984
Norris, M., *Beasts of the Modern Imagination*, London and Baltimore: Johns Hopkins University Press, 1985
Ormond, R., *G.F. Watts: The Hall of Fame*, London: HMSO, 1976
Paley, W., *Natural Theology: or Evidences of the Existence and Attributes of the Deity, Collected from the Appearance of Nature*, London: R. Faulder, 1802
Palgrave, F.T., *Handbook to the Fine Art Collections in the International Exhibition of 1862*, London and Cambridge: Macmillan, 1862
Pater, W., *The Renaissance*, ed. K. Clark, London: Collins, 1961
Patten, R.L., *George Cruikshank: A Revaluation*, New Jersey: Princeton University Press, 1974
Pevsner, N., *High Victorian Design: A Study of the Exhibits of 1851*, London: Architectural Press, 1851
Phythian, J.G., *G.F. Watts*, London: Methuen, 1906
Piozzi, H.L., *Anecdotes of the Late Samuel Johnson LL.D during the Last Thirty Years of his Life*, first published in 1786, ed. S.C. Roberts, Cambridge: Cambridge University Press, 1925
Plato, *Collected Dialogues*, ed. E. Hamilton and H. Cairns, Princeton, New Jersey: Princeton University Press, 1961
Pottle, F.A. (ed.), *Boswell in Holland: 1763–4*, Yale Edition of the Private Papers of James Boswell, London: Heinemann, 1952
Potts, A., *Flesh and the Ideal: Winckelmann and the Origins of Art History*, New Haven: Yale University Press, 1994
Pugin, A.W.N., *True Principles of Pointed or Christian Architecture*, London: J. Weale, 1841
Rabin, L., *Ford Madox Brown and the Pre-Raphaelite History Picture*, New York: Garland Publishing Company, 1978
Rathbone, P.H., *Realism, Idealism and the Grotesque in Art: Their Limits and Functions*, Liverpool: Lee and Nightingale, 1877
Read, B., *Victorian Sculpture*, New Haven and London: Yale University Press, 1982
Read, B., and Barnes, J., *Pre-Raphaelite Sculpture: Nature and the Imagination in British Sculpture, 1848–1914*, London: Lund Humphries, 1991

Redgrave, R., *Supplementary Report on the Exhibition of 1851*, London: HMSO, 1852
Reed, C. (ed.), *A Roger Fry Reader*, Chicago and London: The University of Chicago Press, 1996
Reid, J.C., *Thomas Hood*, London: Routledge, and Kegan Paul, 1963
Reitlinger, G., *The Economics of Taste*, II, *The Rise and Fall of Objets d'Art Prices Since 1750*, London: Barrie and Rockliff, 1963
Robinson, J.C., *A Treasury of Ornamental Art: Illustrations of Objects of Art and Vertù, Photographed from the Originals and Drawn on Stone by F. Bedford with Descriptive Notices by J.C. Robinson, FSA Curator of the Museum of Ornamental Art of Marlborough House*, London: Day & Son, 1858
Roget, J.L., *A History of the 'Old' Water-Colour Society*, London: Longmans Green and Co., 1891
Roots, I., *Speeches of Oliver Cromwell*, London: J.M. Dent, 1989
Rose, P., 'The Grotesque Ceramic Sculpture of Robert Wallace Martin (1843-1923)', *Journal of Decorative Arts*, 3, 1978, pp. 40–54
Rosenberg, J.D., *Carlyle and the Burden of History*, Cambridge, Mass.: Harvard University Press, 1985
Rosenberg, P., *The Seventh Hero: Thomas Carlyle and the Theory of Radical Activism*, Cambridge, Mass.: Harvard University Press, 1974
Rudoe, J., *Decorative Arts 1850–1950: A Catalogue of the British Museum Collection*, London: British Museum, 1994
Ruskin, J., *The Stones of Venice*, 3 vols, London: Smith, Elder and Co., 1851–1853
Ruskin, J., *Works*, 39 vols, ed. E.T. Cook and A. Wedderburn, London: George Allen, 1903–1912
Russo, M., *The Female Grotesque*, London and New York: Routledge, 1994
Sachs, A., *The English Grotesque*, Jerusalem: Israel University Press, 1969
Sanders, C.R. (ed.), *Collected Letters of T. and J. Carlyle*, Durham, N. Carolina: Duke University Press, 1970–1981
Schapiro, M., *Late Antique, Early Christian and Medieval Art*, New York: Braziller, 1979
Schlegel, A.W., *A Course of Lectures on Dramatic Art and Literature*, trans. Rev. A.J.W. Morrison, London: H.G. Bohn, 1846
Scott, W., *Collected Novels*, 26 vols, London and Edinburgh: Adam and Charles Black, 1895
Scott, W., *The Miscellaneous Works of Scott*, Edinburgh: Whittaker and Co., 1834–1836
Scudder, V.D., *The Grotesque in Gothic Art*, privately printed, 1887
Seigel, J.P., *Thomas Carlyle: The Critical Heritage*, London: Routledge, 1971
Sennett, R., *The Fall of Public Man*, London: Faber and Faber (first published in 1974), 1993
Shrewsbury, H.W., *The Visions of an Artist*, London: C. Kelly, 1918
Slater, J. (ed.), *The Correspondence of Emerson and Carlyle*, New York: Columbia University Press, 1964
Smiles, S., *The Image of Antiquity: Ancient Britain and the Romantic Imagination*, New Haven and London: Yale University Press, 1994
Smith, L., *Victorian Photography, Painting and Poetry*, Cambridge: Cambridge University Press, 1995
Smith, P.J., 'Ajax by any Other Name Would Smell as Sweet', in A. Lascombes (ed.) *Tudor Theatre: Emotion in the Theatre*, Bern: Peter Lang, 1996
Snodgrass, C., *Aubrey Beardsley, Dandy of the Grotesque*: London and New York: Oxford University Press, 1995

Snodin, M., *Ornament: A Social History Since 1450*, New Haven and London: Yale University Press, 1996
South Kensington Museum, *Guide to the South Kensington Museum*, London: South Kensington Museum, 1857
Spielmann, M.H., 'The Work of G.F. Watts', *Pall Mall Extra*, 1886
Sprinkler, M., *Imaginary Relations*, London: Verso, 1987
Staley, A., *Victorian High Renaissance*: Minneapolis: Minneapolis Institute of Art, 1979
Stallybrass. P., and White, A., *The Politics and Poetics of Transgression*, London: Methuen, 1986
Stead, W.T., 'Interview with G.F. Watts', *Review of Reviews*, **150**, June 1902, pp. 567–77
Steig, M., 'George Cruikshank and the Grotesque: A Psychodynamic Approach', in Patten, R. (ed.), *George Cruikshank: A Revaluation*, Princeton: Princeton University Press, 1974, pp. 189–213
Stephen, L., *The History of English Thought in the Eighteeenth Century*, 2 vols, London: Smith, Elder and Co., 1876
Stephen, L., *Samuel Johnson*, English Men of Letters, London: Macmillan, 1878
Stephen, L., *The Science of Ethics*, London: Smith, Elder and Co., 1882
Stephen, L., *Swift*, English Men of Letters, London: Macmillan, 1882
Stephen, L., 'Carlyle', *Dictionary of National Biography*, 1886
Stewart, D., 'Theosophy and Abstraction in the Victorian Era', *Apollo*, November 1993, pp. 298–303
Stove, D., *The Plato Cult and other Philosophical Follies*, Oxford: Basil Blackwell, 1991
Strong, R., *And When did you last see your Father?* London: Thames and Hudson, 1978
Surtees, V. (ed.), *The Diary of Ford Madox Brown*, New Haven and London: Yale University Press, 1981
Sussman, H.L., *Fact into Figure*, Columbus: Ohio State University Press, 1979
Sweeney, J.L. (ed.), *The Painter's Eye: Notes and Essays on the Pictorial Arts by Henry James*, London: Rupert Hart-Davis, 1956
Symons, J.A., 'Caricature, the Fantastic, the Grotesque', in *Essays Speculative and Suggestive*, London: Chapman Hall, 1890
Tallis, J., *Tallis's History and Description of the Crystal Palace and the Exhibition of the World's Industry in 1851*, 3 vols, illus., London: John Tallis & Co., 1852
Taylor, J. et al., *Beatrix Potter 1866–1943: The Artist and Her World*, London: F.Warne & Co., 1987
Thomas, E.L., *Victorian Art Pottery*, London, Guildart, 1974
Thomson, P., *The Grotesque*, London: Methuen, 1972
Thorpe, J., *E.J. Sullivan*, London: Art and Technics, 1948
Tilly, H., 'Burmese Art and Burmese Artists', *The Magazine of Art*, October 1892, pp. 415–20
Treuherz, J., *Pre-Raphaelite Paintings from the Manchester City Art Gallery*, London: Lund Humphries in association with Manchester City Art Gallery, 1980
Trevelyan, R., *A Pre-Raphaelite Circle*, London: Chatto and Windus, 1978
Trevelyan, R., *Wallington*, London: National Trust, 1994
Trodd, C., 'The Laboured Vision and the Realm of Value: Articulations of Identity in Ford Madox Brown's Work', in Harding, E. (ed.) *Re-framing the Pre-Raphaelites*, Aldershot: Scolar Press, 1996
Trodd, C., 'The Authority of Art: Cultural Criticism and the Idea of the Royal Academy in mid-Victorian Britain', in Pointon, M., and Binski, P. (eds), *National Art Academies in Europe 1860–1906: Educating, Training, Exhibiting*, Oxford: Basil Blackwell, 1997

Vance, J.A., *Boswell's Life of Johnson: New Questions, New Answers*, Athens, Georgia: University of Georgia Press, 1985
Vasari, G., *The Lives of the Painters, Sculptors and Architects*, 4 vols, Everyman series, London: Dent, 1963
Vaughan, W., *German Romanticism and English Art*, New Haven and London: Yale University Press, 1979
Victoria and Albert Museum, *Art and Design in Europe and America: 1800–1900*, London: Herbert, 1987
Waagen, G., *Galleries and Cabinets of Art in Great Britain*, London: John Murray, 1857
Wainwright, C., 'Principles True and False: Pugin and the Foundation of the Museum of Manufactures', *Burlington Magazine*, **CXXXVI**, no. 1095, June 1994
Ward-Jackson, P.W., 'Some Mainstreams and Tributaries in European Ornament from 1500 to 1750', *Victoria and Albert Museum Bulletin*, **III**, nos. 2–4, 1967
Watts, M.S., *G.F. Watts, Annals of an Artist's Life*, 3 vols, London: Macmillan, 1912
Wellek, R., *Confrontations*, Princeton, New Jersey: Princeton University Press, 1965
West, S. (ed.), *Guide to Art*, London: Bloomsbury, 1996
Wildridge, T.T., *The Grotesque in Church Art*, London: Andrews, 1899
Williams, R., *Drama from Ibsen to Brecht*, Harmondsworth: Pelican, 1973
Williams, R., *Keywords: A Vocabulary of Culture and Society*, London: Fontana, 1983
Wills, W.G., *Charles the First: an Historical Tragedy*, Edinburgh and London: William Blackwood, 1873
Woolner, A., *Thomas Woolner RA, Sculptor and Poet: His Life in Letters*, London: Chapman Hall, 1917
Woolner, T., *Pygmalion*, London: Macmillan, 1881
Woolner, T., 'Where to Draw the Line: A Word to Students', the *Magazine of Art*, November 1891, pp. 7–11
Wright, T., 'The Domestic Manners of the English in the Middle Ages', the *Art Journal*, April 1851, pp. 113–15
Wright, T., *A History of Caricature and Grotesque in Literature and Art, with Illustrations from various sources, drawn and engraved by F.W. Fairholt*, London: Virtue, 1865
Wright, T., *A History of Caricature and Grotesque in Literature and Art*, with an introduction by F. K. Barasch, New York: Frederick Ungar, 1968
Wrighte, W., *Grotesque Architecture, or Rural Amusement*, London: Taylor, 1802
Wyatt, D., *The Industrial Arts of the Nineteenth Century, a Series of Illustrations of the Choicest Specimens Produced by Every Nation at the Great Exhibition of Works of Industry*, London: Day and Son, 1851

Index

Page references in *italic* type indicate illustrations.

Aesthetic Movement, 2, 17, 158
Albert, Prince, 149, 151
Alberti, Leon Battista, 18
Alexander, Patrick Proctor, 38
Allderidge, Patricia, 138
Animal Products Museum, 149–50
antiquarianism, *see* grotesque
Aristotelian biology, 122, 137, 139
Armstrong, Isobel, 44, 54, 75, 87, 137
Arnold, Matthew, 10, 12, 15, 38, 188
  Culture and Anarchy, 12, 15
  On the Study of Celtic Literature, 12–15
  On Translating Homer, 12, 14
Axton, W. F., 130, 139
Augustan aesthetics, 21, 55

Bagehot, Walter, 10, 12–13, 17, 65, 74, 110, 112, 121–23, 126, 127, 136, 137
Bahktin, Mikhail, 22–4, 26, 30, 32, 33, 36, 84
  Rabelais and his World, 22–3, 32
Barasch, Frances K., 3, 4, 5–7, 22–3
Barber, Lynn, 150
Bardili, Christoph Gottfried, 52–3
Baroque structures, 42, 49, 54, 107
Barrell, John, 92
Barrington, Mrs, 175, 182, 184, 187
Beardsley, Aubrey, 2, 17, 56, 98
beauty, *see* grotesque
Beer, Gillian, 9, 19, 120, 126, 133, 138
Bell, John, 158, 162
Blake, William, 15–16, 175
Bonington, Richard Parkes, 72
Booth, Wayne C., 32, 36

Boswell, James, 21–35
  Journal of a Tour to the Hebrides, 26, 34
  Life of Johnson, 21, 22, 25, 27, 34
Brown, Ford Madox, 8, 9, 37, 39, 53–4, 61–77, 99, 110, 174, 186
  Body of Harold brought before William the Conqueror, 75
  Cromwell, Protector of the Vaudois, 67–71, 79
  St Ives 1630: Cromwell on his Farm, 67–71, 78
  Work, 37, 53–4, 99, 110, 111
Browning, Robert, 6, 12, 65–6, 110, 112, 119–27, 132, 135, 136, 137, 178
  Caliban upon Setebos, 112, 123–7, 133, 137
  Deaf and Dumb: A Sculpture by Woolner, 110
  Dramatis Personae, 110, 121, 123
  Sibrandus Schnafnaburgensis, 121
Brunswick, Duke of, 50
Burke, Edmund, 6, 47–8, 51, 55
  On the Sublime and Beautiful, 6, 8, 18
  Reflections on the Revolution in France, 47–8, 55
Burmese art, 16–17

cabinets of curiosities, *see* grotesque
Callot, Jaques, 74
Cameron, Colin, 45, 48, 55
caricature, *see* grotesque
Carlyle, Thomas, 2–3, 4, 6, 7, 8, 9, 11, 14, 23, 24, 27–8, 37–56, 61–77, 120, 186
  ETA Hoffmann, 27
  Latter Day Pamphlets, 38, 39, 53
  Oliver Cromwell's Letters and Speeches, 62, 63

On Heroes, Hero Worship and the Heroic in History, 69, 70
On History, 40, 47
On History Again, 54
Past and Present, 39, 54, 55
Sartor Resartus, 10, 37–46, 47, 48, 51–3, 55
Signs of the Times, 48, 54
The French Revolution, 38, 46–51, 54, 55, 56
Carroll, Lewis, 144, 159
Cattermole, George, 71–2, 76, 77
  Cromwell Consulting the Lawyers, 71–2
  Cromwell Viewing the Body of Charles I, 71–2
Cattermole, Richard, 76
Celtic culture, 13–14, 101, 111, 157, 184–5, 188
  and confusion, 13–14, 103–4, 144, 188; and barbarism, 98, 101, 104–5
Chambers, Robert, 9, 129
  Vestiges of the Natural History of Creation, 9, 129
Chambers, William, 26
Charles I, 67, 71–2, 77
Chesterfield, Lord, 34
Chesterton, G.K., 64, 174–7, 178, 186, 188
Chiarelli, Luigi, 18
Christ, Carol, 121
civilization, 97–110, 177
  and barbarism, 98, 101–5; and primitivism, 98
Classicism, 5, 9, 21, 24–5, 33–4, 97–8, 174, 105–6, 110, 184–5
  'Phidian' tradition, 174, 184; Ideal form, 99, 174, 177; and the body, 34, 108–9; and sculpture, 34, 97, 105–6
Cole, Henry, 7, 153–5, 158, 161
Coleridge, Samuel Taylor, 112
Comte, Auguste, 32, 36
Cowley, Abraham, 21
Cranach, Lucas, 54
Crisp, Sir Frank, 159
Cromwell, Oliver, 8, 55, 61–77, 174
Cruikshank, George, 55, 56

Dadd, Richard, 8, 120, 121, 127–36, 138–9
  Bacchanalian Scene, 131
  Come unto these Yellow Sands, 127
  Contradiction: Oberon and Titania, 128, 138
  Crazy Jane, 131
  Elimination of a Picture and its Subject, 128, 131–2, 134
  Mercy: David Spareth Saul's Life, 138
  Sketch to Illustrate the Passions: Grief or Sorrow, 131
  Songe de la Fantasie, 128, 131, 141
  The Fairy Feller's Master-Stroke, 127–8, 130–36, 140
  Titania Sleeping, 127
Dadd, Robert, 129
Danton, Georges, 51
Darwin, Charles, 9, 10, 18, 19, 108, 119–39, 158, 180
  and Browning, 120–26; and Dadd, 127–37; and design, 158; and social Darwinism, 28–9, 175, 184, 186; and Woolner, 108
  Descent of Man, 10, 19, 108
  Journal of Researches, 136
  Origin of Species, 9–10, 19, 113, 119–23, 130, 137
Davey, Samuel, 73
de Bay, Auguste Hyacinthe, 100–101, 111, 112
Decadents, 17, 56
Delaroche, Paul, 71
Derham, William, 136
Dibdin, T. F., 63
Dickens, Charles, 2, 7, 9, 10–12, 19, 39, 65, 74, 77, 92, 120, 154–5, 160, 161–2
  Barnaby Rudge, 77
  Hard Times, 155
  Martin Chuzzlewit, 160
  Pictures from Italy, 92
  The Old Curiosity Shop, 7
dinosaurs, 19, 150
Dix, Otto, 56
Doré, Gustave, 7, 56
Doyle, Arthur Conan, 7
  The Adventure of Wisteria Lodge, 7
  The Hound of the Baskervilles, 10
Dresser, Christopher, 147, 155–9, 162
Dürer, Albrecht, 15, 54

Emerson, Ralph Waldo, 62
Ernst, Max, 56
evolutionary theory, 9, 29, 119–39, 177–8, 181, 185, 186; *see also* Darwin
  and Creationism, 19–20, 158, 162; and vitalism, 174, 175, 186

Fairholt, Frederick William, 7, 102–3, 111, 112, 146, 160
  Pilgrimages to English Shrines, 112
  Eccentric and Remarkable Characters, 7
  Gog and Magog, 7

Grotesque Design, 111, 146, 160
On a Grotesque Mask of Punishment, 103, 112
Fielding, K. J., 54, 161
Florio, John, 6
Floud, Peter, 148
Forster, John, 74
Foucault, Michel, 28, 160
fragmentation, *see* grotesque
Froud, James, 63
Fry, Roger, 187, 188

Gargantua, 22, 23–4, 31, 51
gargoyles, 5, 97, 111, 145, 160
Garrick, David, 35
Gilchrist, Alexander, 15–16
Gillray, James, 34, 56, 103
Giotto, 12
Gosse, Philip, 19–20, 162
Gothic design, 4–5, 8, 18, 21, 37, 53–4, 81, 86–92, 102, 157
Grandville, J.J., 19, 159
Gray, Tim, 47
Great Exhibition, 100, 150
Greenslade, Sydney, 159
Griset, Ernest, 19, 159, 161
Grosz, Georg, 56
grotesque
  and aberrance, 8, 52, 65–6, 92–3, 155; and antiquarianism, 6–9, 18–19, 72, 77; and barbarism, 10, 20, 98, 101–5; and beauty, 15, 40, 86, 97, 109, 123, 182–3; and bodies, 17, 22, 34, 38, 50, 84, 101, 108, 148, 160; and bourgeois culture, 12–13, 66; and cabinets of curiosities, 7–8; and caricature, 4, 6, 9, 10, 12, 16, 20, 37, 48, 50, 54, 76, 102–5, 144–5, 183; and commodities, 9, 46–7; and contradiction, 3, 16, 23, 38, 102–5, 151; and the demonic, 4, 16, 17, 18, 56, 102, 103, 128, 162; and disease, 12, 15, 22, 25, 27, 30, 34, 38–9, 54, 66, 101; and fantasy, 9, 10, 73, 76, 87, 120, 133, 145, 152, 154, 158; and hybridity, 65, 153, 181; and fragmentation, 2, 4, 9, 13, 40–41, 63, 69, 105, 130, 183; and grotto-esque, 4, 106, 112; and humour, 8, 10, 16, 19, 28, 38, 50, 52, 73, 74, 146, 152; and monstrosity, 7, 15, 17, 40, 50, 108, 145, 156; and natural history, 5, 19, 108, 119–39, 150, 158; and orientalism, 16–17, 19, 26, 74, 175, 186; and ornament, 15, 20, 21, 23, 33, 64, 87, 122, 149–50, 154–7, 185, 188; and picturesque, 9, 18, 38, 39, 44, 74; and physical excess, 9, 10, 20, 22, 84, 108, 177; and popular culture, 9, 10, 13, 16, 65, 83, 183, 188; and realism, 24–5, 30, 54, 147, 150, 152; and sublime, 40, 42–4, 64, 104; and taste, 10, 13, 41, 145–6, 154–5; and the uncanny, 11, 14, 17, 62, 63–4, 73, 145; and violence; 5, 9, 65, 98, 102, 174, 177, 179, 182–3, 186
grottoes, 4, 5, 18–19, 33, 106, 112, 144

Hall, Samuel Carter, 8, 54
Hall, Mrs Samuel Carter, 112
Halliburton, Thomas Chandler, 160
Hamerton, P.G., 185
Hartford, John, 107
Haweis, Mrs, 147
Hawkins, John, 34
Heffer, Simon, 54
Hegel, G.W. F., 51–3, 64–5
  Lectures on Aesthetics, 64–5
Henault, President, 49
Hindson, Paul, 47
Hirst, Damien, 160
Hoffmann, E.T.W. (E.T.A.), 8, 27, 65, 74
Hogarth, William, 9, 26, 54, 65, 75, 103, 183
  The Analysis of Beauty, 54
  John Wilkes, 26
Holbein, Hans, 56
Holliday, Henry, 159
Hollington, Michael, 23, 146
Holmes, Sherlock, 7, 9, 159
Homer, 15
Hood, Thomas, 2, 77
Hopkins, Gerard Manley, 120
horror, 3, 121, 123, 126, 135–6, 145–6, 151, 155–6, 159, 160
Horror victorianorum, 145, 146
Hueffer, Ford Madox, 66, 69, 76
Hugo, Victor, 8, 64, 72
Hume, David, 29–30, 51, 55, 63
humour, *see* grotesque
Hunt, William Holman, 15, 53, 75
hybridity, *see* grotesque

Impressionism, 175, 186
Ingram, Allan, 25

James, Henry, 187, 188
Japanese art, 156
Jeffrey, Lord, 38

Jenks, Edward, 54
Jennings, Lee, 8
Johnson, Samuel, 21–36
Jones, Owen, 18, 20, 154
Jordanova, Ludmilla, 35

Kafka, Franz, 3, 17
Kant, Immanuel, 84, 85, 88, 93
  Critique of Judgement, 88
Karr, Jeff, 126
Kayser, Wolfgang, 8, 36
Kierkegaard, Søren, 45
Kroker, A. and M., 54

Landseer, Edwin, 151
Lavater, J.K., 35
Le Bon, Gustav, 188
Lear, Edward, 19, 144
Leighton, Frederic, 179
Leonardo da Vinci, 143, 153
Lewes, George Henry, 10–12, 13
  Dickens in Relation to Criticism, 10–12
Linnaeus, Carl, 122, 137
Lippincott, Louise, 138
Longfellow, Henry W., 112
  Hiawatha, 112
Louis XIV, 67
Louis XV, 49
Louis XVI, 50
Lyell, Charles, 120
  Principles of Geology, 120, 129

Macaulay, Thomas Babbington, 31, 63
Maclise, Daniel, 77
MacDonald, Flora, 26
Manchester, 9, 102, 186
Maoris, 10, 20
Marat, Jean Paul, 56
Marie Antoinette, 56
Martin, Robert Wallace, 5, 56, 143–5, 151, 158, 159
Marvell, Andrew, 67, 71
Marx, Karl, 3, 9, 46–7, 49, 51–3, 55
  Capital, 47
  The Eighteenth Brumaire of Louis Napoleon, 53
Maurice, Frederic Dennison, 53
McQueen, Alexander, 160
Michelangelo, 12, 106–7, 112–13, 183
Millais, John Everett, 15
Miller, Naomi, 4
Milne, John, 145

Milton, John, 67, 69–70, 76
Mirabeau, Comte de, 51
modernity, 3, 9, 12–14, 26, 39, 41, 45–6, 48, 90, 97–8, 110, 185
Monkhouse, Cosmo, 144–5, 159
Morley, Henry, 152–3, 154–5, 161
Morris, William, 156
Mulready, William, 107, 113
Munro, Alexander, 145, 159

Napoleon III, 52
natural history, *see* grotesque
Norton, Charles Elliot, 31

Omar Khayyám, 56
Orientalism, *see* grotesque
O'Shea, James and John, 5, 102–3, 109, 111, 144, 159
  Punishment Capitals, 102–3, 111, 117
ornament, *see* grotesque

Paley, William, 123, 124, 133–5
  Natural Theology, 123, 133, 138
Palissy, Bernard, 5, 18, 143–5, 152–3, 161, 162
  Palissyite design, 152, 153–5
Pater, Walter, 17, 110
Patmore, Coventry, 97, 98, 110
picturesque, *see* grotesque
Piozzi, Hester, 34
Pirandello, Luigi, 18
Platonism, 84–5, 106–7
Ploucquet, Henri, 150
Pope, Alexander, 15
popular culture, *see* grotesque
Postmodernism, 39, 54, 160
Potter, Beatrix, 158
Potter, Robert, 34
Potter, Walter, 150–51, 158, 161
Pre-Raphaelites, 15, 53, 75, 91, 97, 99, 106–7, 110, 176
Primitivism, 10, 20, 98, 101–5, 112, 156, 186
Pugin, Augustus Welby Northmore, 153, 154, 156
  Puginite design theory, 153–5, 162
Punch magazine, 55

Rabin, Lucy, 76
Rabelais, François, 22–4, 28, 30, 32, 35, 36, 74, 101, 108
Raphael, 4, 5, 9, 15, 18, 156
Redgrave, Richard, 161
Reynolds, Joshua, 14–15, 25

Rhodes, Cecil, 175, 186
Richards, Alfred Bate, 77
Richter, Jean Paul, 8
Roberts, David, 128
Robespierre, Maximilien, 50
Rococo, 56
Romanticism, 8, 14, 22, 40, 44–5, 64, 72, 98
   Romantic grotesque, 8, 24, 26, 32, 64
   Romantic Theism, 180
   Tory Romantic literature, 63, 65
Rosenberg, John D., 73
Rossetti, Christina, 111
   Goblin Market, 111
Rossetti, Dante Gabriel, 2, 92, 111
Ruskin, John, 4, 5, 10, 11, 16, 17, 18, 66, 74, 75, 76, 81–94, 99, 103–4, 106, 110, 112, 113, 143–4, 146–7, 156, 159, 161, 162, 185
   Modern Painters, 76, 81–94, 103, 146
   Seven Lamps of Architecture, 103–4
   Stones of Venice, 75, 81, 85, 87, 103, 161
Russo, Mary, 18

Saint Mark's Church, 81–5, 90, 92
Sachs, Arieh, 33
Sartre, Jean Paul, 55
Schlegel, A. W., 8, 97
science, 5, 7, 29, 41, 46–7, 49, 52–3, 55, 74, 119–20, 122–7, 150, 158, 160, 180, 187
science-fiction, 159
Scott, Walter, 7, 19, 50, 63, 72, 74
   The Antiquary, 7
   Ivanhoe, 50, 55
   Old Mortality, 19
   Waverley, 74
   Woodstock, 63
Scott, William Bell, 99
Sedgwick, Adam, 9, 19, 108, 113
Shakespeare, William, 6, 22, 23–4, 40, 47, 55, 89
Smith, Lindsay, 83–4, 86
South Kensington Museum, 149–50, 156, 162
Spencer, Herbert, 184
Stephen, Leslie, 7, 9, 23, 24, 26–33, 38, 51
   Science of Ethics, 29
   The History of English Thought in the Eighteenth Century, 29–32
Sterne, Laurence, 43
   A Sentimental Journey, 43
   Tristram Shandy, 43, 55
Stothard, Thomas, 71
Stove, David, 145, 146, 149, 160
Strand magazine, 7–8, 19, 151

Strong, Roy, 76
Stuart, Charles Edward, 26
sublime, *see* grotesque
Sullivan, Edmund Joseph, 56
Swift, Jonathan, 30, 43
Symbolism, 17

Tennyson, Alfred, 12, 65, 121, 122
   Enoch Arden, 121
Thackeray, William Makepeace, 38, 55
Thomson, Phillip, 2, 3, 4, 17, 146
Tiger chair, 151, 155, 166
Tilly, Harry, 16–17
Titus baths, 4, 18
Trevelyan, Pauline, 99, 109, 110
Turner, J. M. W., 14, 91–2
typology, 28, 67–8, 72, 122–3, 126, 129, 137

Utilitarianism, 41, 54, 154–5, 174

Vasari, Georgio, 4, 5, 33
Venice, 66, 81–5
Veronese, Paolo, 92
Victoria, Queen, 149
Vitruvius, 4, 21

Waagen, Gustav, 76–7
Wallis, George, 162
Waterhouse, Alfred, 102, 111
Watts, George Frederick, 9, 92, 173–88
   Chaos, 55
   Eve Repentant, 174, 180, 193
   Evolution, 174, 182, 194
   Experientia Docet: Tasting the First Oyster, 174, 177, 180, 190
   House of Life, 176
   Love and Death, 174, 178, 180, 187, 191
   Mammon, 186
   Our Race as Pioneers, 173
   She Shall be Called Woman, 174, 177, 179, 189
   The Genius of Greek Poetry, 174, 182, 183, 195
   The Sower of the Systems, 178, 192
Waugh, Evelyn, 160
Wilde, Oscar, 17, 56
Wilkes, John, 26, 35
Wilkinson, John Gardener, 128
Williams, Raymond, 3, 5, 17–18, 54
Wills, W.G., 77
Winckelmann, Johann Joachim, 110
Wood, Dr, 128
Woodward, Benjamin, 159

Woolner, Thomas, 5, 10, 97–113, 159
  Adam Sedgwick, 108
  Civilization, 98–113, 115–16
  Constance and Arthur, 110
  Puck, 97–8, 108, 110, 114
  Pygmalion, 106, 112, 159
Wotton, Henry, 6
Wordsworth, William, 12, 65

Wornum, Ralph, 153
Wright, Thomas, 4, 6–7, 9, 16, 18, 75, 102, 106, 111
  History of Caricature and Grotesque in Literature and Art, 6, 75, 102
  Domestic Manners of the English in the Middle Ages, 111
Wrighte, William, 18

For Product Safety Concerns and Information please contact our EU
representative GPSR@taylorandfrancis.com
Taylor & Francis Verlag GmbH, Kaufingerstraße 24, 80331 München, Germany

www.ingramcontent.com/pod-product-compliance
Lightning Source LLC
Chambersburg PA
CBHW052108300426
44116CB00010B/1583